Louis Mallet, Bernard Mallet

Free Exchange

Papers on political and economical Subjects

Louis Mallet, Bernard Mallet

Free Exchange
Papers on political and economical Subjects

ISBN/EAN: 9783337071585

Printed in Europe, USA, Canada, Australia, Japan

Cover: Foto ©Suzi / pixelio.de

More available books at **www.hansebooks.com**

FREE EXCHANGE

FREE EXCHANGE

PAPERS ON POLITICAL AND ECONOMICAL SUBJECTS
INCLUDING CHAPTERS ON THE

LAW OF VALUE

AND

UNEARNED INCREMENT

BY THE LATE

RIGHT HONOURABLE SIR LOUIS MALLET, C.B.

EDITED BY BERNARD MALLET

"If, as an economist and a Liberal, I did not believe that the free operation of natural economic laws tended to raise the condition of the masses and to bring about a less unequal distribution of wealth, I should take very little interest in political economy or in public affairs."—*From a Letter*

LONDON

KEGAN PAUL, TRENCH, TRÜBNER & CO., Lt.

1891

INTRODUCTION.

I have been led to think that the publication of this volume, which contains all (except some letters to the newspapers) that the late Sir Louis Mallet wrote for the public, as well as some important but hitherto unprinted work, would be welcomed by many besides his personal and official friends, from the fact that in it is to be found the sum and substance of the teaching of the most original school of politics which this country and century have produced—the school founded by Richard Cobden.

Many who are familiar only with the usual travesty of Cobden's opinions may be surprised to find that the policy inaugurated by that statesman was a carefully thought out scheme, embracing every department of the national life. It was, moreover, a policy of which the guiding principles were so much in harmony with modern social conditions in England, and with economical laws founded upon the most durable of human instincts, that so far from being, as we are constantly assured, already obsolete, it has to a large extent been accepted by common consent.

Those, on the other hand, who understand and

appreciate Cobden's work, will perhaps be interested in a statement by one of his most distinguished and devoted followers of the ideas which animated the leaders of the party—a statement in many ways more complete and comprehensive than is to be gathered from anything hitherto published.

Before endeavouring to point out the consistency and development of my father's opinions, as shown in the various papers included in this volume, I may be allowed to quote the judgment of one of his friends as to how far he represented Cobden's own ideas.

"You are not only a Cobdenite *pur sang*, but, unless I am much mistaken, you have realized more perfectly and completely than Cobden did himself the higher and more ideal side of the Cobdenic creed. I have searched in vain through Cobden's writings for much that I have heard you quote as established Cobdenic doctrine, and I account for my failure by a fact which I believe to be universally true about all the faiths, great and small, that have shaken mankind, viz. that the disciple is in many ways above his master. . . . It is easy to see how this happens in cases like that before us. You were filled with a great enthusiasm and a personal admiration and love for Cobden. You were constantly with him at one of the most important periods of his life, and must have over and over again discussed the great questions on which your own mind had long been working, and respecting which your own faith has since become definitively fixed. There must have been the keenest sympathy between you, and the intercourse must have been as great a delight to him as it was to you. . . . In such intercourse it is absurd to assign to the disciple a passive part. What the disciple afterwards gives out as the faith of the master is really a joint product of their two minds, and their two individualities."

I cannot omit his own answer :—

". . . There may be, no doubt, a certain amount of truth in this view, but far less, I think, than you suppose. Cobden had no time to elaborate a system or trace all his opinions to their logical results, but he spent his life in talking and writing letters, and those who habitually lived with him or who corresponded with him will, I think, bear me out in saying that I have done little more than put into a connected shape ideas which they have heard from him over and over again. So much was this the case that, among the little set of his intimate friends, there was a kind of freemasonry, which, almost without discussion, ensured an extraordinary degree of political sympathy on nearly all questions."

One of the commonest charges against the so-called "Manchester school" is that, as a party of capitalists, they were unmindful of, if not indeed hostile to, the interests of the labouring classes. Of any such charge as affecting the leaders of the movement—assuming as it does a necessary antagonism between capital and labour—the whole tenor of these papers is a sufficient refutation—if, indeed, such were needed, in the face of the actual effects of the free trade policy. But personal utterances are always interesting, and the following words show how wide of the mark in my father's case would have been any suggestion of want of sympathy.

"I suppose that the first question which every one who is placed above want asks himself, when he begins to speculate upon social questions, is, Why have I so much, and others so little? While the poor man asks, Why have I so little, and others so much? I say at once that a man who meddles in public affairs without having satisfied himself as to the relation in which these two phenomena stand to each other is a 'charlatan,' and is not entitled to have any share in the work of statesmanship.

"Certainly, for my own part, I remember the torment of this question, and, even as a boy, I could never rest until I had found some solution of this terrible enigma which my reason and conscience could accept. But it was only after the weary round of thought and inquiry through every form of social heresy that I reached solid ground at last in the free trade creed, and with it a necessary belief in the gradual emancipation of the millions, both materially and morally, and, therefore, politically."

To the view of economical science here indicated, upon which Sir Louis Mallet based his belief—a belief so remarkably justified by the history of the last fifty years—in free trade rather than in socialistic methods in politics, I shall return later. I will first say a few words on the foreign policy of the Manchester school.

The accusations of those who find in the Cobdenic policy an indifference to England's position as a great power, are based on a conception of national duties and responsibility so opposed to that held by free-traders, and betray so inadequate a comprehension of the real meaning and consequences of the repeal of the corn laws, that it would be impossible to attempt to answer them here. The answer can, moreover, be easily gathered from many of the following papers. It cannot, however, be denied that there were certain exaggerations in the utterances of some members of the party which have obscured the merit of their work, and laid them open to criticism. From "peace at any price" opinions,* for instance, the following passage sufficiently dissociates the writer :—

"I entirely repudiate the method of laying down a hard-and-fast rule in foreign policy. If one must formulate such a policy at all, I should say that, as our knowledge and our power and our interest in the affairs of other countries must be limited, so also should our interference be limited to cases in which these three elements are so combined as render it not only a positive, but (at the same time) a relative duty. I believe that, by a steady adherence to this rule, the chances of war would be reduced to the 'minimum.'"

His general view is clearly stated in the essay on Cobden, and in the letter to M. de Laveleye, written during the "Jingo" agitation of 1878; but I may be allowed to quote the following extracts from a private letter written about the same time, as they still further explain his position :—

"It puzzles me how an economist and a Liberal can fail to see that the kind of way in which Europe has hitherto been governed, in which the people have been the mere tools and victims of governments and governing classes, is absolutely incompatible with democracy and free trade, and that the choice lies between two courses in deciding on the future foreign policy of England.

"The first programme would be a return to a system of

---

* On another occasion he thus expressed himself on "peace at any price:" "This is a foolish charge brought against those who denounce unnecessary or unjust wars. Probably there are quite as few people, or fewer, who desire peace at any price, as those who desire war at any price. But there is this difference : peace is a good in itself, and an end in itself; war is an evil, and can never be desired by good men except as a means to peace."

foreign alliances, territorial extension, and the further subjugation of inferior races, which could only be successful if by infinite skill and extraordinary luck, by swagger, audacity, reckless expenditure, the sacrifice of all consistent principle, and the abandonment of all liberal progress at home, we threw back the moral and material condition of our people to that which prevailed fifty years ago, *i.e.* the restoration of a state of things which was not only a reproach and a scandal, but an imminent peril to all our institutions; for there can be no greatness or security to any people unless they rest on the material well-being of the population.

"The second course is not without risk either, but the cause is so sacred and the aim so great, that to my mind they would justify and glorify even failure, if fail we must. This is, to cast in our lot broadly and heartily with the interests of the people, by which I mean the working millions of the human race, beginning with our own. It is upon them that the real cost of wars invariably falls. It is all very well for you or me to talk about sacrificing our lives and fortunes for the sake of some notion about honour and prestige, which, when analyzed, resolves itself into little more than a reflected self-glorification; but should we feel the same, should we accept, without much deeper and closer examination, a proposal which involved this sacrifice, if the result would be to send our wives to the workhouse, and turn our children on the streets? and this is what it really means to vast numbers of our countrymen."

And again—

"From a purely national point of view, the one thing which I feel most deeply and keenly is, that England, by a rare combination of accidents, and by the efforts of some of her greatest men, has achieved a unique position, and has a chance of pulling through the grandest political experiment that the world has seen. This chance will be imperilled and probably lost if we get into another era of wars. We shall then merely add another page to the history of the great empires which have risen and fallen in recorded time, in which national greatness and supreme physical power were the aim, and not the assertion of great principles."

From the comments on the subject in the paper on the "National Income and Taxation," with its grave and eloquent warnings as to the complacency with which this country, regardless of the claims of posterity, continues to accumulate Imperial responsibilities, it will be seen that, in the opinion of the author, England had in 1885 already thrown away the chance of "associating her name in history with the peaceful solution of social problems which affect the permanent interests of humanity"—a chance of which he had spoken with hopefulness in 1880. Apathy as to foreign policy has now taken the place of clamour, and it cannot be denied that we are very far removed from realizing any such conceptions as are here described of international relations; but it would not be difficult to point to signs which seem to afford the hope that, in this respect at any rate, Cobden's teaching may be destined to future triumphs.

I have reprinted the pamphlet on the "National Income and Taxation," which is important as a weighty exposition of general policy, and as insisting on the intimate connection between general and financial policy; and which is also noteworthy for an economical discussion as to whether the interest on the national debt should be estimated as forming part of the national income.

b

Another good specimen of the kind of logical reasoning in which the writer delighted, is the statement of the "Theory of Bimetallism," which has already been widely circulated and has never been disproved. Sir Louis Mallet's well-known advocacy of bimetallism is in itself an answer to the doubt lately expressed by Mr. Gladstone as to whether an instructed disciple of Cobden could be a bimetallist. It would, indeed, be singular if the removal of one of the obstacles to the healthy growth of international trade—the existence of different standards of value in groups of countries with a large interchange of commodities—had not been an object of special interest to an adherent of Cobden's international principles.

I have obtained permission to reprint an official memorandum, written in 1866 (the interest of which is now, it is to be feared, mainly historical), on the policy of commercial treaties—a policy which, as recent controversies have reminded us, was never frankly accepted by the Liberal party. I regret the necessity of passing over with so slight a mention the work of some of my father's best years, but it is perhaps impossible to deal as yet with the large correspondence, official and private, connected with the various Treaty negotiations in which he was engaged, containing as it does much of great interest and value to students of commercial policy.

About the second part of the volume, consisting of the chapters on the "Unearned Increment," something more must be said. Sir Louis Mallet devoted much time, after his retirement from official life in 1883, to thought and study on economical questions, which finally took shape in an intention to write upon the prevalent socialistic theories on the land question. The work was unhappily interrupted—as the event proved for ever—by the long and difficult labours imposed upon him by his appointment to the Gold and Silver Commission, and although the material was ready, collected in many notes and essays, the final task of arrangement, except in the case of one most important chapter, that on "Value," was never accomplished. It is from these materials that the work has been compiled. I am only too conscious that the result is not a treatise which my father, who was most critical about his own work, would have printed in its present unexpanded form. It is to a large extent a mosaic pieced together from various note-books, and I can only claim that the argument is clear and logical, and that the chapters indicate, in his own words, the direction which the writer's speculations took. The originality and importance of the considerations suggested, and the imminence of the danger from erroneous or subversive teaching on this subject, will, I hope, be considered to have justified my action in preparing these chapters for publication.

The felicitous use made by socialist writers of Mill's arguments upon the land question might have been expected to awaken more doubt than it seems to have done in the mind of the public as to the soundness of his views, which have apparently survived the damaging criticism of economists like Professor Jevons and Mr. Macleod. From an early period Sir Louis Mallet dissented from the assumptions upon which Mill and his followers argued.* His connection with Cobden probably first turned his attention to Bastiat, and through him to Condillac and his successors; and his later studies led him definitely to range himself with Jevons in his expression of the opinion that the " only hope of attaining a true system of economics is to fling aside once and for ever the mazy and preposterous assumptions of the Ricardian school;" that "our English economists have been living in a fool's paradise;" and that "the truth is with the French school."

It is characteristic of the actual condition, at all events in England, of the science of Political Economy, of which De Quincey wrote in 1844, that "anarchy even as to its earliest principles is predominant in it," and which Jevons, in 1879, described as a "shattered science," that any one who desires to consider a practical question like the proposal to nationalize the land, should find it necessary first to criticize and analyze the standard writers, and reconstruct or restate for himself a theory of value. Nothing less than this is the task of the chapter on " Value."

But it is unnecessary to say more upon a subject which is discussed in the first chapter, on " The Shattered Science." I will only add that the way in

---

* His suspicions had perhaps been aroused by the very lukewarm support afforded to the free trade policy by Mill. See Appendix B. to Chapter II. of the second part. See also p. 312 of the chapter on " Unearned Increment."

which the common economic errors on the land question are there traced to their source, and the application which is made in succeeding chapters of a corrected theory of value to the fact of private property in land, whether agricultural or urban, place on a scientific basis the opposition to schemes of ill-considered reform, and ought so far to be of practical weight in present controversies. For, as the writer said, "to many minds, and mine is among them, there is something peculiarly repugnant in any conclusion which fails to satisfy the requirements of sound theory as well as of policy."

A point of considerable interest—which is brought out very clearly in this treatise as well as in the earlier writings—is the manner in which Sir Louis Mallet developed the policy of Free Trade into something very much wider than is commonly denoted by that phrase. In his view it was something more important than a question of tariff reform;* it was a distinct bid for the solution of what is called the social problem; and he preferred to it the more comprehensive expression "Free Exchange," which the French economists have always used as "asserting in the broadest sense the principle of private property, of which free exchange is only an attribute." I have, therefore, adopted it as the title of the book. The following note will help to show how wide a field of

* "You in England," as an American observer once said, "have the protective idea permeating the whole of your internal policy. You are only free traders externally. I think the paternal or protective system does more mischief when applied internally than when applied externally."

speculation and controversy is opened by the use of this term :—

"Free Trade, or Free Exchange, to use the better expression of the French economists, is a form of words in every one's mouth, but it is one to which it may be doubted whether many persons attach a very precise and definite meaning; while among those who have formed a clear conception of the sense in which they understand it, there are probably very few who would agree in its practical application.

"When men speak of a system or policy of Free Exchange, do they mean it should apply to all exchanges, or only to some? Are all commodities and services—everything, in short, which is exchangeable between man and man material and incorporeal—to be freely exchanged, or only some things? If any limitations are to be placed on the exercise of a function so essential as this appears to be to human progress, what are they to be, and on what principle are they to be determined? Ought a distinction to be made between products and services upon which competition freely operates, and those which are the subject of natural monopolies? Is freedom to prevail in the relations of capital and labour, as well as in the exchange of commodities? Is a distinction to be observed between the products of past or present industry, and those of the future? Is credit to be restricted if labour and capital are free? Again, is Free Trade only a geographical or a political expression confined to the people of particular countries at particular stages of progress, or is it a universal international principle, and a bond of union between all the nations of the earth?"

Sir Louis Mallet would have been the last to claim for the following scattered papers the dignity of a system of political philosophy, or to describe the teachings of Cobdenism as the "last word on human society." But this volume will at least show how study of economic conditions in relation to human nature as it is led him to advocate, with a fervour strengthened by his characteristic aversion to compromise in opinion, the widest extension of the principles of free exchange and free competition. He held that the incentives to production must continue to be either competition or coercion, whatever the forms of social or industrial organization which may be destined to prevail; and he did not share the belief of some modern leaders of opinion, that another system might be devised, by which men should be induced to surrender their personal liberty in freely exchanging their services, and be relieved of their responsibility for providing for themselves and their children, without their motives to exertion being thereby impaired.*

It would, I need hardly say, be a mistake to assume that the author was indisposed to recognize any limitations on the absolute freedom of the relations between labour and capital—limitations such as those imposed by the Factory Acts, and defensible on moral and humane and indirectly even on economic grounds.

* He sometimes quoted a memorable passage from Sir Henry Maine's "Popular Government," p. 52: "There are two sets of motives, and two only, by which the great bulk of the materials of human subsistence and comfort have hitherto been produced and reproduced. One has led to the cultivation of the Northern States of the American Union from the Atlantic to the Pacific. The other had a considerable share in bringing about the agricultural and industrial progress of the Southern States, and in old days it produced the wonderful prosperity of Peru under the Incas. One system is economical competition; the other consists in the daily task, perhaps fairly and kindly allotted, but enforced by the prison or the scourge. So far as we have any experience to teach us, we are driven to the conclusion that every society of men must adopt one system or the other, or it will pass through penury to starvation."

He would not have denied that the better organization of industry may in some instances be beneficially assisted by statute law, giving effect to previously existing changes in public sentiment. Nor is there anything in this book to discourage the philanthropic efforts of society to deal with the "residuum," and raise it if possible to the ranks of legitimate and self-supporting labour. But his general attitude was one of distrust towards restrictive and protective legislation. In his view, as is shewn in the chapter on "Unearned Increment," the interference of the State, now beginning to be so loudly invoked on behalf of the labouring classes, affords a parallel to the laws by which other classes when possessed of political power have endeavoured to secure exclusive privileges for themselves. Socialism, corn laws, and protective tariffs all alike mean privilege and compulsion. It was to freedom and equal rights that he looked as the only means of ensuring the supreme object of the largest possible production, an increasing share of which, as the facts prove beyond all controversy, go under such a system to labour. But I cannot do better than quote here the words * which my father has himself used in this connection:—

"Wherever it is found that the accumulating wealth of a country is not accompanied by a progressive augmentation of that portion of the annual product which falls to the share of the direct producers, or working classes, it is a sure sign that the economic mechanism of the nation is disordered, and that imperious social laws have been infringed.

* From a preface to a Cobden Club republication of a report on the revenues of the United States of America by the Hon. David A. Wells. 1870.

" In onè of the last letters which Bastiat wrote to Cobden, he quotes the following remarkable passage from an essay by M. de Fontenay :—

"' *Le capital est le signe caractéristique et la mesure du progrès ; il en est le véhicule nécessaire et unique. Sa mission spéciale est de servir de transition de la valeur à la gratuité. Par conséquent, au lieu de peser sur le prix naturel, son rôle constant est de l'abaisser sans cesse.*'

" Upon this observation, Bastiat emphatically says that it 'comprehends and resumes the most fruitful of the economic phenomena' which he had spent his life in investigating, and adds—

"' En elle est le gage d'une réconciliation inévitable entre les classes propriétaires et prolétaires. Puisque ce point de vue de l'ordre social n'est pas tombé, puisqu'il a été aperçu par d'autres qui l'exposeront à tous les yeux mieux que je ne pourrais faire, je n'ai pas tout à fait perdu mon temps, et je puis chanter, avec un peu moins de repugnance, mon "*Nunc Dimittis*."'

" These words of the great economist cannot be too often remembered and repeated. To enable capital to fulfil this mission, to provide, as far as possible, that its growing accretions shall act directly on the productive labour of the world by removing all national and international restrictions on production and exchange, and that the joint results of capital and labour shall thus be distributed in more just proportions between those whose services have contributed to them, is the most urgent and the most important task to which the statesmen of all countries can address themselves.

" But the one indispensable condition of this result is international co-operation. No nation, however rich in resources, or strong in political power, can ever accomplish the task, unaided and alone. The causes which prevent the international circulation of capital are diminishing year by year. It is essential that the causes which obstruct the free exchange of the products of labour should equally disappear. The great law of the mutual dependence of nations is asserting its claims to allegiance, and enforcing obedience under intolerable penalties."

Sir Louis Mallet was discouraged in later years by the apparent progress of tendencies opposed to all the principles he had advocated—tendencies which in 1869 and 1873 he had foreseen and combated with every hope of success. It is, indeed, becoming clear that, if we are not, as Mr. Goldwin Smith anticipates,* to witness the "renewed ascendency in fiscal"—and it may be added, in social—"legislation of the blind cupidity of the Dark Ages," the free trade battle will have to be fought over again in presence of an electorate very different from that appealed to by Peel and Cobden. It is too often assumed that the free trade bid for the solution of social problems has failed ; and there is a tendency due to obvious causes to give prominence to the worst features of our social system, —the circumstances attendant on local congestion in the great cities,—and to overlook the astonishing record of the progress of the last half-century. Free-traders are therefore compelled to repeat that this record, which is attested by all economists and statisticians, is one which may well be weighed against socialistic counsels of perfection or of despair. As Professor Marshall has stated it, "the average money income of the people has more than doubled, while the price of almost all important commodities except

* See his article in *Macmillan's Magazine* for September, 1890, on the American Tariff.

animal food and house-room has fallen by one-half, χ
or even further." Mr. Giffen has given it as his
opinion that the "poor have had almost all the benefit
of the great material advances of the last fifty years," χ
and has summed up the case by saying that what has
happened to the working classes in Great Britain "is
not so much what may be called an improvement,
as a revolution of the most remarkable description."
Finally, Mr. David A. Wells concludes a powerful
passage,* pointing out the reality of this advance, and
the difficulties in spite of which it has been made, by
asking if it is reasonable to expect that further progress
in this direction is to be arrested.

Surely "no" must be the answer, unless mistaken and reactionary ideals, against which the present
volume may in one aspect be considered a protest, gain
the upper hand in this country. That there is nothing
new in such fears, that complaints of the failure
of the free trade policy and "morbid cravings after
other agencies" were no less prevalent twenty years
ago, it is well to be reminded as we are by the admirable preface to the essay on Cobden; but it is less
encouraging to observe that progress in sound opinion

---

* From "Recent Economic Changes." New York: 1889. Mr. Wells' arguments, and, I may add, the considerations set forth by M. LeRoy-Beaulieu in his
"Répartition des Richesses," certainly cannot be met by mere imputations of
"shallow economic optimism." The well-known labours of Mr. Wells and Mr.
Atkinson are a standing proof that the free trade creed (to use that expression in
its widest sense) has a vigorous life in the United States, whatever may be the
case in this country. The statistical investigations of the last-named economist
(see, for instance, his work on the "Industrial Progress of the Nation," published
during the last few months) also illustrate and confirm in the most remarkable
way, by means of the new facts drawn from American experience, the conclusions
enforced in this volume.

and reform has not made it impossible to meet these criticisms with the words which Sir Louis Mallet then used, certainly in no spirit of complacent optimism.

"Before accusing Economic Science and Free Exchange, I would ask whether, with our present laws as they affect our land, our currency, our fiscal and colonial systems, our foreign relations, and our military and naval administration, we may not rather trace our failure in civilization to a systematic and deliberate violation of their most imperious precepts? whether the success of what is called practical statesmanship is such as to justify its cynical contempt of principles? and whether it is wise to condemn and discredit as ineffectual a policy which has never yet been tried."

It will be clear from the foregoing observations that a more personal account of my father's life, such as some of his friends may have looked for, does not fall within the scope of this book.* The publication of a volume dealing with the opinions with which his name is associated seemed to me to be the most fitting tribute I could pay to the memory of one whose great characteristic was his whole-hearted devotion to public interests. Inadequate such a record will doubtless appear to those who remember the peculiar power and charm of my father's conversation, still more to those whose happiness and privilege it was to live in constant and affectionate intercourse with him. But I believe it would be impossible for any one to read

---

* It may at some future time seem possible and desirable to print a selection from my father's letters, which certainly contain some of his most valuable and interesting work, and I should be very grateful if any of his friends who may possess letters would communicate with me.—B. M.

these papers without gaining some idea of the qualities of mind and character which so deeply impressed all who were brought into contact with him, whether in official or in private life.

BERNARD MALLET.

November, 1890.

CONTENTS.

PART I.

		PAGE
I.	THE POLITICAL OPINIONS OF RICHARD COBDEN	3
II.	THE POLICY OF COMMERCIAL TREATIES ...	72
III.	FREE TRADE AND FREE ENTERPRISE	95
IV.	NOTE ON STATE RAILWAYS...	104
V.	EGYPT. A LETTER TO M. DE LAVELEYE ...	109
VI.	RECIPROCITY. A LETTER TO MR. T. B. POTTER, M.P.	122
VII.	A STATEMENT OF BIMETALLIC THEORY	150
VIII.	THE NATIONAL INCOME AND TAXATION ...	154

PART II.

THE LAW OF VALUE AND THE THEORY OF THE UNEARNED INCREMENT.

CHAPTER		PAGE
I.	THE SHATTERED SCIENCE	225
II.	VALUE	245
III.	NATURAL MONOPOLIES	272
IV.	THE UNEARNED INCREMENT	298

PART I.

B

THE POLITICAL OPINIONS OF RICHARD COBDEN.

(PUBLISHED IN 1869.)

PREFACE.

THE following paper was written for the *North British Review* in 1867, and has been reprinted, with a few alterations, by permission of the editor, at the request of the Committee of the Cobden Club.

I originally wrote it with reluctance, because I was conscious of my inability to do justice to its subject, but I thought that, as a contribution towards a better understanding of Cobden's political character, it might serve a useful purpose; and in the same hope I have consented to reprint it now.

I have done so the more readily, because it is impossible not to feel that Cobden's principles are even now constantly misrepresented; and are, in some directions, losing their hold on the public mind of England.

Is it in ignorance, or in irony, that the charge of aiming at nothing more than mere material prosperity

is so often brought against the one statesman who
vindicated with a peculiar wisdom the morality of
Economic Science; in other words, the veiled but
eternal harmony between material progress and the
highest civilization of our race?

Is it in deeper ignorance, or in more subtle irony,
that one whose whole life was an unceasing protest
against a narrow and selfish patriotism, and who will
take his place in history as the "International Man,"
has been identified with the policy which, under the
name of "non-intervention," confounds, in a coarse
and common condemnation, political meddling and
international co-operation?

I have said that Cobden's principles are in some
directions losing their hold on the public mind. This
is especially the case with respect to what we call
"Free Trade;" which, between its so-called friends
and its enemies, is drifting more and more into irre-
trievable confusion as a principle of imperial policy.

In its domestic aspect "Free Trade," or rather
"Free Exchange," has been forgotten in the chorus
of congratulation at the downfall of protection in its
grossest form; and in our Foreign policy, while dis-
carding reciprocity of restrictions, we have failed
to appreciate the importance of the reciprocity of
freedom.

We have obtained enough Free Trade to enable
our upper and middle classes to acquire more wealth
than, with their present education, they can either
employ wisely or spend innocently; and to stimu-

'late unproductive consumption in vulgar luxury and wasteful charity; but we have not obtained enough Free Trade to feed and clothe and house our people, or to inspire confidence in other countries, and to establish those international relations without which all hope of internal progress is a foolish and idle dream.

It is painful to perceive the inferiority of the political utterances of our day on social and economic questions, to those of the Anti-Corn-Law League, in grasp of principles, in command of facts, and, above all, in moral feeling.

The men who took part in the labours of the League dwell naturally more on that which they have done, than on that which we have to do; and a generation has succeeded to a large share in our political life, which consults for the solution of our social problems far other oracles than those which inspired Cobden.

The sinister reaction set in motion by the Crimean War, fostered by the wars in China, and culminating in the Parliament of 1857, has gone far to neutralize the impulse given to our productive forces by the partial liberation of our trade, and left us with increased wealth indeed, but with a distribution of it more unequal and more unnatural than before, and with a large population, whose chronic wretchedness and degradation is a standing reproach to our civilization, and a sullen protest against our laws. And while the cry of suffering multitudes is the morning and the evening sacrifice of our proudest cities, our Government and our people alike are calling on each other helplessly in turn for a policy of deliverance.

Can we wonder, then, that those who have been taught to believe that they are living under a Free Trade dispensation, and who have never taken the pains to compare the doctrines of its apostles with the practice of our lawgivers, should accuse it of disastrous failure ; and that while on one hand we are advised to desist from further action till, by the free play of consciousness, we have discovered an intelligible law of things ; on the other, we are urged to tamper with the laws, and assail the rights of labour and of property, and to revive discarded systems which are only innocent so long as they are impossible ?

But before accusing Economic Science and Free Exchange, I would ask whether, with our present laws as they affect our land, our currency, our fiscal and colonial systems, our foreign relations, and our military and naval administration, we may not rather trace our failure in civilization to a systematic and deliberate violation of their most imperious precepts ? whether the success of what is called practical statesmanship is such as to justify its cynical contempt of principles ? and whether it is wise to condemn and discredit as ineffectual a policy which has never yet been tried ?

It is because I believe that the work of Governments lies in providing for the full and undisturbed action of the forces of freedom, instead of interfering themselves with their operation ; and that our social disorders can only be remedied by pressing along the lines of progress, laid for us by Cobden and the League ; that I view with pain and fear the morbid craving of our time after other agencies, in most of which may be detected, disguise it as we may, the germ of Communism, a fatal poison, tainting at their common source two of the most sacred springs of social life, personal liberty and personal responsibility.

L. M.

June, 1869.

THE POLITICAL OPINIONS OF RICHARD COBDEN.

THE time has not yet arrived for writing Cobden's life.

The great political struggles in which he engaged are still too fresh in the memory of the present generation, to admit of a faithful record of his political career, without including much which affects too closely the characters of public men still on the scene, or but recently removed from it ; and of the last great achievement of his life, and his solitary official act, the Commercial Treaty with France, it is impossible yet to speak freely.

But it is on this account only the more important,— and especially at a time when upon the conduct and intelligence of the Liberal party in this country it depends, whether the years before us are to bring with them a repetition of the inconsistencies and hesitations which have too often deformed and paralyzed our recent course, or are to be a fruitful and brilliant period of rational and consistent progress, —that the policy of which Cobden was the foremost representative, should at least be thoroughly understood and widely known.

It is therefore with a peculiar satisfaction that we

hail the work * before us, and we trust that it may be shortly followed by a republication of his principal speeches, both in and out of Parliament, so far as these can be collected, and if possible by a selection of his letters, on the great practical questions of the day.

In bringing together, in a connected form, these political essays, written on various subjects, on different occasions, and at wide intervals of time, but unsurpassed in cogency of reasoning, and in their truthful and temperate spirit, Mrs. Cobden has rendered a great service both to her husband's memory and to the rising generation of Englishmen.

Presented originally to the public in the ephemeral form of pamphlets, thrown out in sharp opposition to the prevailing passions and prejudices of the hour, and systematically depreciated as they were by the organs of public opinion which guide the majority of our upper classes, we suspect that they are well-nigh forgotten by the elder, and little known to the younger men among us. Yet do these scattered records of Mr. Cobden's thoughts contain a body of political doctrine more original, more profound, and more consistent, than is to be found in the spoken or written utterances of any other English statesman of our time, and we commend them to the earnest study and consideration of all who aspire to exert an influence on the future government of our country.

* "The Political Writings of Richard Cobden," published by Ridgway (2 vols.), which formed the subject of the article in the *North British Review* referred to in the text.

Whatever may be thought of his political character, it will be admitted that no man has made a deeper impression on the policy of this country during the last thirty years than Richard Cobden.

This will, we believe, be acknowledged by many of his countrymen, who would be slow to allow that the impression thus made had been for good, and who still regard him with open aversion or concealed suspicion, as one of the foremost and most powerful advocates of changes in our system of government, designed, as they believe and fear, to affect the security of vested interests, which they have been in the habit of identifying with the greatness and welfare of the State. But it cannot, we think, be denied even now that, in spite of the resistance of class interests, and of the avowed or tacit opposition of the great political parties, our national policy has been gravitating more and more in the direction of his views, and that, so far at least, whatever progress has been made in the national prosperity has been principally due to the steps which have been taken in fulfilment of his principles.

The false judgment so commonly passed upon this statesman is to be traced, we believe, in a great measure to that which constitutes his great and his distinguishing merit, viz. his steady adherence to general principles, and his consequent freedom from class and party views, and his indifference to the popular clamour of the hour, which in turn brought him into collision with all classes and with all parties, and, on some memorable occasions, with the body of the people themselves.

It is thus that he has been constantly charged with narrowness, and with hostility to the institutions of his country, too often confounded with its conservative forces, and cherished as such by many who are entitled to our respect, as well as by the ignorant and selfish ; but it will be found that the charge is usually brought on the part of some class whose special interests he denounced or thwarted, or on the part of the nation at large, when the assumed national interest has been opposed to the larger interest of humanity. He has been accused of want of patriotism and indifference to the national honour and greatness, when, on the contrary, a deeper examination of his views will show, we think, that he was one of the few leading statesmen of our time who have exhibited a real practical faith in the future of England.

The public estimate, however, of this political leader has undergone, and is undergoing, a very remarkable change ; and it is in the hope of aiding in a better understanding of principles which, from their soundness and close logical coherence, appear to us to afford the only consistent and intelligible ground for the policy of the Liberal party, that the following pages are written.

Mr. Cobden's political character was the result of a rare and fortunate combination of personal qualities and of external circumstances.

Sprung from the agricultural class, and bred up (to

use his own expression) "amidst the pastoral charms of Southern England," imbued with so strong an attachment to the pursuits of his forefathers, that, as he says himself, in the volumes before us, " had we the casting of the *rôle* of all the actors on this world's stage, we do not think that we should suffer a cotton-mill or manufactory to have a place in it ; " trained in a large commercial house in London, and subsequently conducting on his own account a print manufactory in Lancashire, Mr. Cobden possessed the peculiar advantage of a thorough acquaintance and sympathy with the three great forms of industrial life in England. Nor were the experiences of his public career less rich and varied than those of his private life.

The first great political question in which he bore a conspicuous part, the Anti-Corn Law agitation, and his consequent connection with the powerful producing class, which, by a fortunate coincidence of interest with that of the people at large, originated and led this great and successful struggle, gave him a thorough insight into this important element of our body-politic, in all its strength and in all its weakness ; his knowledge of other countries—the result of keen personal observation, and much travel both in Europe and America, his intimate relations with some of their best and most enlightened men, as well as with their leading politicians, and the moderating and restraining influences of twenty years of Parliamentary life, during which he conciliated the respect and esteem even of his strongest opponents, combined with the entire absence in his case of all sectarian influences and prejudices,—gave to his opinions a comprehensive and catholic character, which is perhaps the rarest of all the attributes of English statesmanship.

Mr. Cobden entered Parliament, not, as is the fate of most of our public men, to support a party, to play for office, or to educate himself for professional statesmanship, still less to gratify personal vanity or to acquire social importance, but as the representative of distinct principles, and of a great cause.

Mr. Cobden belonged to the school of political thinkers who believe in the perfect harmony of moral and economical laws, and that in proportion as these are recognized, understood, and obeyed by nations, will be their advance in all that constitutes civilization.

He believed that the interests of the individual, the interests of the nation, and the interests of all nations are identical ; and that these several interests are all in entire and necessary concordance with the highest interests of morality. With this belief, an economic truth acquired with him the dignity and vitality of a moral law, and, instead of remaining a barren doctrine of the intellect, became a living force, to move the hearts and consciences of men. It is to a want of a clear conception of this great harmony between the moral and economic law, or to a disbelief in its existence, that are to be traced some of the most pernicious errors of modern times, and the lamentable condition of Europe at the present moment.

We believe that the main cause of the hopeless
failure of the great French Revolution, in the creation
and consolidation of free institutions in Europe, was
the absence, on the part of its leading spirits, of all
sound knowledge of the order of facts upon which
economic science rests, and the prevalence of false
ideas of government, derived from classical antiquity.

Rousseau, who exercised a greater influence in
bringing about the Revolution than any other man,
and after him Mirabeau and Robespierre, the two
great figures which represent and personify that
mighty upheaval of society, were all fundamentally
wrong in their conception of the right of property.
This, instead of regarding as a right preceding all
law, and lying at the root of all social existence, they
considered simply as a creation of the law, which
itself again derived its rights from a social compact,
opposed in many respects to the natural rights of
man.   Society was thus made to rest upon the quick-
sand of human invention, instead of being fixed on
the rock of God's providence ; and law was made the
source, instead of the guardian, of personal liberty and
of private property.

Hence the disastrous shipwreck of a great cause,
the follies and the crimes, the wild theories, the
barren experiments, and the inevitable reaction.   The
principle invoked, the State, was stronger than those
who appealed to it, and swallowed them up in a
military despotism.

This false direction of ideas survived the Restora-

tion, and when, after 1830, the intellect of France
again addressed itself to social questions, it was with
the same result. Saint Simon, Fourrier, Louis Blanc,
and Proudhon are there to attest the deep-rooted
perversion of thought which has hitherto made all
free government impossible in France, and brought
upon her again, for the second time, the stern hand of
a military ruler, who, wiser than his uncle, while setting aside for a time other forms of liberty in France,
has had the sagacity to perceive that, by entering
upon even a partial and tentative course of material
reform, he could evoke forces which have hitherto
been strong enough to maintain him on his vantage-
ground, against all the political parties opposed to
him, dynastic and socialist, whose common hatred to
him has been rendered impotent by the only other
common bond between them, viz. their still deeper
hatred of some of the most sacred rights of the human
race—the rights of labour and of property. And even
to this day what do we see ? In spite of the terrible
experience of nearly a hundred years of failure, French
so-called liberal leaders still ranged on the side of
industrial monopoly and commercial privilege, and
while clamouring for constitutional freedom, proving
in the same breath their incapacity for using it, by
denouncing that in which, at all events, the Emperor
is entitled to the sympathy of the friends of progress,
—his commercial policy. Until the bourgeois class in
Europe has learnt that no country can be free until
the rights of its people are secured by free exchange,

they will have to choose between the rival alternations
of autocratic and socialistic misrule.*

The great founder of the English school of political
economy, who had witnessed himself in France the disorders which preceded the Revolution, and speculated
on their causes, viewed them from another side. He
instinctively perceived that, as all human society must
rest upon a material foundation, it was to the laws of
material progress that inquiry must be first directed,
and that, before and beneath all systems of government and all schemes of public morality, there must
lie the science of the "wealth of nations." To the
investigation of this science Adam Smith devoted
those years of patient and conscientious thought, to
which we owe the treatise which has made his name
immortal, and which, in spite of much that has been
added and much that has been taken from it since,
remains as a great storehouse of knowledge to the
students of economic laws.

It is easy, however, to trace the habitual connection
in the mind of Smith, between the dry facts of science
and the great social laws which alone give them life
and meaning, and a belief in the steady natural gravi-
tation of all the interests of our race towards order
and moral progress.

The school of English economists who succeeded
him appear to us to have too much lost sight of this

* It is interesting to see, from the remarks in Part II. Chap. I., how the progress of events and of opinion in France and England caused the writer to change
his opinion as to the comparative social stability of the two countries.—ED.

necessary connection, and to have dwelt too exclusively on the phenomena of economic facts, as distinct and separate from their correlative moral consequences. To this cause, as well as to their partial and often inaccurate observation of those phenomena, we attribute the absence of adequate political results which has attended their teaching, the repugnance which their doctrines have too often excited in generous and ardent natures, and the consequent discredit of a science indispensable to the progress and prosperity of nations, and destined, perhaps more than any other branch of human knowledge, to reconcile the ways of God to man.

The mission of man in this world is to possess the earth and subdue it, and for this purpose to summon to his aid, and bring under his control, the external forces of nature. This task, hard and ungrateful at first, becomes lighter as it proceeds. Every natural force successively subdued to man's uses adds to the stock of gratuitous services which are the common possession of the race, and when the rights of property and labour are thoroughly established by universal freedom, and the services of man have thus secured their just remuneration, the inequalities which prevail in the conditions of human life, so far as they are the result of artificial, and not of natural, causes, will diminish and disappear more and more, till even the lowest classes in the social scale will be raised to a level of well-being hitherto unknown and unimagined.

The first great law of humanity is labour. "By

c

the sweat of thy brow shalt thou eat thy bread."
From this there is no escape. The burden will be
lightened, and reduced to a minimum, inconceivable
to us at present, as the forces of nature are brought by
science and industry more under the control of man;
and it may be shifted, as it is, from the whole to a part
of society, but the law remains.

It is this law, then, the law of labour, which lies at
the root of all human life. Upon this foundation rests
the whole fabric of society, religion, morals, science,
art, literature—all that adorns or exalts existence.
But if the law of labour is thus paramount and sovereign, it follows that its rights are sacred, and that
there can be no permanent security for any society in
which these are not protected. The rights of labour
involve and comprehend the right of personal liberty,
and the right of property. The first implies the free
use of each man's powers and faculties; the second,
an inalienable title to the products of his labour, in use
or in exchange.

It is to the violation of the rights of labour and of
property, thus identified, in all the various forms of
human oppression and injustice, by force or by fraud,
in defiance of law or in the name of law, that is to be
traced the greatest part of the disorders and sufferings
which have desolated humanity, and the unnecessary
and unnatural inequalities in the conditions of men.

It is to the assertion of these rights, and to the
gradual ascendency of the opposing and equalizing
principles of justice and freedom, that the coming

generations alone can look for a future which shall be better than the past.

"Il n'y a que deux moyens," says Bastiat, "de se procurer les choses nécessaires à l'embellissement, et au perfectionnement de la vie,—la production et la spoliation." And again, " Propriété et spoliation, sœurs nées du même pére, Génie du Bien, et Génie du Mal, Salut et Fléau de la Société, Puissances qui se disputent depuis le commencement, l'empire et les destinées du monde."

These truths are of comparatively recent acceptance even in theory among us, and in practice still are far indeed from being applied. Such, moreover, is the confusion of thought, engendered by historical association, political prejudice, and class interest, that many of the forms of spoliation are hardly recognized when disguised in the garb of a British institution, a party principle, or a vested right ; in which artificial costume they still impose on the credulity of many of our countrymen.

It is true that war is generally admitted to be an evil, and slavery to be a wrong ; that the Reformation has dealt a heavy blow at theocracy, and Free Trade at monopoly.

But the spirit of war is still fostered and stimulated, by false ideas of national honour, patriotism, and policy, and to the art of war we still devote our mightiest efforts, and consecrate our costliest sacrifices. The grosser forms of slavery have indeed disappeared, but its taint is still to be traced in some of our

institutions, and in our feeling towards subject races ;
while our Reformed Church, with its temporalities,
and its exclusive pretensions and privileges, is still
too often the enemy of the foundation of all freedom,
liberty of thought.

The last, and perhaps the most insidious, of the
leading forms of "spoliation," commercial monopoly,
though driven from its strongholds, and expelled from
our national creed, is still regarded by many among
us with secret favour, and by most of us rather as a
political error than as a moral wrong.

It was to a struggle with this last great evil that
Cobden devoted his life, and it is with the most decisive victory ever achieved in this field of conflict that
his name and fame will be always identified ; but it is
significant and interesting to know that, in selecting his
work in life, it was to "Education," and not to "Free
Trade," that his thoughts were first directed.

Two reasons decided him to prefer the latter as
the object of his efforts :— *Firstly*, his conviction
(referred to above) that the material prosperity of
nations is the only foundation of all progress, and that
if this were once secured the rest would follow.
Secondly, his consciousness that no direct attempt to
obtain a system of national education which deserved
the name, could lead to any clear result in the life of
his own generation, and that, measured with those at
his command, imposing as were the forces of resistance
arrayed against him on the question of Free Trade,
they were less formidable than those which would be

brought to bear against a measure which united in a common hostility the Established and the Dissenting Churches.

It was Cobden's fate or fortune to find himself, in taking up the cause of Free Trade, in the presence of one of the worst laws which the selfishness or folly of Governments have ever imposed on the weakness or ignorance of a people.

When the soil of a country is appropriated, the only means whereby an increasing population can limit the encroachments of the proprietors, is by working for foreign markets. Such a population has only its labour to give in exchange for its requirements, and, if this labour is constantly increasing, while the produce of the soil is·stationary, more of the first will steadily and progressively be demanded, for less of the last.

This will be manifested by a fall of wages, which is, as has been well observed, the greatest of misfortunes when it is due to natural causes—the greatest of crimes when it is caused by the law.

The Corn Law was the fitting sequel to the French war. The ruling classes in England had seized on the reaction of feeling created by the excesses of the French Revolution, to conceal the meaning of that event, and to discredit the principles of popular sovereignty which it asserted. They had before them a people impoverished and degraded by the waste of blood and treasure in which years of war had involved their country ; and seeing the prospect before them, which the peace had opened, of a fall in the prices of agricultural produce, under the beneficent operation of the. great laws of exchange, they resorted to the device of prolonging by Act of Parliament the artificial scarcity created by the war, and of thus preserving to the landed interest the profits which had been gained at the expense of the nation.

It is thus that, as the forces of progress are invariably found to act and react on each other, the forces of resistance and of evil will ever be side by side, and that as protection, which means the isolation of nations, tends both by its direct and indirect effects to war, so war again engenders and perpetuates the spirit of protection. Free Trade, or, as Cobden called it, the International Law of the Almighty, which means the interdependence of nations, must bring with it the surest guarantee of peace, and peace inevitably leads to freer and freer commercial intercourse; and therefore, while there is no sadder page in the modern history of England than that which records the adoption of this law by the British Parliament, there is, to our minds, none more bright with the promise of future good than that on which was written, after thirty years of unjust and unnecessary suffering, its unconditional repeal.

But as the intellect and conscience of the country had failed so long to recognize the widespread evils of this pernicious law, and the fatal principles which lay at its roots, so did they now most dimly and imperfectly apprehend the scope and consequences of its abolition.

It was called the repeal of a law ; admitted to be the removal of an intolerable wrong; but we doubt whether in this country, except by a few gifted and far-seeing leaders of this great campaign, it was foreseen that it was an act which involved, in its certain results, a reversal of the whole policy of England.

This was, however, clear enough to enlightened observers in other countries. By one of those rare coincidences which sometimes exercise so powerful an influence on human affairs, it happened, that while Cobden in England was bringing to bear on the great practical questions of his time and country the principles of high morality and sound economy which had been hitherto too little considered in connection with each other, Frederic Bastiat was conceiving and maturing in France the system of political philosophy which has since been given to the world, and which still remains the best and most complete exposition of the views of which Cobden was the great representative.

It appears to us that these two men were necessary to each other. Without Cobden, Bastiat would have lost the powerful stimulant of practical example, and the wide range of facts which the movement in England supplied, and from which he drew much of his inspiration. Without Bastiat, Cobden's policy would not have been elaborated into a system, and, beyond his own immediate coadjutors and disciples, would probably have been most imperfectly understood on the Continent of Europe.

More than this, who can say what may not have
been the effect on the minds of both these men, of
the interchange of thoughts and opinions which freely
passed between them ?

In his brilliant history of the Anti-Corn-Law
League, "Cobden et la Ligue," Bastiat thus describes
the movement of which England was the theatre
during that memorable struggle :—

"I have endeavoured to state with all exactness the question which is being agitated in England. I have described
the field of battle, the greatness of the interests which are
there being discussed, the opposing forces, and the consequences of victory. I have shown, I believe, that though
the heat of the contest may seem to be concentrated on
questions of taxation, of custom-houses, of cereals, of sugar,
it is, in point of fact, a question between monopoly and liberty,
aristocracy and democracy—a question of equality or inequality in the distribution of the general well-being. The
question at issue is to know whether legislative power and
political influence shall remain in the hands of the men of
rapine, or in those of the men of toil ; that is, whether they
shall continue to embroil the world in troubles and deeds of
violence, or sow the seeds of concord, of union, of justice, and
of peace.

"What would be thought of the historian who could
believe that armed Europe, at the beginning of this century,
performed, under the leadership of the most able generals, so
many feats of strategy for the sole purpose of determining
who should possess the narrow fields that were the scenes of
the battles of Austerlitz or of Wagram ? The fate of dynasties
and empires depended on those struggles. But the triumphs
of force may be ephemeral ; it is not so with the triumphs
of opinion. And when we see the whole of a great people,
whose influence on the world is undoubted, impregnate itself

with the doctrines of justice and truth ; when we see it repel
the false ideas of supremacy which have so long rendered it
dangerous to nations ; when we see it ready to seize the
political ascendant from the hands of a greedy and turbulent
oligarchy,—let us beware of believing, even when its first
efforts seem to bear upon economic questions, that greater
and nobler interests are not engaged in the struggle. For if,
in the midst 'of many lessons of iniquity, many instances of
national perversity, England, this imperceptible point of our
globe, has seen so many great and useful ideas take root
upon her soil,—if she was the cradle of the press, of trial by
jury, of a representative system, of the abolition of slavery, in
spite of the opposition of a powerful and pitiless oligarchy,—
what may not the world expect from this same England
when all her moral, social, and political power shall have
passed, by a slow and difficult revolution, into the hands of
democracy—a revolution peacefully accomplished in the
minds of men under the leadership of an association which
embraces in its bosom so many men whose high intellectual
power and unblemished character shed so much glory on
their country, and on the century in which they live ? Such
a revolution is no simple event, no accident, no catastrophe
due to an irresistible but evanescent enthusiasm. It is, if I
may use the expression, a slow social cataclysm, changing all
the conditions of life and of society, the sphere in which it
lives and breathes. It is justice possessing herself of power ;
good sense of authority. It is the general weal, the weal of
the people, of the masses, of the small and of the great, of the
strong and of the weak, becoming the law of political action.
It is the disappearance behind the scene of privilege, abuse,
and caste-feeling, not by a palace-revolution or a street-rising,
but by the progressive and general appreciation of the rights
and duties of man. In a word, it is the triumph of human
liberty ; it is the death of monopoly, that Proteus of a
thousand forms, now conqueror, now slave-owner ; at one
time lover of theocracy and feudalism, at another time assum-

ing an industrial, a commercial, a financial, and even a philanthropic shape. Whatever disguise it might borrow, it could no longer bear the eye of public opinion, which has learned to detect it under the scarlet uniform or under the black gown, under the planter's jacket and the noble peer's embroidered robe. Liberty for all! for every man a just and natural remuneration for his labour! for every man a just and natural avenue to equality in proportion to his energy, his intelligence, his prudence, and his morality! Free Trade with all the world! Peace with all the world! No more subjugation of colonies, no more army, no more navy, than is necessary for the maintenance of national independence! A radical distinction between that which is and that which is not the mission of government and law; political association reduced to guarantee each man his liberty and safety against all unjust aggressions, whether from without or from within; equal taxation, for the purpose of properly paying the men charged with this mission, and not to serve as a mask under the name of outlets for trade (*débouchés*), for outward usurpation, and, under the name of *protection*, for the mutual robbery of classes. Such is the real issue in England, though the field of battle may be confined to a custom-house question. But this question involves slavery in its modern form; for as Mr. Gibson, a member of the League, has said in Parliament, ' To get possession of men that we may make them work for our own profit, or to take possession of the fruits of their labour, is equally and always slavery; there is no difference but in the degree.' "

This passage, all due allowance made for the tendency to brilliant generalization which Bastiat shared with so many of his gifted countrymen, remains on the whole a most powerful, condensed, and accurate analysis of the great principles involved in the political conflict then passing in England, and is a testimony to the rare insight and sagacity of the writer. It also affords a striking illustration of the power which a clear and firm grasp of principles gives to the political student, in guiding his speculations on the most complicated problems which society presents.

The system of which the Corn Laws were the corner-stone, traced to its source, rested on the principle of spoliation, and on the foundation of force.

That which was inaugurated by the overthrow of that law, rested on the principle of freedom, and on the foundation of justice.

Monopoly of trade, involving, as it must, the violation of rights of property and of labour, both in the internal and external relations of a State, and implying, when carried to its logical consequences, national isolation, contains within itself the germs of inevitable stagnation and decay. To avoid these results, it is necessary that a Government which maintains it should resort to all the expedients of force and fraud, —to conquest, colonial aggrandizement, maritime supremacy, foreign alliances, reciprocity treaties, and communism in the shape of poor-laws,—and should perpetually appeal to the worst and most contemptible passions of its people, to national pride, to false patriotism, to jealousy, to fear, and to selfishness, in order to keep alive its prestige and to conceal its rottenness.

We are far from imputing the marvellous skill which the ruling classes in England displayed in the use of these expedients to a conscious and deliberate policy. We know that good and able men, and an honest though misguided patriotism, have been too often the blind instruments of the retributive justice which always avenges the violation of moral principles; but there was a point beyond which even these expedients would not suffice to arrest the national decay, and with a debt of £800,000,000, an impoverished starving people, the universal distrust, and the avowed or concealed hostility of foreign nations, who had imitated our policy too closely, while growing communities of our own blood, with boundless material resources and free institutions, were outstripping us in the race of progress, and making the future competition of force impossible, a state of things had been engendered which called for prompt and vigorous remedy.

To Cobden, and his colleagues of the League, belongs the merit of having traced the disease to its source, of having stayed the progress of the poison which was slowly, but surely, undermining our national greatness, and of changing the current of English policy.

Mr. Bright has recently told us the occasion, and the manner, of Cobden's invitation to him to join him in this beneficent work.

At a moment of severe domestic calamity, Cobden called on him and said, " Do not allow this grief, great as it is, to weigh you down too much. There are at this moment, in thousands of homes of this country, wives and children who are dying of hunger, of hunger made by the laws; if you will come along with me, we will never rest until we have got rid of the Corn Laws." The appeal was not made in vain, and we know with what results.

By the repeal of the Corn Laws, the false idea of isolated progress was for ever dispelled, our foreign trade became a condition of our existence, and the great law of international co-operation assumed its rightful place as the animating principle of our future course.

But though the edifice of protection was shaken at the base, and the fabric irrevocably doomed to destruction, the work was only begun ; the ideas which the system had created had taken too deep root in the minds of the governing classes, and the forces of reaction were still too powerful, to allow of speedy or logical progress.

The gradual breaking-up of the protective system after the repeal of the Corn Laws was a work which must in any case have proceeded, under the pressure of the irresistible force of circumstances ; but we think that justice has never been done to the Government of Lord John Russell, and his colleagues Lord Grey and Mr. Labouchere, in this respect.

The equalization of the Sugar Duties, the repeal of the Navigation Laws, the reform of our "Colonial System," were all accomplished by this Administration, and few indeed have been the Governments of England which can point to such substantial services as these in the cause of progress. This course of useful domestic reform was, however, rudely interrupted by one of those events which ought to teach us the hopelessness of all permanent progress by

isolated action, and the absolute necessity of always
considering our position as a member of the comity
of nations. The Crimean War brought once more
into life and activity all the elements of the national
character, the most opposed to the silent and beneficent forces of moral and material progress, fatally
arrested the agencies of peace which the Anti-Corn-
Law League had set in motion, and has gone far to
deprive us of the fruits of the great reforms which
those agencies had effected. In looking back, it is
impossible not to feel how different might have been
our recent history, but for the mysterious dispensation, under which one great Minister died too soon,
while another ruled too long, and which removed
from us, at a time when his influence was too much
needed, the wise Prince who had, we believe, learned
to value Cobden, as Cobden had learned, we know, to
respect and appreciate him.

We all remember the long parliamentary duel
between Peel and Cobden, by which the great
struggle of the two contending principles of privilege
and freedom was brought to a final issue; the impres-
sive advocacy and the imposing fallacies of the powerful Minister; "the unadorned eloquence" and the
pitiless logic of the tribune of the people; and some
of us remember how Cobden, as he watched night after
night his great antagonist, writhing under his unanswerable arguments, saw by the working of his face, long
before his public avowal, that reason and conscience
had done their work, and that the victory was won.

But there was a moment when, unnerved by Drummond's tragical death, and stung by the intention which he attributed to Cobden of wishing to fasten upon him individually the responsibility of further resistance, he referred to some expressions in speeches at conferences of the League, in a way which made a deep impression at the time, and which Cobden could not easily forget. He lived, indeed, to make a full reparation, by the generous tribute which he paid to Cobden's services, in his memorable speech on quitting office for ever, in words which have often been repeated, and which it is well again to repeat—

"I said before, and I said truly, that, in proposing our measures of commercial policy, I had no wish to deprive others of the credit justly due to them. I must say with reference to honourable gentlemen opposite, as I say with reference to ourselves, that neither of us is the party which is justly entitled to the credit of them. There has been a combination of parties, generally opposed to each other, and that combination, and the influence of Government, have led to their ultimate success; but the name which ought to be associated with the success of those measures is not the name of the noble lord, the organ of the party of which he is the leader, nor is it mine. The name which ought to be, and will be, associated with the success of those measures, is the name of one who, acting, I believe, from pure and disinterested motives, and with untiring energy, made appeals to our reason, and has enforced those appeals with an eloquence the more to be admired because it was unaffected and unadorned,—the name which ought to be chiefly associated with the success of those measures is the name of Richard Cobden."

It was, however, we believe, the fact that, in spite of this public testimony, no private intercourse took place at that time between them, and that Peel retired from office, with the execration of his party, and the gratitude of his country, and Cobden entered on his international work, in mutual silence.

But later, when Cobden had returned to the House of Commons, and was standing one day behind the Speaker's chair, Peel rose from his seat, and came towards him, and said to him, holding out his hand, " Mr. Cobden, the time has come, I think, for you and me to be friends."

And still later, amidst the throng of anxious inquirers, who, in those long days of June, besieged Whitehall, and lingered round the doors of the dying statesman, there was no sincerer sorrower than the leader of the League.

The Royal Commission which, under Prince Albert's auspices, organized the first great Exhibition, had brought together at last, in a common and inter-national work, the three men who seem to us to have been eminently designed to co-operate for the public good, and we cannot doubt that, if the lives of Prince and Minister had been spared a few years longer, and Peel had returned to office in 1852, he would have received the cordial support of Cobden, either in or out of office. But this was not to be ; and in 1846, on the occasion of the repeal, to make Cobden Minister would have been an act of political justice and wisdom for which the times were not ripe, while to accept the subordinate office which was offered him, from men who had so recently, and so reluctantly, espoused his

views on Free Trade, and who so imperfectly apprehended or accepted its ulterior consequences, would
have fatally compromised his future usefulness.

He knew that there were several necessary measures which the general intelligence of the Liberal
party would immediately force upon the Parliament,
and his work at this moment lay in another direction.
He had been the chief instrument in giving the death-
blow to a mighty monopoly, in redressing a grievous
wrong, and in giving food to suffering millions at
home. His services as an Englishman being thus far
accomplished, he entered upon his mission as an
" international man."

He knew, and had measured accurately, the obstacles presented by the laws of other countries, often
the too faithful reflection of our own, to the fulfilment
of the grand aim of his life, the binding together of
the nations of the earth by the material bonds which
are the necessary and only preparation for their moral
union. These laws had raised around us innumerable
barriers to intercourse, and as many stumbling-blocks
in the way of peace.

In a tour through Europe, which often resembled a
triumphal progress, he was everywhere received with
interest and attention ; but the sudden recantation of
a policy, bound up with all the traditions of England,
was open to too much suspicion to inspire confidence,
and he was obliged to be content with sowing the
seeds of much which has since borne fruit, and with
inspiring new zeal and hope in the minds of the good

D

and enlightened men who, in each centre which he visited, were labouring in the cause.

No stronger proof can be afforded of the fundamental misconception of Cobden's political character which has prevailed in England than the judgments and criticisms which it was the custom to pass upon him with reference to the class of questions to which he addressed himself on his return to public life at home.

It seems to have been expected that he would have exclusively devoted himself to commercial questions, and when it was found that he proceeded to attack systematically our foreign policy, our system of government in India, our national expenditure, our military and naval administration, and our maritime laws, he was accused of going beyond his province, and discredited as an enthusiast incapable of dealing with the great mysteries of statecraft.

Those who used this language either knew too well, or not at all, that Cobden aimed at something very different and very much deeper than mere commercial reforms.

In each and all of these he took, as was natural, a sincere and consistent interest, but he knew, unless aided and consolidated by collateral measures, that, incalculable as would be the results to the wealth and prosperity of the country, they would not suffice to raise the lower classes of this country from their condition of moral and material degradation, and thus to rescue England from the reproach of failure in the highest ends of civilization, and to assure for her a permanent place in the front rank of nations.

It was, therefore, that, instead of entangling himself in the snares of office, and devoting his time to the details of practical legislation, he undertook the harder and more ungrateful, but far nobler office, of endeavouring to open the eyes of his countrymen to the necessity under which they lay of preparing for fundamental changes in many of the essential principles upon which our national policy had previously been conducted, in its three great divisions,—Foreign, Colonial, and Domestic.

Cobden saw clearly that, unless our system of government, in all its branches, were adapted to the altered conditions of our national existence, not only would our commercial reforms be shorn of their most valuable and complete results in the elevation of the masses of the people, but that we should also incur the risk of very serious dangers. Nothing is so fatal to success in the life of individuals or of nations as a confusion of principles in action.

Under the system of monopoly, it was logical enough to keep alive the chimæra of the balance of power, to seek, in foreign alliances and artificial combinations of force, the security which we could not hope to derive from legitimate and natural causes. In the government of our foreign possessions, it was logical to annex provinces and extend our empire, and by the display of force and the arts of diplomacy to coerce and despoil ; and for both these purposes, it was necessary to maintain costly and imposing forces by sea and land, and to cast on the people the burden of a proportionate taxation.

By means such as these we might have prolonged, for two or three generations, a false and hollow supremacy, and warded off for a while the inevitable doom which awaits all false principles.

But with a policy of free exchange, these things are not only inconsistent, they are dangerous.

They are inconsistent, because a policy of Free Trade rests on the principle that the interests of all nations lie in union and not in opposition; that co-operation and not competition, international interdependence and not national independence, are the highest end and object of civilization, and that, therefore, peace, and not war, is the natural and normal condition of civilized communities in their relation to each other.

They are dangerous, because a country which is unable to feed its own population without its foreign trade, and of whose prosperity, and even existence, peace is thus a necessary condition, cannot afford, without tremendous risks, to encounter the hazards of war with powerful enemies. If such a country trusts to the law of force, by that law will it be judged, and the result must be crushing failure, disaster, and ultimate defeat. There were those who clearly foresaw and apprehended this, and deprecated the repeal of the Corn Law accordingly, but who did not perceive that the alternative was an inadequate supply of food for a third of our population.

From this point of view, the "balance of power" can only be sought in the free development of the natural forces, whether of morality, intelligence, or material wealth, residing in the different countries of the earth, and the balance will always be held (to use the expression of William III., in his address to Parliament, quoted by Mr. Cobden in his paper on "Russia"), so far as any one State can pretend to do so, by the country which, in proportion to its powers, has economized its material resources to the highest point, and acquired the highest degree of moral ascendency by an honest and consistent allegiance to the laws of morality in its domestic policy and in its foreign relations.

The acquisition of colonies and territories, formerly required to afford new fields for monopoly, and defended on the plea that outlets were necessary for our trade; while our ports were closed to our nearest and richest neighbours, appeared in its true light as a waste of national influence, and a costly and useless perversion of national wealth, when all the countries of the earth became our customers, and England the metropolitan *entrepôt* of the world.

Large standing armies and navies, with their necessary accompaniment of heavy, and because heavy, unequal, and indirect taxation, are only rational in countries which are constantly liable to war, and cannot therefore be equally required under a system which relies on moral influence and on international justice, as under one which depends on force and monopoly.

To summon into existence a principle, which in all
human relations shall assert the right of property, in
mind and in matter, in thought and in labour, and
to secure this right on its only true foundation—the
universal rule of justice and freedom—is to evoke
a force which is destined to root up and destroy the
seeds of discord and division among men; to bind
up the nations of the earth in a vast federation of
interests; and to bring the disorders and conflicting
passions of society under the domain of law.

To promote all the agencies through which this
force can act, and to repress all those which oppose
its progress and neutralize its operation, and for this
purpose to analyze and expose to view these several
agencies, both in their causes and in their effects,
eternally acting and reacting on each other, was the
task which Cobden set himself to accomplish.

It was inevitable, with these objects in view, that
Cobden was often obliged to raise discussion upon
questions which, to ordinary minds, appeared somewhat chimerical, and to propose measures which were
in the nature of things premature; that he should
give to many the impression of wasting his strength
on matters which could not be brought to an immediate
practical issue, and in the agitation of which he could
not hope for direct success.

It will be found, however, that although there
often existed no possibility of realizing or applying his
projects at the time of their enunciation, these were
always themselves of an essentially practical character,

and inseparably connected with each other ; and that, although presented as occasion served, from time to time, and as the nature of his mission required, in a fragmentary and separate form, they each and all formed the component parts of a policy coherent and complete, and destined, we trust, to a gradual but ultimate fulfilment.

In characterizing this policy as complete, one exception must be made.

There was one branch of the national economy on which Cobden's views were not, at least, in his earlier years, in accordance with what appears to us sound scientific doctrine. We refer to the laws for the regulation of a paper currency.

In his evidence before the Committee of the House of Commons on Banks of Issue, 1840, he virtually adheres to the main principle of the Bank Act of 1844, and advocates the limitation of all paper issues unrepresented by a corresponding amount of gold to a fixed amount issuable on securities. This view arises, we think, from an imperfect apprehension of the nature and functions of credit, and of the law of value. We cannot but think, therefore, that if Cobden retained it in his later years it must be attributed to the absorbing character of his practical labours, which precluded the possibility of a deeper and more scientific investigation of a subject confessedly among the most complex problems in the range of economic speculation.

The programme which Cobden appears to have

set before him in the construction of a policy embraced the following objects :—

1. Complete freedom of trade throughout the British Empire with all the world, exclusive for the present (as a practical necessity) of restrictions indispensably requisite for fiscal purposes.

2. The final and unqualified abandonment of a policy of conquest and territorial aggrandizement in every quarter of the world.

3. The adoption of the general principles of *non-intervention* and arbitration in our foreign policy, publicity in all the transactions of diplomacy, and the renunciation of all ideas of national preponderance and supremacy.

4. The reduction of military and naval forces by international co-operation.

5. A large reduction of taxation.

6. A reform in the laws affecting land.

7. Freedom of the press from all taxes, happily stigmatized by Mr. Milner Gibson as taxes on knowledge.

8. A reform of maritime law.

We do not include in this programme the two great measures of National Education and Parliamentary Reform, because, although essential to the progress and security of government, and as such of course enlisting Cobden's sympathy, they are, after all, the means and not the end of good government; and we are disposed to think that he felt that his peculiar powers could be more usefully devoted to the assertion of the principles on which governments should be conducted than to the construction of the machinery out of which they should be elaborated. We will endeavour to give briefly an outline of what appear to have been Cobden's views on the leading divisions of national policy which the foregoing programme was designed to affect. We have said that the central idea of the national policy represented by Cobden was "Free Exchange" in the most comprehensive meaning of that term as the necessary complement of personal freedom, and the full assertion of the rights of property and labour. The realization of this idea logically involves all the consequences which Cobden aimed at promoting by direct or indirect efforts.

Foreign Policy.—In the field of foreign policy these consequences were immediate and obvious. The principle of foreign policy under a system of monopoly is national independence—in other words, "isolation;" under that of free exchange it is international interdependence. We have already observed upon the bearing of this latter principle on the doctrine of the balance of power, and pointed out the fundamental difference between a policy which proceeds on principles of international morality, and appeals to the common interests of all nations of the earth, and one which rests on ideas of national supremacy and rivalry. But in the practical application of the Free Trade foreign policy, there has been so much misunderstanding of Cobden's views, and, as we think, so much confusion of thought even among advanced Liberals, that a few further remarks may be useful. This policy is ordinarily characterized by the name of *non-intervention*. In some respects this designation has been an unfortunate one. It has given colour to the idea that what was desired was a blind and selfish indifference to the affairs of other countries, and a sort of moral isolation, as foreign to the principle of international interdependence as it is impossible in connection with increased material intercourse.

Cobden never, so far as we are aware, advanced or held the opinion that wars other than those undertaken for self-defence were in all cases wrong or inexpedient.

The question, as we apprehend it, was with him one of relative duties. It is clear that the duty and wisdom of entering upon a war, even in defence of the most righteous cause, must be measured by our knowledge and by our power; but, even where our knowledge is complete and our power sufficient, it is necessary that, in undertaking such a war, we should be satisfied that, in doing so, we are not neglecting and putting it out of our reach, to fulfil more sacred and more imperative duties.

The cases are rare in the quarrels of other nations, still rarer in their internal dissensions, in which our knowledge of their causes and conditions, and our power of enforcing the right, and assuring its success, in any degree justifies us in armed interference—the last resort in the failure of human justice.

But even if these difficult conditions of our justification in such a war were satisfied, the cases must be rare indeed in which, with a population of which so large a part is barely receiving the means of decent existence, and another part is supported by public charity at the expense of the rest, and at a charge of nearly £10,000,000 per annum, this country would be justified in imposing on our labouring classes (on whom, be it remembered, the burden must chiefly fall) the cost of obtaining for another people a degree of freedom or a measure of justice which they have so imperfectly secured for themselves.

Such a course is certainly not defensible unless the people have a far larger share in the government of their country than they possessed during Cobden's life in England.

When we add to these considerations the singular inaptitude of the governing classes of this country to comprehend foreign affairs, the extraordinary errors which are usually to be observed in their judgments and opinions on foreign questions, and the dangerous liability to abuse in the hands of any government, of the doctrine of " Blood and Iron," even if it be sometimes invoked in a just cause, we shall, we think (without asserting that it must be inflexibly enforced), acknowledge the sober wisdom of Cobden's opinion, that, for all practical purposes, at least for this generation, the principle of non-intervention should be made, as far as general principles can be applied to such questions, the rule of our foreign policy.

Let those who sneer at what they consider a sordid

and ungenerous view, reflect on the history of the past, and ask themselves what is to be the hope of humanity if the motives which have hitherto regulated the policy of our country are in future to determine the intercourse of nations.

Let them look back upon the great French war, not as it is interpreted by Cobden in his most instructive paper in the work before us, but read by the light of those teachers of history who see in it a proud record of England's glory and power in vindicating the liberties of mankind, and satisfy their conscience, if they can, of the righteousness of a cause which required the aid of Holy Alliances, the legions of despots, and a campaign which terminated in the Congress of Vienna; and which ended in the suffocation of popular rights for half a century, the enactment of the English Corn Law and all that it represents, and a condition of Europe which even now almost precludes the hope of real civilization.

Colonial Policy.—There is no branch of the national economy in which the neglect of Cobden's principles has led to more glaring and lamentable results than in that between the mother country and what are called its "foreign possessions." The inability even of the Government which was borne to power on the shoulders of the Anti-Corn-Law League to apprehend the scope and importance of Free Trade is in no direction more strikingly manifested than in the colonial policy.

Would it not have been possible, when the right

of self-government was conferred upon our colonial possessions, to have stipulated, as a necessary condition, and as a great and fundamental rule of imperial policy, the complete absence of protection throughout the dominions of the Crown ?

Instead of this, the most confused idea prevailed, and still prevails, as to the limits of colonial self-government in adopting a commercial policy, opposed to the principles and interests of the mother country.

The colonies have been allowed to impose protective duties on British manufactures, and on those of foreign countries ; but they are not allowed to discriminate between the two. They are allowed to protect : would they be allowed to prohibit ? for it must be remembered that protection, so far as it restricts a trade, is nothing more nor less than prohibition to that extent ; and if not to prohibit, where is the line to be drawn, at duties of 20, or 30, or 50, or 100 per cent. ?

Again, the colonies are allowed to tax and restrict our trade, but are compelled to give perfect freedom to our ships, both in their foreign and coasting trades, and then, as if to destroy and efface all trace and remnant of principle in our policy, they are compelled to admit foreign ships in their foreign trade, but allowed to exclude them from their coasting trade (thus violating the rule of equality between British and foreign trade laid down with respect to goods), but are not allowed to admit them to that trade on less favourable terms than British ships : in other words, they are allowed to inflict the greater, but not the less, injustice!

Can any conceivable confusion be more hopelessly confounded?

Does self-government apply to trade and not to shipping? Does it apply to a coast trade and not to a foreign trade? And is it not out of place to talk of self-government at all, as a principle, when every Colonial Act must be sanctioned by the Crown before it becomes law?

The truth is that we have here another instance of the evil effects of a displacement or dislocation of responsibility.

It is clear that the right of absolute self-government involves the corresponding duty of self-support and self-defence; and as the colonies are far from having undertaken the latter, it is surely not too much to call on them to admit such a degree of interference with their self-government as imperial interests require.

It is estimated that the military and naval expenses borne for the colonies by the mother country amount to £6,000,000 a year—more than the revenue derived from our sugar duties! If such sacrifices as these are imposed on the British taxpayer, has he not a right to be allowed to trade on equal terms with his colonial fellow-subjects? Cobden never lost an opportunity of protesting against this last misappropriation of the money of the old country, and of exposing the secret connection of this feature in our policy, with the perpetuation of pretexts for increased armaments.

But to return to our commercial policy. Has a colonial Minister ever asked himself what is the difference between entering into a compact with a foreign Government for the regulation of international trade, and entering into a similar compact with a colonial Government? Does the fact that the first would probably be recorded in a treaty and the second in an Act of Parliament affect the essence of the agreement, and render the one a legitimate and the other an illegitimate form of international action? If so, it would be better that our colonies should become in reality, as well as in name, "foreign possessions," so that we might then be allowed to treat with them.

It is painful to think of the contrast between our present position and prospects as a nation, and that which it might have presented, had the foundations of our colonial empire been laid broad and deep in commercial freedom. Is it yet too late? Is no effort yet possible towards such a consummation?

Eastern Policy.—The British rule in India was to Cobden a subject of the deepest anxiety and apprehension. His paper in the present volumes entitled, "How Wars are got up in India," is an honest and indignant criticism upon an episode in our Indian history which has only too many parallels, and gives expression to one of his strongest convictions, viz. the retribution which one day awaits the lust of power and of territorial aggrandizement, and the utter disregard of morality so often exhibited in our dealings with the races of this great dependency. But in our Eastern policy much progress has been made since Cobden's time, and we have seen, we trust, the dawn of a better day in the administration of Lord Lawrence in India, and in the policy of Sir F. Bruce at Pekin.

Reduction of Military and Naval Expenditure.— The changes advocated by Cobden in our foreign and colonial policy necessarily involved a large reduction in our military and naval establishments, and to this object his most strenuous efforts were constantly directed; but here the difficulties which he had to encounter were enormous, and the Crimean War and its results throughout Europe have rendered all attempts at reform in this branch of our national economy hitherto unavailing.

In attacking our "Services" he not only had to contend against powerful interests, connected with almost all the families of the upper and middle classes of the country, but also against many honest, though mistaken, opinions, as to the causes of national greatness and the sources of our power. It was the widespread prevalence of such opinions, combined with the selfish influence of the worst element in British commerce, which led, on the occasion of the Chinese War in 1857, to the rejection of Cobden by the West Riding, and of Bright and Gibson by Manchester. The class of ideas symbolized by the "British Lion," the "Sceptre of Britannia," and the "Civis Romanus," irrational and vulgar as they are, have nevertheless a side which is not altogether ignoble, and are of a nature which it requires more than one generation to eradicate.

Cobden approached this question of reduction by two different roads. He endeavoured to bring to bear upon it international action, by arrangements for a general limitation of armaments, in which, as regards France, there appeared more than once some possibility of success, and in which he was cordially supported by Bastiat in the years succeeding the repeal of the Corn Laws ; he also sought, by every means in his power, to urge it on his countrymen, by appeals to their good sense and self-respect. He exposed, firstly, our policy ; and secondly, our administration ; and showed, with irresistible arguments, that, while the one was unsound, the other was extravagant ; and that thus the British people were condemned, not only to provide for what was useless and even dangerous, but at the same time to pay an excessive price for it.

He tells us in his article on Russia, vol. i. p. 309—

" If that which constitutes cowardice in individuals, viz. the taking excessive precautions against danger, merits the same designation when practised by communities, then England certainly must rank as the greatest poltroon among nations."

It is incontestable that the extent of our precautions against danger should be proportioned to the degree of that danger, and it cannot, we think, be

E

denied, even by those who are the most disposed to connect the greatness and security of England with the constant display of physical force, that as our liability to war has diminished, our preparations for it should also diminish; and that it is as irrational to devote to our "Services" in a period of "Free Trade," colonial self-government, and non-intervention, the sums which were wrung from our industry in an epoch of monopoly, of colonial servitude, and of a "spirited foreign policy," as it would be to pay the same insurance on a healthy as on a diseased life.

For what are the causes (under her own control) which render a country liable to war?

They may, for present purposes, be classed under the following heads :—

1. The disposition to engage in wars of conquest or aggression.

2. The necessity of maintaining, for the purpose of repressing liberty at home, large standing armies, which a Government may be compelled to employ in foreign wars, either to gratify the military spirit engendered by the existence of a powerful service, or to divert public attention from domestic reforms.

3. The habitual violation of the rights of labour and property in international relations, by prohibitive and protective laws of trade.

4. The policy of providing outlets for trade, and of introducing what are called the agencies of civilization, by means of consuls and missionaries, supported by gun-boats and breech-loaders.

5. The pretension of holding the balance of power, and of interfering, with this object, in the affairs of other nations, with its result, the theory of armed diplomacy, which aims, by a display of force, at securing for a country what is assumed to be its due influence in foreign affairs.

All these motives would be absolutely removed under a system of government such as that which Cobden advocated, and even now, they are, we believe, very generally discredited, with the exception, perhaps, of the last, which must, however, be so cut down and modified in order to be a pretext for military armaments, as to lose its general character, and to require re-statement. The doctrine of the " balance of power" is, we hope, consigned to the limbo of exploded fallacies, with the "balance of trade," and we refer any remaining believers in the balancing system to the history and analysis of this phenomenon, in the essay on Russia in the work before us, as we think it cannot fail to dispel any lingering faith in this delusion.

With the rejection of the doctrines of the " balance of power," a fruitful source of dangerous meddling in the affairs of foreign countries has been cut away. There only remains, therefore, the limited form of armed interference in foreign affairs to which we have already adverted, and which it is still thought by many among us, and even by a large section of the Liberal party, we should be prepared to exert in certain events, and for which, if the principle be admitted, some allowance must be made in estimating the extent of our military and naval requirements.

We refer to the supposed duty of England to resort to war in possible cases for the purpose of defending the principles of free government or international law, or of protecting a foreign country from wanton or unjust aggression. On this subject we have already stated what we believe to have been Cobden's view; but, whatever margin may be left for this consideration, it must be admitted by candid reasoners, that the liability of the country to war under a policy such as that of which the general outlines have been traced, would be reduced within narrow proportions.

Cobden was often blamed for not devoting more time and labour to the task of minute resistance to the "Estimates" in the House of Commons. This was the result of his perfect conviction, after years of experience and observation, that such a course was absolutely useless, and that no private member, however able or courageous, could cope in detail with the resources at the disposal of Government in evading exposure and resisting reductions. He therefore always insisted that the only course was to strike at the root of the evil, by diminishing the revenue and the expenditure in the gross.

Taxation.—This brings us to our next topic, which is inextricably bound up with the last, viz. the reduction of the national expenditure, and the consequent diminution of taxation, objects the importance of which is becoming yearly more vital. Cobden knew that no material reform in our financial system could be effected (for all that has been hitherto done has been to shift the burden, and not to diminish it) until our external policy was changed, and hence his incessant efforts in this direction; but he also knew that the surest method of accomplishing the latter object was to diminish the resources at the disposal of Government for military and naval purposes.

The first object in financial reform was, therefore, in Cobden's opinion, the gradual remission of indirect taxation.

In a letter to the " Liverpool Association " he made use of the remarkable expression that he considered them to be *the only body of men in the country who appeared to have any faith in the future of humanity.*

His objections were threefold, and they are to our mind conclusive :—

" 1. The dangerous facilities which they afford for extravagant and excessive expenditure, by reason of their imperceptibility in collection, and of the consequent readiness of the people to submit to them, and also of the impossibility of insuring a close and honest adaptation of the revenue to the expenditure.

" 2. Their interference with the great law of free exchange, one of the rights of property, and (so far as customs duties are concerned) the violation of international equity which they involve ; for it is obvious that the conditions of international trade are essentially affected by taxes on imports and exports, and it is impossible to apportion them so as to insure that each country shall pay neither more nor less than its own due share.

"3. The enhancement of the cost of the taxed article to the consumer, over and above the amount of the tax."

The root of the evil may again be traced to the infringement in the case of indirect taxes, of the great law of "free exchange of services, freely debated." A tax is nothing more than a service contributed to the State by the people, in return for a corresponding service rendered to the people by the State. The great object, therefore, in imposing a tax should be to connect it as closely as possible with the service for which it is required, and to facilitate as far as possible a close comparison between the two. The superiority of a direct tax, like the income-tax and the poor-rate, over taxes on consumption and on trade, from this point of view, is apparent; but such is the distorted view of large classes in the country on this subject, that they consider what we have characterized as the great vice of indirect taxation, as its chief and distinguishing merit, and that the supreme art of government consists in extracting from the pockets of the people, by a sort of "hocus pocus," the largest possible amount of money without their knowing it.

Do those who with so much *naïveté* repeat this argument whenever this question is discussed, ever reflect, that to drug the taxpayer before he pays his money will in no degree diminish the evil to a country, of excessive taxation, and that ignorance and irrespon-

sibility are not the best securities for an efficient and
conscientious administration of our public affairs ?

If it be objected that indirect taxation is the only
method by which the masses of the people can be made
to contribute their share to the revenues of the State,
we reply, that if the condition of the masses of the
people in any country is such as to place them beyond
the reach of direct taxation, it is the surest proof that
the whole national economy is out of joint, and that,
in some form or other, resort will be had to "communism." In England we have too clear and disastrous
evidence of this in our Poor Law system, and in our
reckless and prodigal almsgiving. In withholding
from our children the bread of justice, we have given
them the stone of enforced and sapless charity.

We hail, therefore, with pleasure the movement
which is beginning in Germany and Belgium, in favour
of a gradual abolition of all customs duties; and are
convinced that there is none, perhaps, among all the
articles of the Liberal creed which, both in its direct
and indirect effects, contains the promise of so much
future good.

The fulfilment of this policy should, we think, be
rigorously exacted from every Liberal Government,
till no tax of customs or excise remain upon the
statute-book, save those on tobacco and spirits, which
our heritage of debt has placed it beyond the pale
of hope to remove by any scheme of practical and
proximate reform.

Land.—Cobden held that the growing accumulation,

in the hands of fewer and fewer proprietors, of the soil of the country, was a great political, social, and economical evil, and as this tendency is unquestionably stimulated by the system of our government, and some of our laws, which give it an artificial value, he foresaw that one of the principal tasks of the generation which succeeded him, must be to liberate the land from all the unnecessary obstacles which impede its acquisition and natural distribution, and to place it under the undisturbed control of the economic law.

We cannot here attempt to enter upon a due examination of the causes which in this country neutralize and subvert this law in the case of landed property, but the general principle involved may be very shortly suggested.

The more abundant the supply of land in a country, the cheaper, *cæteris paribus*, will it be, the larger will be the return to the capital and labour expended on it, and the greater the profits to be divided between them.

It is obvious that laws which keep land out of the market,—laws of entail, laws of settlement, difficulties of transfer, as well as a system of government which gives to the possession of land an artificial value, for social or political purposes, over and above its natural commercial value,—must have the inevitable effect of restricting the quantity, of enhancing the price, and of diminishing the product to be obtained. Land thus acquires a monopoly price, small capitals are deterred from this form of investment, competition is restricted, production is diminished, and the condition of those who live by the land, as well as of those who exchange the produce of their labour for the produce of the land, is necessarily impaired.

To illustrate our meaning by an extreme case : let us suppose that the State were to connect with property in land the highest titles and privileges, on the condition that it was entirely diverted from all productive uses, and kept solely for purposes of ornament and sport, and that the honours and advantages so conferred were sufficiently tempting to induce many persons to accept these conditions. It must follow that the stock of available land in such a country would be diminished to whatever extent it was so appropriated, and its material resources proportionately reduced.

In a less degree, who can deny that these causes are operating among us, and are a source of incalculable loss and waste of the national wealth ? The suggestion last year that our coal-beds would be exhausted in one hundred years, almost startled Parliament from its propriety. Yet we acquiesce year after year, without a murmur, in a curtailment of our supply of land, and those who warn us of our danger are denounced as the agents of revolution.

In his speech at Rochdale, in November, 1864, which was his last public utterance, Cobden especially left this task as a legacy to the younger men among us, and told them that they could do more for their country in liberating the land than had been achieved for it in the liberation of its trade.

Maritime Laws.—On the question of " Maritime law," it is well known that he advocated the largest extension of the rights of neutrals, and the greatest possible limitation of the rights of belligerents, as a necessary and logical accompaniment of a Free Trade policy.

His views on this subject will be seen from a letter addressed to Mr. H. Ashworth, in 1862, in which he recommends the following three reforms :—

1. Exemption of private property from capture at sea during war by armed vessels of every kind.

2. Blockades to be restricted to naval arsenals, and to towns besieged at the same time by land, except as regards contraband of war.

3. The merchant ships of neutrals on the high seas to be inviolable to the visitation of alien Government vessels in time of war as in time of peace.

In this letter he observes—

" Free Trade, in the widest definition of the term, means only the division of labour by which the productive powers of the whole earth are brought into mutual co-operation. If this scheme of universal independence is to be liable to sudden dislocation whenever two Governments choose to go to war, it converts a manufacturing industry such as ours into a lottery, in which the lives and fortunes of multitudes of men are at stake. I do not comprehend how any British statesman who consults the interests of his country and understands the revolution which Free Trade is effecting in the relations of the world, can advocate the maintenance of commercial blockades. If I shared their views I should shrink from promoting the indefinite growth of a population whose means of subsistence would be liable to be cut off at any moment by a belligerent power, against whom we should have no right of resistance, or even of complaint.

" It must be in mere irony that the advocates of such a policy as this ask—Of what use would our navy be in case of war if commercial blockades were abolished? Surely, for a nation that has no access to the rest of the world but by sea, and a large part of whose population is dependent for food on foreign countries, the chief use of a navy should be to keep open its communications, not to close them!

" I will only add that I regard these changes as the necessary corollary of the repeal of the Navigation Laws, the abolition of the Corn Laws, and the abandonment of our colonial monopoly. We have thrown away the sceptre of force, to confide in the principles of freedom—uncovenanted, unconditional freedom. Under the new *régime* our national fortunes have prospered beyond all precedent. During the last fourteen years the increase in our commerce has exceeded its entire growth during the previous thousand years of reliance on force, cunning, and monopoly. This should encourage us to go forward in the full faith that every fresh impediment removed from the path of commerce, whether by sea or land, and whether in peace or war, will augment our prosperity, at the same time that it will promote the general interests of humanity."

In most of the foregoing questions, Cobden, as we have said, was contented to preach sound doctrine, and to prepare the way for the ultimate adoption of principles of policy and government, which in his time he could not hope to see prevail.

But he was destined, before the close of his career, once more to engage in a great practical work, and to identify his name with an accomplished success, scarcely inferior in its scope and results to the repeal of the English Corn Law.

This was the Commercial Treaty with France.

As the Corn Law was the great stronghold of monopoly in England, so was the prohibitive system in France the key-stone of protection in Europe, and Cobden selected these accordingly, with the unerring instinct of real statesmanship, as the first points for attack, and fastened upon them with a tenacity and resolution which insured success.

Fifteen years had elapsed since England had renounced, in principle at least, the false system of commercial monopoly, and, in Cobden's words quoted above, "thrown away the sceptre of force, to confide in freedom."

She had trusted to the teaching of her example, and to the experience of her extraordinary success, in leading the countries of Europe to answer to her appeal for co-operation in liberating trade, and vindicating the rights of labour; but she had met with slight response.

Our conversion was perhaps too recent, our course still too inconsistent, and our motives too much open to suspicion, to make this surprising, and, so far as France was concerned, we had unfortunately contrived in all our reforms to retain in our tariff restrictions upon the staple articles of French production, wine and silk.

The time had come when, unless some new impulse could be given to international intercourse, the forces of reaction might have again acquired the ascendency, and European progress have been thrown back for years.

Our relations with France were those of chronic distrust and rivalry. The cry of *Perfide Albion* in France too often resounded in our ears ; and the bugbear of French invasion was successively invoked on this side of the Channel no less than three times in the period we are considering.

This was a state of things fraught with danger. Monopoly had borne as usual its deadly fruits, in alienating two great nations destined by nature for the closest relations of friendship and mutual dependence, and in fostering in both the spirit of war.

It was under circumstances such as these that Cobden set his hand to the great work of co-operation which led to the Commercial Treaty.

Bastiat, who would have hailed with delight this tardy reparation of the defects in our reformed commercial system which he always deplored, was no longer alive to aid the cause ; but to one of the most distinguished of modern French economists, Michel Chevalier, is due, in concert with Cobden, the merit of the scheme which the Governments of England and France were induced to adopt, which has opened to us the prospect of a new era of progress, in the gradual union of the nations of Europe in a great commercial confederation, and in laying the foundations of a civilization, which may yet keep pace with that now dawning on our race in the Anglo-Saxon republics of the Western world.

It was pleasant to see how his old friends rallied around him on this occasion, and how many, who had been often unable to comprehend or follow him in his political career, rejoiced to see him once again in the field, against his old enemy, Protection. But, on the other hand, he was assailed by an influential class among us with a bitter animosity, which all but made his task impossible, and which revealed too clearly the strength and vitality of the reactionary forces still at work in our midst.

As Cobden saw in his beneficent work the hope of a new era of peace, and of liberal progress in Europe, as its certain fruit, so did his opponents instinctively perceive that his success would carry with it the doom of the traditions of hatred and of fear, which the Governments of Europe had too often successfully invoked, to plunge the people into wars of which they are the invariable victims, and to keep alive the rumours of wars, which have deprived them of the solid fruits of peace.

So long as the political condition of Europe is such as to render necessary or possible the large armaments, which are a reproach to our age and boasted civilization, while 4,000,000 men, in the flower of their age, are taken from productive industry, and supported by the labour of the rest of the population, no real and permanent progress can be made in the emancipation of the ˙ people, and in the establishment of free institutions.

At the time of which we are speaking, even still more than at present, all direct attempts to mitigate this monster evil appeared hopeless; and although

Cobden never ceased to urge, both in England and France, the wisdom of a mutual understanding, with a view to reduced armaments, he knew that the only certain and available method of undermining this fatal system, and preparing for its ultimate overthrow, was to assist in every way the counter-agencies of peace.

It was in the consciousness that by breaking down the barriers to commercial intercourse between England and France, a greater impulse would be given than by any other event to the forces of progress in Europe, that the men who in both countries undertook and completed this international work entered upon their task. We have said that the time has not arrived when it is possible to speak freely of this episode in Cobden's life, but it is necessary to vindicate his policy from charges, which, although forgotten and overwhelmed in its extraordinary success, were brought against it too commonly, and from quarters whence it ought least to have been expected, at the time.

In France he was reproached by many of his earlier friends, whose sympathies were bound up with the Orleanist or Republican *régimes*, and who viewed with a natural aversion the Second Empire, for contributing to a work which, if successful, might do more than anything else to consolidate the Imperial reign. He replied, that what the immediate effect might be he neither knew nor cared, but that all the forces of freedom were "solidaires," and that the ruler who gave "Free Trade" to the nation, whether King,

President, or Emperor, was doing that which, more than anything else, would assure the future liberties of France.

The same causes operated in many quarters to make the Treaty unpopular in England ; but he was also assailed in a more insidious form. He was accused of having forgotten or forsaken the sound doctrines of political economy, of which he had in his earlier life been the uncompromising advocate, and of having revived the discarded policy of " reciprocity treaties."

It would perhaps be unnecessary to revert to this charge, were it not that a suspicion of unsoundness still lurks in many minds as to the principles of the French, and subsequent, Treaties of Commerce. It may be well, therefore, to say that, so far as this charge was honest, and something more than a convenient method of discrediting a measure which it was desired to obstruct, it proceeded on a very imperfect knowledge of the policy of the Treaty, and on an erroneous and confused idea of the principles of Free Trade itself.

The system of reciprocity treaties and tariff bargains was one of the natural but most pernicious developments of the doctrine of protection. The most notorious of such treaties in our history is, perhaps, the famous Methuen Treaty, from the effects of which we are still suffering in England, in the shape of adulterated wine. These arrangements aimed at the extension of the limits of monopoly, by securing for our products protection in a foreign country, against the competition of all other countries, and always proceeded on the supposed interest of the producer, to the injury of the consumer. They were logical, when it was believed or professed that the reduction of a duty was a sacrifice on the part of the country making it to the country in whose favour it was made. From this point of view, it was natural, in making such reductions, to demand what were thought to be equivalent concessions from the country with which we were treating, and the supreme art of negotiation was held to consist in framing what had the appearance of a " nicely adjusted balance of equi-valents," but in which each country secretly desired, and sought to obtain, the maximum of reductions from the other, against the minimum of its own.

But from the Free Trade point of view, in which all reductions of duties, at least so far as productive duties are concerned, are an admitted and positive gain to the country making them, it becomes absurd and impossible to use them as the ground of a claim on a foreign country for compensating or equivalent remissions.

The French Treaty had no affinity, except in form, to treaties such as these.

Instead of a bargain in which each party sought to give as little and to get as much as possible, it was a great work of co-operation, in which the Governments of England and of France were resolved, on both sides, to remove, within the limits of their power, the

F

artificial obstacles to their commercial intercourse presented by fiscal and protective laws.

England had already spontaneously advanced much further than France in this direction, and hence alone, if for no other reason, all idea of "equivalent" concessions was out of the question. She contributed her share to the work, by sweeping from her tariff, with some trifling exceptions, all trace and remnant of protection, and by reducing her fiscal duties upon wine and brandy.

France, unable at one stroke to destroy the whole fabric of monopoly, nevertheless made a deadly breach in the edifice, by substituting moderate duties for prohibition, in the case of the chief British exports.

If these reforms had been made exclusively in each other's favour, they might have been justly open to the charge of unsoundness, but they were made equally for the commerce of all the world, on the side of England immediately, on the side of France prospectively, and thus, instead of reverting to a system of monopoly, the prohibitive and differential policy of France was annihilated, and the equal system of England maintained and consolidated.

There were, however, two objections made to the treaty of a more plausible kind, and which we will, therefore, briefly notice :—

First, that a work of this description need not assume the form of a treaty, which tends to disguise its real character, but should be left to the independent legislation of each country.

Secondly, that, although it might be well to abolish protective duties by this method, it was impolitic to fetter ourselves by treaty with respect to fiscal duties.

As regards the first objection, it is sufficient to reply, that at the time we are considering, for political reasons, a treaty was the only form in which such a measure could be carried in France ; but a more permanent justification is to be found in the fact that a treaty is nothing more than an international statute-law, and that, in a matter of international concern, it is necessary that there should exist an international See p. 6 guarantee of permanence. Without such a security, what would be the condition of trade ?

The second objection is more subtle, but has no better foundation. A tax which, from whatever cause, dries up an important source of national wealth, and thus takes from the fund available for taxation more than the amount gained by the revenue, is a bad tax, and ought never, if possible, to be imposed or maintained.

The tax on French wine and spirits had the effect of restricting most injuriously one of the most important branches of our foreign trade, and would, if maintained, have deprived us, by preventing the conclusion of the Treaty, of an addition of at least £20,000,000 sterling per annum, to the value of our general exchanges with France. No wise legislation could retain such a tax in the face of such consequences. There is probably no other form of tax to which it would not have been preferable to resort, rather than to maintain these obstacles to our trade with France.

But the consequences of the Treaty with France were not confined to that country and to England. It was an act which, both by its moral effect and its direct and necessary influence on the legislation of the other Continental countries, has set on foot a movement which grows from year to year, and will not cease till all protective duties have been erased from the commercial codes of Europe.

It was thus the rare privilege of the man who had been the foremost in giving the death-blow to monopoly in England, to be also among the first to storm the citadel of protection on the Continent, and to give to the work which he commenced at home, a decisive international impulse, destined to afford new securities for the most sacred of human rights—the right of labour, and to add " new realms to the empire of freedom."

Cobden had yet another success awaiting him, to our mind the most signal triumph of his life. He lived to see the great moral and economic laws, which he had enforced through years of opposition and obloquy, asserting their control over the forces of reaction, and moulding our foreign policy.

It must have been with a superb and heartfelt satisfaction that Cobden watched the conflict of public opinion at the time of the Danish War.

The diplomatic intervention of the Government had

brought us to the verge of war, and made it more than usually difficult to retreat.

The old instincts of the ruling classes of the nation were thoroughly aroused, and, unless they had been neutralized and overpowered by stronger and deeper forces, we should, under a fancied idea of chivalry and honour (if anything can deserve these names which is opposed to reason and duty), have squandered once more the hard-earned heritage of English labour, in a war of which the causes and the merits were for the most part unknown among us, and could never have been made intelligible to the nation, and in which our success, if possible, might have thrown back all liberal progress for years, both in England and on the Continent.

But it soon became manifest that a nobler and larger morality had been gaining ground in the heart of the nation, had at last found its expression in the Councils of the State, and had enforced its control over those who still believed that the mission of England is to hold by force the balance of power in Europe.

The memorable debate which decided the course of our policy in this critical moment decided far greater issues ; and the principle of "non-intervention," as it has been explained above, the only hope for the moral union of nations and the progress of freedom, became the predominating rule of our foreign policy, and, with different limitations and qualifications, a cardinal point in the Liberal creed.

We must here close a hasty and imperfect sketch of Cobden's political life and principles, in the hope that the outline which we have traced may be filled up by other hands. Our object will have been attained, if we have succeeded in leading some of our readers to suspect the erroneous and superficial nature of the prevalent opinion of Cobden, in the upper ranks of English society, and to believe that the verdict of history will rather confirm the judgment of his humbler countrymen, with whom his name has become a household word.

In reviewing the political programme given in the preceding pages, we shall see that while much has been done, far more remains to do ; and that, although there is great cause for hope, there is also much ground for fear.

Of all the dreams in which easy-going and half-hearted politicians indulge, the idlest appears to be that in which it is fondly imagined that the days of party strife are over, and that no questions lie before us, on which the majority of moderate and honest men are not agreed. It is useless to shut our eyes to the fact that, before the future greatness and prosperity of our country can be assured, great issues must be raised, and fierce political struggles traversed. We have a firm and confident belief that the forces on the side of progress are sufficient to achieve what is required for this consummation, by peaceful and constitutional reforms; but the cause will not be won without strenuous efforts.

It will not be won without the aid of men who, in the measure of their gifts, will bring to bear upon the task the qualities of which in Cobden's life we have such enduring proofs : pure morality, keen intelligence, perfect disinterestedness, undaunted courage, indomitable tenacity of purpose, high patriotism, and an immovable faith in the predestined triumph of good over evil.

That the principles of public morality which Cobden devoted his life to enforce will ultimately prevail in the government of the world, we think that no one who believes in God or man can doubt. Whether it be in store for our country first to achieve by their adoption the last triumphs of civilization, and to hold her place in the van of human progress, or whether to other races, and to other communities, will be confided this great mission, it is not for us to determine.

But those who trust that this may yet be England's destiny, who, in spite of much which they deplore, delight to look upon her past with pride, and her future with hope, will ever revere the memory of Cobden, as of one whose lifelong aim it was to lay the foundations of her empire in her moral greatness, in the supremacy of reason, and in the majesty of law,—and will feel with us that the "international man" was also, and still more, an Englishman.

II.

THE POLICY OF COMMERCIAL TREATIES.

(An Official Memorandum on the Commercial Treaty with Austria, 1865, now Published for the First Time.)

The policy of England under her Free Trade system with respect to Commercial Treaties has been so strangely misunderstood or misrepresented, and there appears to exist in the public mind so much confusion of thought upon the subject, that it is important upon an occasion which has already revived a controversy which ought never to have arisen, to record in a brief outline the principles upon which it has proceeded, and the results which it has achieved.

The conclusion of the Treaty with Austria is a peculiarly suitable moment for such a review, as it is the first successful application of that policy in a form which leaves no room for cavil or doubt as to its entire conformity with the so-called " Free Trade principles " which have guided our commercial legislation during recent years.

First, then, let us define what is commonly meant by " Free Trade principles."

All that has ever been meant in this country by

" Free Trade," in connection with any question of practical legislation, is the liberation of trade from all protective duties. The term may some day mean a great
deal more; but it is not among the opponents of
modern Commercial Treaties that we shall find the
advocates of its wider application.

The leading principle, then, of the recent commercial policy of England is war against protection in
every form.

I propose to consider in what way this principle
has been infringed by the French or the Austrian
Treaty; but it will first be necessary to recall the
course of legislation which preceded this last development of the Free Trade movement.

Until the repeal of the Corn Laws in 1846, the
doctrine of protection, though damaged and under-
mined, still retained a firm hold on the minds of the
governing classes in that country.

There still prevailed an illogical idea that the conditions of production ought to be artificially equalized,
and that the consumer ought to be made to support
the burden of industries which were supposed to be
unable to prosper without public subsidies; in other
words, that the nation ought not to be allowed a free
exchange of its products precisely in those cases
where it would derive the greatest advantage from
such exchange.

It was not surprising that under this order of ideas
reductions of duty upon the produce of a foreign
country came to be regarded as national sacrifices,

which entitled the country making them to corresponding concessions, and hence the policy of tariff bargains,
which more or less will be found to have pervaded
the commercial negotiations of the period, and which
survived even so late as the Reciprocity Treaty between the United States and the British provinces of
North America.

It was probably owing to a perception of this
fallacy, and also in some degree to the gradual and
fragmentary introduction in this country of Free Trade
measures, that the British Government proceeded to
carry through these reforms, without any reference to
the legislation of foreign countries, and without any
attempt to obtain their co-operation in a common
effort to root out a form of human oppression, which,
though resting on cunning instead of force, and applied
to the produce of labour instead of to the person of
the labourer, is no less opposed to justice, and no less
a violation of the rights of property, than slavery itself.

Had it been possible at any one time, by adopting
in one great policy of commercial reform the measures
which were successively introduced, and by an appeal
to the conscience and interests of Europe, to obtain
simultaneously the removal of corresponding restrictions in the continental countries, it is difficult to see
on what grounds of principle or expediency such a
course could have been impugned.

It is one thing to make internal reforms which are
dictated by national interest and demanded by justice,
conditional on the co-operation of foreign countries;

it is another to take the occasion of those reforms to found an appeal to foreign countries resting upon international equity, and grounded in reason, to make common cause with you in a great work of freedom and progress.

More than this, the two principles are not only different, they are directly opposed to each other. The first rests upon the fallacy that to liberate trade without reciprocity is an evil; the second, on the incontestable truth that Free Trade in all countries is better than in one alone.

But such a course was probably not possible, and it may perhaps have been on the whole better that England was left to work out her commercial salvation in her own time, and in her own way. She was enabled, moreover, the better to do this from her comparative independence of European trade: the great markets of America and of her Colonial possessions being sufficient for many years to absorb her productions. If she has thereby forfeited the power of offering tariff reductions as material bribes to other countries for commercial reforms, she has certainly acquired the right of presenting herself in the councils of Europe as the representative of a great principle.

It is this right which is questioned by the opponents of the recent commercial policy; we shall hereafter examine upon what grounds.

But admitting that this course was not only the best that was possible, but in itself the best, it must not be forgotten (and I think it has been too much

forgotten) that these national reforms, however fruitful in good results, must not be regarded as constituting
a complete and fulfilled policy, but as the first act in
a great drama, in the playing out of which England is
deeply interested, both on moral and material grounds.

It is a law of nations no less than of individuals
that complete development cannot be attained alone.
England, of all countries, can ill afford to disregard
the policy of other countries on this vital question.
Her greatness, even her existence, depends upon her
foreign trade; and to place that trade upon sound
foundations must be one of the most important of her
interests.

To prohibit trade is to violate one of the first
principles of international ethics—it is a hostile act ;
a restriction * is a prohibition, to whatever extent it
operates ; and is, therefore, also a hostile act.

Thus England has not only the strongest motive,
but the clearest right, to protest against the protective
laws of foreign countries, from the injury which they
inflict on her trade, and the injustice which they cause
to her people.

The rapid progress of our industry and commerce
during recent years has led us to overlook, too much,
the magnitude of the injury which we sustain from the
hostile policy of foreign countries.

The full rewards of labour cannot be attained until
the right has been established for all, whether white or

---

* Of course this does not apply to duties imposed equally on native and
oreign goods for fiscal purposes.

black, to the produce of their own industry in use or
in exchange.

Bastiat has well said—

"L'échange est un droit naturel comme la propriété.
Tout citoyen qui a acquis ou créé un produit doit avoir
l'option ou de l'appliquer immédiatement à son usage ou de
le céder à quiconque, sur la surface du globe, consent à lui
donner en échange l'objet de ses désirs. Le priver de cette
faculté uniquement pour satisfaire aux convenances d'un
autre citoyen, c'est légitimer une spoliation, c'est blesser la
loi de justice."

To whatever extent British products are exchanged
against the products of countries where protection is
maintained, still more to whatever extent they are not
so exchanged in consequence of that protection, the
British consumer will bear the enhanced cost which is
the result of his being debarred from buying in the
cheapest market. It is true that in practice this effect
may be more or less neutralized by the operation of
the laws of international supply and demand ; but it
is nevertheless broadly and unquestionably true that
whatever impairs the producing power in a country
from which we draw our supplies is an injury to the
British consumer, whose interests always represent the
interests of the nation at large.

And it must not be forgotten that, while the
interests of British labour are thus injuriously affected
by restrictions on the exchange of its products, no
such restrictions are imposed on the transfer of British
capital to countries which exclude the products of
British industry, and that this capital is constantly

diverted from its natural channel and withdrawn from employment at home to suck profit out of these monopolies, and help to retard their doom by supplying foreign Governments with funds which they can no longer raise from the impoverished resources of their own people.

Unless, therefore, by the exchange of our products we can extend the area of our production, and thus neutralize the effects of our limited territorial resources, the day will come when our people will follow our capital, and we shall enter upon the period of our decline.

Nor is it the destiny of the working classes alone which is involved in the fulfilment of this policy. The only economical justification of the right of property in land in a country where the soil is limited as in England, is in the perfect freedom of exchange with countries where the soil is comparatively free. This is shown, I think, conclusively in Bastiat's Essay, "Propriété et Spoliation," and indirectly proved, I think, by the English economists—Ricardo, McCulloch, Senior, etc., in their theory of "Rent."

A direct connection is thus established between the full development of the Free Trade policy and the condition of the working classes of England, the great problem of our time, which, unless solved, will solve itself by the decay of England.

The only possible foundation of all progress, and the only hope of the future of the human race, lie in the material emancipation of the people. Free Trade

between all nations is certainly one of the most powerful of the agencies at the command of Governments
in this consummation, which is the only possible
foundation of all schemes and systems of social or
political improvement.

It was under the influence of these convictions
that those who both in France and England had
devoted their lives to the cause of Free Trade, set
themselves to the work which ended in the conclusion
of the Treaty of 1860.

It is not surprising that these measures should
have roused the hostility of that party in England
which has acquiesced in Free Trade as a political
necessity, but never accepted the principles from
which it springs or the consequences which must flow
from it.

It is not so easy to comprehend the fierce opposition
which they have met with from some professed Free-
Traders, still less the hesitating defence of them made
by some of their friends who have always assumed a
semi-apologetic tone in speaking of them. It is thus
that the French Treaty has been justified as an exceptional measure resting on grounds of general
political expediency rather than as the first step in a
great commercial policy.

That Treaty was denounced as a departure from
Free Trade principles—as a return to an exploded
theory—and as involving an unsound financial policy.

It is easy to show that it is open to none of these
objections, and that it can only so be considered by

those who have never taken the trouble to understand the idea which inspired it, or the principles out of which it grew both in England and France.

Those principles may be briefly stated.

The commercial intercourse of these two countries, separated only by a few miles of sea, was so restricted and hampered by perverse laws as to be a scandal to our times, and a source of loss and danger.

The Governments of both countries resolved to remove on both sides within the limits of their power the obstacles to this intercourse.

That power was very different in the two countries, England having advanced so much farther than France in liberating her trade from protective laws; hence alone, if for no other reason, all idea of *equivalent* concessions was out of the question.

England contributed her share to the work, by sweeping from her tariff, with some trifling exceptions, all trace and remnant of protection, and by binding herself to reduce to moderate rates her fiscal duties on two of the staple products of France—wine and brandy.

France, unable to destroy at one blow the whole fabric of monopoly, nevertheless made a deadly breach in the edifice, by substituting moderate duties for prohibition on the chief English exports.

If these reforms had been made exclusively in each other's favour, they might justly have been called unsound, but they were made equally for all the countries of the world; on the side of England at once, on the side of France prospectively; and thus, instead of reverting to a system of monopoly, the differential policy of France was for ever destroyed, and the equal system of England maintained and consolidated.

If, then, without the sacrifice of a single Free Trade principle, we were able to break up the prohibitory and differential system of France, and obtained a large increase of commercial freedom, by what law of Free Trade can such a course be impugned, or by what true Free-Trader regretted ? *

---

* In a speech in the House of Commons, on the 17th March, 1865, Mr. Lowe attempted to show that as a Free-Trader he must disapprove this "new-fangled plan of carrying into effect Free Trade principles." He said, " Are these Commercial Treaties which we are now negotiating, teaching the nations around us the true principles of political economy? . . . Political economy says—Lower your duties, in order that you may get the productions of other countries as cheaply as possible, *i.e.* for the sake of the consumer; and it is sound doctrine. But what do we virtually say when we negotiate a Commercial Treaty? We say, the end of commerce is not what political economy would teach you, the obtaining of imports, but the sending out of exports. The *summum bonum* is to send out as much as possible."—*Vide* " Hansard," vol. cxvii. p. 1861.

Does Mr. Lowe suppose that a merchant exports goods for the pleasure of exporting? Does not every export imply and involve an import and a profit on the exchange? Is it possible to increase your export trade profitably, without increasing your imports? Is not the science of political economy the science of the laws of exchange? · Can a foreign country lower her import duties without improving her conditions of exchange with other countries, and is not the British consumer principally and vitally interested in the reduction of foreign tariffs? It cannot be repeated too often, or insisted on too strongly, that this question is a *consumer's* question. The reduction of an import duty in a foreign country must (*cateris paribus*) enable the countries with which it trades to exchange their products with it more advantageously, *i.e.* they obtain by an equal amount of labour a larger result, and under a system of free competition increased cheapness must be the consequence, and the consumer must be the ultimate and principal gainer.

It is, of course, unnecessary to add that the language attributed by Mr. Lowe to the British Government and its agents in these negotiations is directly opposed to that which has been invariably used in addressing foreign Governments. The prevailing argument has been, " We want your produce for our consumption. We

G

The fiscal objection remains to be considered. It had been said that it is unsound financial policy to tie your hands with regard to the amount of your fiscal duties, such as wine and spirits, as you thus deprive yourself of a resource which you may one day require.

The answer (and it is a conclusive one) is this :—

A tax which from whatever cause dries up an important source of national industry and wealth, and thus takes from the fund which is available for taxation far more than the amount gained by the revenue, is a bad tax, and ought never, if possible, to be imposed or maintained.

The tax on French wines and spirits had the effect of restricting injuriously one of the largest branches of our foreign trade, and would, if maintained, by preventing the conclusion of the treaty, have deprived us of an accession of something like £20,000,000 per annum to the value of our general exchanges with

cannot buy from you, unless you will take our produce in exchange." The object in all cases being to remove all obstacles to a free exchange.

The fallacy into which Mr. Lowe has fallen will be best shown by an extreme illustration, but which is nevertheless governed by precisely the same law as that which he tries to explain.

Suppose that there are only two countries in the world, A and B, of which one, A, prohibits the trade of the other, B. Mr. Lowe would say to B, political economy teaches us to reduce our import duties for the benefit of our consumer. B therefore reduces all her import duties on the produce of A, but finds that in spite of the soundness of her doctrine she can import nothing from A, until A will take her produce in exchange, and that the consumer in B is no better off than before. This is the *reductio ad absurdum.*

" La grande loi économique est celle-ci.

" Les services s'échangent contre les services. Do ut des, do ut facias, facio ut des, facio ut facias; fais ceci pour moi, et je ferai cela pour toi, c'est bien trivial, bien vulgaire,—ce n'en est par moins le commencement le milieu et la fin de la Science." *

---

* Bastiat, "Sophismes Economiques," p. 407.

France. No wise legislation could advocate the retention of such a tax in the face of such consequences. There is probably no other form of tax to which it would not have been preferable to resort rather than to maintain these obstacles to our trade with France.

Such are the principal objections : it remains to consider the advantages of the policy which has been pursued.

It is unnecessary now to allude to the direct effects of the French Treaty. These are sufficiently known and appreciated, at last, to require no further reference.

It is not so generally known what have been the indirect results upon the commercial progress of Europe.

It is a common form of British self-complacency to talk of the great effect on other countries of the successful example of England's Free Trade policy, but facts do not justify this boast. Twenty years have elapsed since the repeal of the Corn Laws, and until the French Treaty the protective Tariffs of Europe had scarcely been touched; our self-governing Colonies have all more or less adopted protective Tariffs, and the United States of America have lost no occasion of increasing the restrictions upon foreign trade. The French Treaty has given an impulse to Free Trade which it was impossible for England alone to give. Those who are acquainted with the public opinion of other countries on this question know that so long as England was the only great country which had prospered under the modern system, the example produced but little effect. It was said that England had been enabled by a long course of monopoly to bring her industries to such a degree of strength, and to increase her productive power to such a point, as to enable her to face all competition, but that a similar course could only be taken by other countries, when they had, by a similar waste of their productive forces, increased in like manner, by some unexplained and mysterious process, their productive power. As soon as France, however, the great stronghold of protection, had renounced the error of her ways, and committed herself to a course of progressive freedom, the moral effect upon the Governments and upon the public opinion of Europe was irresistible. But this was not all.

We have said that in France the differential system was only abolished prospectively. This course was advisedly taken to enable her, while reforming her own system, to ensure the adoption by other countries of similar measures ; and thus, by the French Treaty, we secured the alliance and co-operation of France in breaking down the whole prohibitory laws of Europe.

Perhaps this policy of France may be censured by some " doctrinaire " politicians as unsound.

I cannot think that any one who desires the substantial progress of Free Trade rather than the assertion of a barren theory can share this view.

If, after reasonable efforts, other countries had refused to reciprocate, it would doubtless have been wiser on the part of France to adhere broadly to her own reforms, and disregard the course taken by others; but it could not have been expected, with the example of England before her eyes, that France, whose foreign trade is far more dependent on European markets than ours, could have entered alone upon this experiment, until she had exhausted every effort to obtain the simultaneous action of other nations. And if, by postponing for a few years the full development of her policy, she has been able to secure the co-operation of every country in Europe, it surely has been wise to wait.

But with this, whether right or wrong, England has nothing to do, except to consider its effect upon her own policy; and certainly it has placed her in a position of peculiar advantage. Without sacrificing her own independent principle, she thus regained the opportunity of obtaining all that France is able to extort by the material bribe of her reformed Tariff, and wherever commercial reforms are commenced, of asserting again her right to an equal share in all their results, if, indeed, she cannot effect even more than this by moulding them by her influence, and by an appeal to the principles and example of her policy, on a sounder and freer model.

It has been questioned whether the continental countries, if left to take their own course, might not have advanced more rapidly in the direction of Free Trade. This view exhibits a profound ignorance of these countries. The Governments always profess Free Trade, but, except under the influence of external pressure, would be often unable to set aside the strong opposition of the protected classes. The policy of France in withholding her Tariff affords a motive which is irresistible even to these classes, and thus strengthens the hand of the Governments effectually in overcoming their interested opposition.*

Thus, in pursuance of her policy, France has already in five years made in Europe alone Treaties with Belgium, the Zollverein, Italy, Sweden and Norway, and Switzerland, by which large reductions have been made in the Tariffs of all those countries.

England has obtained an equal participation in all these reductions by claiming where she had already the right by Treaty, and by obtaining by negotiation,

---

* This view, moreover, entirely overlooks the influence of co-operation and the friendly interchange of opinions and information, which are among the most valuable results of these negotiations. People talk of the example of England's progress and prosperity, but in most of the old countries of the Continent, without free discussion and an independent press, the facts and principles which illustrate and justify that progress and prosperity are most imperfectly known ; and many laws and restrictions which impede trade and distort international relations have their origin far more in ignorance than in deliberate design.

This form of criticism is one of the effects and evidences of the lamentable want of the "international spirit" which is so general in this country.

In every civilized country there are to be found a certain number of men penetrated with modern ideas, and anxious for liberal reforms. These men look to England as the representative of commercial freedom ; and a public act, such as a Commercial Treaty, not only affords a rallying-point for all that is sound and progressive in those countries, but, as it were, crystallizes and consolidates the elements of public opinion, which are required to enable Governments to effect a change of policy.

where such right did not exist, most favoured nation treatment.

Confining ourselves to the effect of these changes on the trade of England alone, these are the results. Taking the special trade with Belgium, France, and Italy (it is impossible to trace it with the Zollverein and Switzerland), the aggregate value exchanged backwards and forwards is as follows :—

			Imports.	Exports.
			£	£
FRANCE	... ...	1860 ...	17,774,000	12,701,000
		1861 ...	17,826,000	17,427,000
		1862 ...	21,675,000	21,765,000
		1863 ...	24,025,000	23,294,000
		1864 ...	25,640,000	23,825,000
BELGIUM	... ...	1860 ...	4,079,000	3,964,000
		1861 ...	3,817,000	4,914,000
		1862 ...	4,876,000	4,550,000
		1863 ...	5,174,000	5,059,000
		1864 ...	6,410,000	5,979,000
ITALY...	... ...	1862 ...	2,618,000	6,167,000
		1863 ...	2,358,000	7,338,000
		1864 ...	2,181,000	6,740,000

But as the indirect effects of this liberation of trade are quite as remarkable as the direct results, it is necessary to compare our European trade generally with that which existed prior to the French Treaty. This comparison gives the following result :—

1860.		1864.	
	£		£
Imports	84,403,000	Imports	98,502,000
Exports	69,644,000	Exports	100,064,000

These results are sufficiently striking to show the advantage which England has derived, both directly

from the French Treaty, and indirectly through the
Treaties made by France with other countries ; but
great as they are, it has been felt, as said before,
by all those who are practically acquainted with the
nature of the continental Tariffs, and the prevalent
ideas on customs' legislation in most European countries, that if England could obtain no more than an
equal participation in all that France secured, far less
progress would be made in commercial reform, and far
less practical advantage be reaped by British trade,
than if she were admitted to co-operate in the reconstruction of European Tariffs.

It is its assertion of this principle that gives a
peculiar value to the recent Treaty with Austria.

That Treaty may be generally described as a most
favoured nation Treaty so far as commerce is concerned, accompanied by engagements on the part of
Austria to revise her Tariff upon British produce and
manufactures within the limits of certain maxima rates
of duty, taking English prices, to be fixed by a Mixed
Commission, as the basis of assessment, and to conclude a supplemental Treaty, for the purpose of
applying specific duties within those limits.

Independently of the great value of the principle
thus asserted, the practical advantages of this Treaty
were considerable.

1st. It provides that the Customs Legislation of
Austria shall be revised in co-operation with England,
i.e. that the external influence brought to bear on this
work shall be that of a country whose policy is that of

commercial freedom in the widest sense, and whose experience enables her to supply the greatest range of facts and arguments, rather than that of countries like France or Prussia, who still cling to the form and phraseology of Protection.

2nd. It annihilates the differential system in Austria, which has heretofore given the Zollverein a virtual monopoly of her markets for many articles of produce.

3rd. It affixes certain limits to the amount of possible protection, and ensures a more equal incidence of duties than now exists, by an improved classification.

The small Tariff changes on both sides provided by the Protocol only require notice, because it may be feared that from an erroneous estimate of the relative value of the stipulations of the Treaty, these mutual reductions may be taken to show that the Treaty is after all a Tariff bargain. To dispose of this objection, it is only necessary to refer to the primary object of the negotiation, viz. the removal, wherever possible, consistently with the principles or policy of either country, of the obstacles to their mutual trade, and to say, that these duties being on both sides of a nature which enabled the two Governments to deal with them at once, and as they all of them created obstacles which it was for the interest of both to remove, this Treaty presented the most suitable occasion for doing so by common agreement. Certainly, on the principle of "equivalent concessions," this Treaty, if a Tariff bargain, must be regarded as a great achievement, for it secures a revision of the whole Customs Tariff of Austria, in return for the abolition of duty on a few Austrian staves, and the equalization of duty on Hungarian wines in bottle and in wood!

It has hitherto been supposed by many * that as England had no further Tariff reductions to offer to other countries, she was debarred from entering upon the negotiation of Treaties involving the reduction of foreign tariffs.

This idea proceeded unconsciously on the doctrine that a reduction of a Tariff is a concession to a foreign country, instead of being, as it is, a measure primarily and principally dictated by national interest.

But, even from this point of view, the necessity which was imposed on all the countries of Europe of reforming their Tariffs, by the policy adopted by France, opened the door to the action of English diplomacy.

The language used to foreign countries has been this: "You are obliged to reform your system in order to entitle you to the French concessions and save you from commercial isolation. It is far better to perform this work with England, which has no special objects to promote, and works in the general interests of freedom, than by the method of Tariff

---

* It is curious to trace the lingering operation of the protective fallacy in this objection. "You have nothing to give," it is said, "therefore you can ask nothing." This argument was well met by Mr. Bonar at Vienna. When asked what England would give in return for a reduction in the duty on herrings, he said, "more herrings."

bargains with France or other countries, to which you can, if you please, proceed from a better diplomatic vantage-ground when you have a more liberal foundation for your negotiations." You will then have more to offer than they will have to give, and "you may bring them down to your level."

The policy of the recent Treaties, however, rests upon much broader foundations.

The Austrian Treaty has been negotiated on the principle that a Tariff of Customs duties is a measure of international taxation, and is therefore a proper subject for international regulation.

It is impossible to impose taxes on commodities on any rational principle without a knowledge of the commodities to be taxed ; where these are, as they must be in the case supposed, of foreign origin, a correct foundation of facts can only be obtained by the co-operation of foreign countries.

England and Austria, therefore, agree to co-operate in framing a Tariff which, while on the one hand it secures the national object of a certain measure of protection (still unwisely thought necessary by Austria), shall nevertheless attain this object in the manner least injurious to English trade, and with such a correct knowledge of the facts upon which it is founded as to insure that no greater protection shall be given than is really intended.

It is strange that in a country like England, which did not hesitate to spend millions and resort to war for the purpose of vindicating her right of trade with

China and Japan, it should be thought unreasonable in the case of European countries with restrictive and prohibitory laws to hold such legislation as affording a ground for remonstrance and a claim for co-operation in reducing to a minimum the injury inflicted.

But it is said that we should not proceed by way of Treaties, that each country should be left to act by independent legislation. To this it may be answered, Why not proceed by way of Treaty? If you are in earnest in your policy and have entire faith in its wisdom, why object to bind yourself to it by an international contract? Independently, however, of the practical necessity of this mode of proceeding caused by the policy of France, my answer is this: A Treaty is nothing more than an international statute law, and it is most important that in a matter of international concern there should exist an international guarantee that the policy adopted shall be maintained and placed beyond the reach of reactionary influences. Where would commerce be without a security?

The argument often used, that it is inconsistent with national dignity and independence to admit a foreign country to interfere in the regulation of a Tariff, of course falls to the ground when the international character of this kind of legislation is admitted. But this argument, it may be observed, is never used by those who really desire commercial reform; it is merely a device of the enemy to rouse the foolish prejudices and passions of the country, and always will be found to emanate from the Protectionist camp.

The Tariff which will be constructed in the spring in co-operation with England will henceforth be the Austrian Tariff, and will doubtless be gradually extended to all other countries by Treaties or otherwise.

Whatever, therefore, may be the direct and immediate effects of the new Tariff upon British trade, and it is not probable from a variety of causes, for some years to come, that these will be very great, it cannot be doubted that the foreign trade of Austria with the countries near her frontiers—the Zollverein, Italy, Switzerland, and her Eastern neighbours—will be rapidly increased, that her consuming power will be developed, and her resources proportionately augmented.

Thus gradually will the rich territories and large population of this great Empire be brought within the ever-widening circle of commercial civilization, and contribute their share to the commonwealth of Europe.

If this be the result, it matters little to England whether Austria's direct exchanges are made with her or not. She is certain sooner or later to obtain her full part in the general accession which will thus be made to the productive forces of the world.

And it must be recollected that every fresh accession to this new alliance is a pledge for its future extension.

Each new Treaty which is made has a double operation. It not only opens the market of another country to foreign industry, but it reacts on those already opened ; and by the universal introduction of the most favoured nation principle, the indispensable condition of all recent Treaties, each new point gained in any one negotiation becomes a part of the common law of Europe.

It is thus that the Austrian Treaty has obtained for France an alteration in the English wine duties, and Austria is at present engaged in obtaining for England a relaxation of the French navigation laws.

It is now certain that in a few years in every country in Europe prohibitions will have been replaced by a system of moderate duties, and a great impulse given to international trade throughout the Continent, and it may reasonably be believed that the results of these changes will lead, at no distant day, to complete and general freedom from protective Tariffs.

With such a prospect in view of the present generation, is it too sanguine a hope that the united example of the old world may lead the Great American Republic and the younger Anglo-Saxon communities still unsevered from us in which the seed of this great wrong is already sown, to turn aside from following in the track of folly and injustice which marks the slow progress of commercial freedom in Europe; that monopoly, like the still darker bondage of slavery, may be proscribed by all civilized nations, and the rights of labour universally secured by equal laws ?

III.

FREE TRADE AND FREE ENTERPRISE.

(Extract from Preface to Report of Proceedings at the Dinner of the Cobden Club, June, 1873.)

Mr. Milner Gibson's remarks were directed to another class of questions closely connected with the Free Trade policy. Both he and all the speakers who followed him adverted to the reactionary tendency which appears to be increasing in this country, to look to the State for the performance of functions which have hitherto been left to private persons and to private enterprise. Such are the theoretical proposals which have been made for the partial or entire appropriation by Government of the rent of land and of minerals, and the more practical schemes for the State purchase of railways, docks, packet services, and other industrial undertakings. Projects of this description have long been only too familiar to economists of other countries; their only novelty consists in their prevalence in England, and especially at a time when the too-hasty critics of the Free Trade policy are confronted with the significant fact of the gradual emancipation of the classes, which it was reproached with having failed in reaching. But it is well that such a tendency should be carefully watched and resisted, by all who believe that it is dangerous to the national economy, and to the progress of society.

The State has been well defined as "the great fiction by means of which every one attempts to live at the expense of every one;" and it will be found that, in the last analysis, all these proposals rest upon the economic fallacy that the State, in substituting itself for private or personal agencies, can evade or control the inexorable law of supply and demand. This it can never do, except on one condition, viz. that, in superseding individual responsibility, it shall at the same time suppress individual liberty; for, after all, the much-denounced law of competition is nothing but the law of liberty, and the essential condition, as it is the only permanent safeguard, of social order and democratic progress.

But it is said that State interference is invoked for the very reason that there is a class of cases to which the rule of free competition cannot apply, and in which to allow private property is to create partial monopolies. So far as this is true, and the effects of international competition render it much less true than is generally assumed, it must be the result of limited conditions of supply, which cannot be materially improved, if, indeed, they would not be still further limited, by State proprietorship. Whatever, then, may be the evil of partial monopolies, it will certainly not be removed by the creation in their place of the absolute and far more dangerous monoply of the State.

Private monoplies can always be controlled and regulated by the power which creates or permits them, but
war or revolution can alone control the abuse of power
by the State itself. This would be so, even if the
State were only another name for the Government;
but it must be observed that, just in proportion as the
representative system is extended, so will it be more
and more impossible for Parliament to control the acts
of an executive entrusted with vast and complex
administrations.

A minister of Land Revenue or of Public Works
may, indeed, be nominally responsible to Parliament;
but it is notorious and self-evident that the real work
of such departments can only be performed by permanent officials, who are not responsible to Parliament,
nor in any practical sense to the minister, who must
always be completely at their mercy. It is a suspicious
fact that this call for State interference coincides with
a widely extended franchise and an ostensible advance
towards a more democratic system. Can it be an
unconscious attempt to escape from the consequences
of this policy, and recover for authority on the one
hand, what has been conceded on the other? If so,
it is a grave political anachronism. The real remedy
for the drawbacks on Parliamentary Government is
not to extend its nominal duties and powers, while
virtually vesting them in an irresponsible executive,
but to contract more and more the functions of the
central power, and entrust the internal administration
of the country more and more to the local institutions,

which are the life and soul of a free and self-governing people.

It is impossible on this occasion to do more than glance at a few of the forms in which the tendency to which reference has been made has manifested itself; but it will be seen that they all involve a dislocation of the forces which, in a free society, regulate and restrain each other, and thus ensure the harmonious working of the body-politic.

To take the case of property in land. The function of rent is to restrain the undue pressure of population on the soil. Where the State, or, in other words, the community at large, is the landlord, it must either (as it ought in justice to do) exact competition rents from the occupants or create a privileged class of tenants, by which a particular portion of the population would be favoured at the expense of the rest.

On the first hypothesis, not only would no benefit accrue to the cultivator, but the constant accretions of rent which would go in reduction of taxation, and to the relief of the people at large, would directly tend to aggravate the demand for land and the pressure of the population on the soil. On the second, the effect would be simply to create again those very private rights of property in land which it was intended to destroy.

How different is the solution offered by the Free Trade policy? Instead of the futile attempt to plant an indefinite and ever-increasing population in a limited area, it would, on the one hand, remove

all the artificial obstacles to the free acquisition and
natural distribution of property in land, and, on the
other, reassert and confirm private property in land,
on the logical grounds, that wherever land is limited,
so must its occupancy be; that unless the State
undertakes to regulate the increase of population, its
limitation can only be enforced by the operation of
private ownership; and that, while trade is free and
the products of labour can be exchanged for the
products of the soil of all the world, it is not
necessary to justice or to the welfare of a nation that
the land itself should be possessed by all its inhabitants.

Free-Traders say to the people, "If you desire
to possess land and cannot afford to purchase it at
home, even when all distinctions between land and
personal property have been effaced, there is land
enough and to spare in other countries for you; but
if you prefer to remain at home, you shall be able
to obtain the products of the soil in exchange for
your labour in all the markets of the world free from
all tax or tribute."

But it will be said that a system which enables
a large proportion of the population to possess the
soil in partial or absolute ownership, is essential to
secure its most profitable use, and the social and
political welfare of a nation.

By no one was this opinion more strongly held
than by Cobden, who regarded the present alienation
from the land of the body of the agricultural class

as one of our greatest dangers. But how did he propose to remedy the evil? Not, certainly, by the nationalization of the land, or by the appropriation by the State of a fanciful unearned increment of rent, but by liberating the land, as he would have liberated trade, from all impediments to free exchange.

If it be urged, as it often is, that the conditions of society in England at the present time, the accumulated wealth of the upper classes, and the keen competition for land, preclude the hope of any effectual progress towards Cobden's ideal, by such an orthodox reform as the assimilation of real and personal property, Free-Traders may well reply that they distrust this sweeping assertion, believing, on the contrary, that by prudence and co-operation on the part of the labouring class, in the face of a decreasing ratio of supply to the demand for agricultural labour, much may be accomplished; in any case, they may insist that this measure shall at least be tried before, on the plea of State necessity, recourse be had to such desperate expedients as the regulation by Government of the terms on which the land shall be held, and of the number of those who live by it.

The policy of Free Trade is to expand and disperse; that of State proprietorship or Communism is to contract and concentrate. The first is identified with progress and civilization; the second can only culminate in stagnation or anarchy.

The case of coal affords a good illustration of the

operation of the two conflicting principles. It is clear that the real and paramount cause of the recent rise of price has been nothing but excessive demand. The only possible remedy is to check this demand by a stern enhancement of price. For this purpose what agency can be so effectual as that of private ownership ? What popular Government, in the face of a fierce demand for an article of first necessity, could resist the pressure which would be brought to bear upon it to exert all its influence as proprietor to keep down prices, and thereby aggravate the evil until it became incurable ? But even if such a Government were found, the increasing rentals derived from the progressive rise in price must be devoted to the remission of taxation ; and thus, by relieving the people from pressure in another direction, neutralize in proportion to such relief the check upon consumption caused by the rise in price.

But it is to the question of the purchase of railways by the State that public attention has been of late especially directed. It will be found that to this proposal also, the economic objection which has been stated equally applies.

Why is this measure urged upon us ? It can, of course, only be urged on the assumption, that by better administration, economy of management and absence of competition, the supply of railroad accommodation will be increased at the same or a diminished cost to the public, and with a profit to the State.

Admitting for the sake of the argument this most doubtful proposition, one of two consequences must follow—

Either the State will act on the commercial principle, and charge the rates which yield the largest profit, or it will not.

If it does, the profits will be devoted to the reduction of taxation, and the relief thus afforded will not only tend to increase the demand for railway accommodation, and thus increase the pressure on a supply which is, on the assumption, limited, but it will be directly given at the expense of that portion of the community which requires railway service. If it does not, which may be safely predicted, the effect would be even more opposed to sound economy and public policy, as it would, by artificially cheapening the cost of transport, of which the supply is limited, dangerously disturb the natural equilibrum of supply and demand, and be tantamount to a subsidy paid by the public at large to the trading and travelling classes.

Mr. Goschen enforced Mr. Milner Gibson's admonition in some observations which merit careful attention. He reminded his hearers that, although in the political struggles in which Cobden engaged he possessed the advantage of having the masses on his side, against the class interests which were opposed to him, the time may come in England, as it has often come elsewhere, when his followers must be prepared to face the masses.

This is an important truth, but it is not only in the misdirected action of the masses that the danger lies. The wage-receiving classes in this country require less and less every year the intervention of the State, to secure for them their fair share in the annual profits of the nation ; and it may be hoped that their practical sense, and love of justice, will in the long run save them, not only from Continental socialism, but also from the errors and excesses which, by driving capital abroad, and stimulating foreign competition, must infallibly recoil upon themselves.

There is perhaps a still greater, because a more insidious, danger, in the counsels of those short-sighted politicians and impatient reformers, who have more faith in the action of an irresponsible bureaucracy, and in what they call " constructive economy," than in the forces of freedom ; and who, abandoning the work begun by Cobden and the League, in liberating exchange from all that impedes the natural distribution of wealth, would call upon Government to undertake duties which it never can properly discharge, with powers which it will assuredly abuse.

IV.

NOTE ON STATE RAILWAYS.

[I have, by permission, printed this extract from an official memorandum written at the India Office in 1882, as it explains at rather more length the position on this subject taken in the preceding paper by Sir L. Mallet, and it is a good instance of the way in which considerations of theory and of political economy, so often regarded as *spéculations oisives*, guided him in his practical work.— ED.]

I DO not know that the general argument in favour of leaving the public works of a country in the hands of private capitalists can be better stated than in the words of Lord Macaulay in a review of "Southey's Colloquies"—

"There are two or three principles respecting public works which, as an experience of vast extent proves, may be trusted in almost every case.

"It scarcely ever happens that any private man or body of men will invest property in a canal, a tunnel, or a bridge, but from an expectation that the outlay will be profitable to them. No work of this sort can be profitable to private speculators unless the public be willing to pay for the use of it. The public will not pay of their own accord for what yields no profit or convenience to them. There is thus a direct and obvious connection between the motive which induces individuals to undertake such a work and the utility of the work.

"Can we find any such connection in the case of a public work executed by a Government? If it is useful, are the individuals who rule the country richer? If it is useless, are they poorer? A public man may be solicitous for his credit. But is he not likely to gain more credit by a useless display of ostentatious architecture in a great town than by the best road or the best canal in some remote province? The fame of public works is a much less certain test of their utility than the amount of toll collected at them. In a corrupt age there will be direct embezzlement. In the purest age there will be abundance of jobbing. Never were the statesmen of any country more sensitive to public opinion and more spotless in pecuniary transactions than those who have of late governed England. Yet we have only to look at the buildings recently erected in London for a proof of our rule. In a bad age the fate of the public is to be robbed outright. In a good age it is merely to have the dearest and worst of everything.

"Buildings for State purposes, the State must erect. And here we think that in general the State ought to stop. We firmly believe that five hundred thousand pounds subscribed by individuals for railroads or canals would produce more advantage to the public than five millions voted by Parliament for the same purpose. There are certain old saws about the master's eye and about everybody's business, in which we place very great faith."

This seems to me to be excellent sense, and a closer examination of the subject will, I think, show that the superior efficiency of private agencies in this respect is the result of economical laws which cannot be evaded, and which will assert their power whatever may be done to evade them.

What is the reason urged for placing railway enterprise in the hands of the State? It is that as railways are in their nature partial monopolies, it is not right that private persons should reap the advantage of them, but that the profits should be shared by the whole community. As a matter of abstract right or justice, I entirely fail to see why the whole of any particular community should reap this profit any more than a particular set of capitalists. This is precisely the same argument as that which is urged in support of the nationalization of the land, and other communistic theories, which I presume that those whom I am addressing will agree with me in thinking thoroughly unsound.

But I prefer to confine my remarks on this occasion to the practical question, viz. : Is it for the advantage of the community that what are called monopoly profits (not always, I may observe, very clear and definable) should be divided among the whole community, instead of being appropriated by private persons or bodies ?

In speaking of monopolies, sufficient care is not always taken to distinguish between natural and artificial monopolies. A natural monopoly is the result of a limitation of supply caused by a law of nature. This may be a misfortune, but it is inevitable, and the only way of meeting it is to allow it to exert its power in limiting the demand. The land of a particular country is in this class. If the population of a purely agricultural country increases to a point at which the land is insufficient to support it, people must go elsewhere or die ; no system of tenant rights, or peasant proprietaries, still less of State proprietorship, can ever avert this, except by restraining the growth of population. An artificial monopoly is the

result of an artificial and arbitrary interference with
the natural law of free competition, and is as unnecessary as it is unjust and mischievous. Wherever
the railways of a country are left, as in England and
America, to private enterprise, they are only monopolies in the former sense, viz. as the result of a
natural law—the limitation of the land, the configura-
tion of the country, etc,—which prevents the free
action of competition. This state of things justifies
certain interference on the part of the State, with a
view to the general convenience, but in a strictly
economic sense affords no hope of alleviation by any
process of State appropriation. On the contrary, the
effect of such appropriation can only be to add to the
evils of a natural monopoly those of an artificial
monopoly as well.

The public object—in other words, the interest of
the community—in a railway system, is that it should
afford the most efficient and the cheapest means of
transit. In private hands the rates and fares must, in
the long run, be governed by the inevitable conditions
of supply and demand. In the hands of the State one
of two things must happen. Either the commercial
principle will be adopted, and the rates will be fixed
with a view to obtain the largest profit, or it will not.
If it is, the profits will be devoted to the reduction of
taxation, and the relief thus afforded will tend to
increase the demand for railway accommodation, and
thus increase the pressure on a supply which is on the
assumption limited, thereby increasing its cost, in

which case it will be directly given at the expense of that portion of the community which requires railway service; or if it is not, which may be safely predicted, for the State will rarely be able to resist popular demands for reduction of rates, the effect will be even more opposed to sound economy, as it would, by cheapening the cost of transport of which the supply is limited, dangerously disturb the natural equilibrium of supply and demand, and be tantamout to a subsidy paid by the public at large to the trading and travelling classes.

Whatever, then, may be the evil of the partial natural monopolies of private enterprise, it will certainly not be removed by the substitution of the absolute and far more dangerous artificial monopoly of the State. Private monopolies can be and are always controlled and regulated by the power which permits them, but it is far more difficult to prevent the abuse of power by the State itself.

On economical grounds, therefore, I do not think that railway profits constitute a safe or legitimate source of public revenue.

V.

EGYPT.

(A Letter to M. de Laveleye.)

10*th March*, 1878.

Dear M. de Laveleye,

I have read with extreme interest your article in the *Fortnightly Review* for February on "England and the War." With its general tenor I have only to express my warm sympathy. It appears to me very able, and conclusive as to the general policy and duty of England on the so-called Eastern Question. But there is one passage on page 164, in which, after accepting Mr. Gladstone's propositions, that we have nothing to fear from Russia in barring the passage of the Suez Canal, and that we have already so many responsibilities and vulnerable points all over the world, that it would be folly, and even madness, to increase their number, you nevertheless impose upon us as a sacred duty the annexation of Egypt!

I confess that I read this passage with very great regret. The course which you advocate is pressed upon us from so many different quarters both at home

and abroad—bondholders, journalists, soldiers, adminis-
trators, and adventurers at home; by Bismarck at
Berlin, by a powerful class in Paris, by Nubar, and
many others abroad—it is a course so congenial to the
vulgar British instinct, and so favourable to the reactionary party now in the ascendant among us, that
I cannot undertake to say the thing may not be done.
But this I do say, and I say it with deliberation and
a strong assurance, that an occupation of Egypt would
be a turning-point in the history of England; and
that whatever fate might then be in store for her, of
which I for one should augur ill, at least this is certain,
that she must renounce all hope of solving the deepest
problems of society and achieving the last triumphs of
a civilized policy.   This crowning glory will be reserved
for a wiser people.

This, however, is only an opinion, whatever it may
be worth.   I proceed to give you some of my reasons,
and I do so, because they are in a great degree the
result of an experience with which you are less familiar,
and which I venture, therefore, to think you may not
sufficiently have taken into your account.   I refer to
considerations derived from my knowledge of the
character and effects of British rule in India.

I am glad to perceive that even you foresee that
the enterprise, to which you so cheerfully invite us,
involves the attempt to civilize the better part of
Africa by missionaries, breech-loaders, and brandy.
We may, therefore, at once assume that we both mean
the practical conquest and possession of a vast con-

tinent by England in the course of the next half-
century. For my own part, I may say at once that
I have not a shadow of a doubt that, unless meanwhile
some decisive check be given to our national progress,
this will be the inevitable result.

From this point of view the experiences of our
Indian Empire become, in some of their aspects,
most important. Have you fully considered them
under the three following heads ? The effects of that
empire upon (1) our national character; (2) our foreign
relations; (3) the people of India.

In Grant·Duff's closing chapter of his "Notes of
an Indian Journey," the advantages and disadvantages
of India to England were summed up with great fair-
ness and his usual ability. Although he takes a less
unfavourable view than I do of our balance-sheet, you
will recollect that even he admits that our national
energy and enterprise might have more profitably
expended itself in other fields, that our position as a
European power is distinctly weakened, and that our
hopes of leaving a permanent impression upon the
people or founding a durable empire in India are at
present of the vaguest and most speculative kind.

I must add to his picture some darker shadows,
which his political temperament has led him to omit,
and which the events of the last two years have
brought into repulsive prominence. I think it is a
serious evil that a not inconsiderable portion of our
educated class should receive their political training
and impressions in governing subject-races under

despotic institutions. This class forms an important auxiliary to the "vested interests" of war, which present one of the most formidable obstacles to moral and material progress. Including India, we spend annually on our military and naval services no less a sum than £45,000,000 sterling. Think for a moment what this means, bearing in mind that there is hardly a family in the upper and middle classes which does not possess some interest, direct or indirect, in the division of this spoil, and also the enormous political power which its dispensation confers upon the Government.

It is not in human nature that any body of men, however patriotic, should look favourably on a policy which, if realized, would destroy their *raison d'être*, and which, at every successive stage of its success, diminishes their number and curtails their importance. The possession of India not only enormously increases and strengthens the military element in our body-politic, but, as I have said before, perverts the political instincts of almost all the civilian class which is connected with its government.

Even where slavery in name does not exist, the habitual contact of a privileged race with an alien and subjugated people is alike degrading to both. The waste of national power in our attempt to hold India has been, I believe, incalculable. What might not we have achieved in consolidating our institutions at home and developing them in our colonial possessions with half the effort made in the thankless task of governing a people who hate us on principles which we do not believe—in a country where we cannot live?

I believe that we do not know how much our national progress is retarded, and our national conscience obscured, by the presence amongst us of so large and powerful a class, the whole current of whose ideas is opposed to social and economic reforms. This class, by the law of its being, is favourable to schemes of Imperial ambition, to a reactionary foreign policy, to personal government and to privilege, to a lavish expenditure and to indirect taxation—in a word, to chauvinism and to socialism.

Thus we are constantly engaged in a task which you in this very article most justly condemn, when you say, " There can be nothing worse than to pursue at once two inconsistent lines of conduct." We are carrying on side by side an Imperial and a Democratic policy : in one part of our dominions proclaiming self-government and free institutions with the widest popular suffrage; in another maintaining our hold on vast populations only by a powerful administrative despotism supported by military force—at once a great Christian nation and the greatest Mahomedan power in the world—in England, so far secure in the strength of a loyal and united people; in India, trembling at the mere whisper of a Russian pedlar in a native bazaar!

These are the conditions under which you invite us to conquer and to govern Africa! It is true that in a former paper you considerately suggested that we might

I

simultaneously abandon India. If this were possible, we might at least have the advantage of a choice between two evils. But, alas! the duties and responsibilities of empire, once assumed, cannot be thrown aside. If we leave India, it will not be to take another continent under our sway, but to confess our failure, to avow our defeat, and to accept too late a humbler destiny. It is not to the deserts of Africa nor to the plains of Hindostan that the friends of freedom and the believers in the future of the human race turn their wistful eyes. " Westward the course of empire takes its way."

What are your reasons for urging on us so insane a course? " Great nations, like great men, have a mission to fulfil which they must accept as a duty. If they refuse it, they are punished. It is not for nothing that England has set the world the example of constitutional liberty, has scattered over the four quarters of the globe her swarms of Anglo-Saxon descent, and has undertaken to govern two hundred millions of subjects. Greatness has its obligations, *honores onera*. The country which has done so much for the civilization of the whole human race cannot satisfy herself with growing rich, with heaping up gold in the hands of her magnates, and slumbering on the pillows of contented opulence. Instinctively the people will seek more work, and if the cravings for action be not satisfied, it will turn to discontent and unwise exertion. Whence arises at this moment in England the secret disquiet, the pugnacious disposition which nothing justifies in the eyes of sensible and reflecting men? Simply because the people is experiencing an unsatisfied desire of expansion. If the present war comes to an end without further complications, by the acceptance in whole or in part of the conditions imposed by Russia, the bulk of the nation will thereupon experience a vague but deep sentiment of humiliation and loss of consequence which may be in the future the cause of actions very far from reasonable."

I can only understand these remarks by again concluding that in writing them you had before you, in a very imperfect manner, the real conditions of our rule in India.

It can hardly be argued that because a country has undertaken, with extraordinary audacity and at infinite risk, to govern two hundred millions of subjects in India, she is bound in honour and duty to take on herself the task of governing another two hundred millions in Africa. On the contrary, such a fact affords the strongest possible reason for her not doing so.

This reason acquires greatly increased strength when it is recollected that so far as we have gone we have certainly not succeeded in our government of India, that all its greatest problems are yet unsolved, and that there is hardly a statesman of mark among us now who does not doubt whether it might not have been better for England if the unscrupulous genius of Hastings, and the daring rapacity of Clive, had been foiled by a kinder fate.

And with this warning before us, can honour or

duty be invoked to bid us embark in another and perhaps more perilous adventure ? Rather should I attribute such a course to the allurements of cupidity and the morbid promptings of an uninstructed philanthropy.

It is true that in the conquest and so-called civilization of Africa we should have a very different work before us from that which we have found in India— different, but not therefore less difficult—in many of its aspects clearly a task requiring even rougher and more brutalizing agencies, involving on a gigantic scale the ignoble conflict of the armed European with the naked savage ; and as English troops are far too few and too costly for such an enterprise, the employment of Sikhs and Ghoorkas to shoot down African negroes, while the duskier cohorts of Africa are retained to stamp out the seeds of disaffection in the provinces of India.

These are the imperial arts to which the policy you advocate would compel us to resort ! These are the exploits which, as the champions of constitutional liberty and the interpreters of Providence, we are called on to perform, that we may appease a craving for action and a desire of expansion on the part of the idlest and most ignorant of our people, or avert a vague and irrational sentiment of humiliation at the dearly bought successes of Russia, while millions of acres unbroken by the plough and of forests untouched by the axe are lying ready in our own possessions to absorb ten times our present population in the peaceful pursuits of a beneficent and fruitful industry. Let us at least people our own solitudes and replenish the waste corners of our own dominions, before we make ourselves the missionaries of blood and plunder in the heart of Africa.

But you say that we must not " be satisfied with growing rich and heaping up gold and slumbering on the pillows of contented opulence," and would urge us to gird up our loins and begin again on a grander scale the career of boundless territorial conquest—which it has been the earnest effort of all our wisest statesmen during the last fifty years to restrain and abandon.

Was it thus to squander the heritage of our toiling millions that Romilly and Horner, Hume and Huskisson, Cobden and Bright, Peel and Gladstone, have taught us a higher morality, liberated the springs of our industry, and laid the lines of our financial greatness ?

Is England to lead the way in transplanting to another continent the miserable traditions and discredited maxims of the past, to bring Africa into the scale to trim a new balance of power, and there to seek new battle-fields for the nations of Europe to add to the bloody record of their own ?

It may be that the bankers and bondholders of Paris may persuade a feeble Government to connive for the time at a British occupation of Egypt ; but with recovered resources can any man believe that the old rivalry would not revive, and that the dying embers of national hatred between France and

England would not glow once more into life in Egypt and Algiers ?

The Italian people would soon follow suit in seeking to found in Tunis another Carthage—and thus it is easy to see how Africa would soon become the centre of a new system of intrigues, of conflicting ambitions, of suspicions and jealousies, of wars and conquests, aggravated by all the incidents of uncertain boundaries, disputed native rights, and certain native wrongs.

It was the boast of Canning that in holding out the hand of fellowship to the young republics of America, he had called a new world into existence to redress the balance of the old. It is to be the task of his degenerate successors to create another world in order to reverse his work, to give a new lease to despotic power and military government, and to repeat in Africa the follies and the crimes of Europe.

And what is the time chosen for this sinister policy ? The interval which has elasped since the peace of 1815 has been spent (with the inauspicious exception of the Crimean War) in building up the fabric of our national greatness by the diligent prosecution of liberal reforms, in developing our material resources, in probing social problems, and in extending the principles of civil, religious, and commercial liberty. Our insular position, our economical conditions, our maritime supremacy, and our colonial possessions have laid the foundations of a system of our own, strong enough to stand aloof from the alliances and political complications of Continental Europe, and if true to ourselves to carry through the greatest experiment in government which the world has ever seen.

To raise the masses of our people to the level of human beings, to force through by allowing the unimpeded action of natural laws the just distribution of wealth, to educate our people and bring them more and more within the pale of responsible and self-conscious citizenship, to co-operate with other nations in the arts of peace, to undermine and neutralize the reactionary forces of Europe by promoting all the material agencies of civilization, and to send out swarms of free men to found English institutions in our foreign possessions,—this is a work which is worthy of a great ambition, and it is a work within our reach.

But if, held back by the baser elements in our national life, we turn our thoughts again to wars and conquests, those who would lightly regard the loss of moral greatness may yet pause in their enterprise, lest they incur the deeper reproach of a political blunder.

The architects of our present fortunes had other ends in view. Their means were adapted to their ends, and will not lend themselves to other uses. The English Empire must in the last resort be defended, as it has been won, by English hands. The expedients of a handful of conquerors will not always suffice to hurl with effect half-willing legions of subject-races against the soldier-citizens of Europe, and our financial resources, great as they are for all legitimate purposes, may one day break under the strain. It is a significant fact that the whole cost of our army and our navy in England (£30,000,000 sterling) is defrayed by taxes upon intoxicating drinks! This is a resource which mainly depends on the degradation of our people, of which it is by a fatal implication at once the cause and the effect. For every shilling spent by a drunken workman, the State takes eight from his helpless wife and children, thus indirectly maintaining a tax on decency and providence.

But the demands of a great military power cannot be met without it, and we shall thus be placed in the dilemma of renouncing all hope of the real emancipation of our working classes, or of submitting to sacrifices which an educated nation with a wide popular franchise may one day refuse to accept.

It is one thing to fight for national existence and to avert a foreign yoke; it is another to drain the heart's blood of a people for a phantom empire, and to dispute with Russia an imaginary claim to an impossible universal dominion. The one thing is a reality, the other an idea. We have seen the incredible efforts made by England at the beginning of the century when stirred by the fear of French invasion, and the heroic stand made by France to defend her soil from a German conquest. We have also seen the first, accepting tardily, but readily

enough, when the real pressure came, the independence of America ; and the second renouncing,
almost without a murmur, the military supremacy of
Europe.

With such issues before us, what shall we choose ?
Shall the final record of history be that England was
unequal to the greatness of her fortunes—that,
tempted by a false ambition, she shrank in moral
cowardice from her half-finished work as the free
mother of free nations, and left it to other leaders,
in a better time, to guide a chosen people into the
promised land ?

VI.

RECIPROCITY.

(A Letter addressed to Mr. Thomas Bayley Potter, M.P., as
Chairman of the Committee of the Cobden Club.)

March 17th, 1879.

Dear Mr. Potter,

I was asked last year by the Committee of the Cobden Club to write a paper for them on the subject of the recent cry for what has been known by the name of " Reciprocity."

The constant pressure of other work has hitherto prevented me from complying with this request—but I am bound to add that I have been deterred by another cause.

Whenever I attempted to address myself to the task, I was confronted with an insuperable difficulty.

In spite of much reading and a very sincere desire to understand the objects and arguments of the advocates of this new commercial policy, I have entirely failed in finding any statement of their case, or any programme of practical measures which will stand the test of serious discussion.

So that whenever I approached my adversary, I found him to be a man of straw.

I wish, therefore, frankly to lay my difficulties before the Committee; and, unless they can help me to a more distinct comprehension of the position which I am asked to assail, to submit to them a proposal which may, I hope, have the effect of eliciting the desired information.

For the present I can only deal with the crude opinions and proposals which have been put forward from time to time in the public press and at public meetings.

I take the following statement of the case on the part of the " Modern Reciprocitarian " from a pamphlet by Lord Bateman, entitled, " A Plea for Limited Protection or for Reciprocity : "—

"Granted that the theory of free and unrestricted commerce with all quarters of the universe is as bold as it is magnificent; granted that the idea, by whomsoever originated (and advocated by no one more consistently than by our good and wise Prince Consort), is both grand and glorious in its conception; granted that to give effect to it has been the aim, as it has been the long-accepted policy, of successive Governments; it cannot be denied that the sting of 'want of reciprocity' has from the first checkmated our philanthropic efforts, and obliged us now to confess, after thirty years of trial, that in practice our Free Trade is at best but one-sided; and that, while we are opening our ports to the commerce and manufactures of the world free and unrestricted, other countries, without conferring upon us any reciprocal benefit, are taking advantage, without scruple, of our magnanimous but disastrous (because one-sided) liberality."

It is necessary here to point out that there is no apparent connection of ideas between the statement of facts (even if they were correct) in this paragraph and the conclusions at which it seems to point, viz. that we are suffering not only from restrictions abroad, but from freedom at home.

No one would, I presume, deny that the system under which British trade is now carried on is not one of Free Trade, nor that a complete system of free trade is better than a one-sided Free Trade; but if, as is alleged, protection is only sought for the sake of reciprocity, it is impossible to understand why a one-sided Free Trade should not be better than no Free Trade at all.

The mutual relaxation of restrictions is a mutual advantage; the mutual creation of restrictions is a mutual injury. If one tariff is bad, two must be worse. It matters nothing whether the barrier be raised in one country or in another, the effect is precisely the same. It would be as rational, if the French railway from Boulogne to Paris doubled its charges, for the South-Eastern to do the same by way of reciprocity, as for the British custom-house to raise the duties on French produce because France raises them on ours.

It will be said, perhaps, that the railway tariff affects the French exports as well as the British imports, and that, therefore, the case is not parallel; but this is a fallacy. A moment's reflection will show that the French tariff affects French exports as well as British imports. If a French wine-grower is made to pay a higher price for his Lancashire cloth, or,

what is the same thing, gets less of it for a " barique "
of his wine, he will raise the price of his wine or give
less of it in exchange ; and his trade, as well as that
of the British manufacturer, will be burdened and
restricted by the tax.

To repeat this process at the English port would
simply double the burden on both the French and
the English trade. As Sir Robert Peel said long
ago, the only way of fighting hostile tariffs is by free
imports.

For what is reciprocity ? The essence of all trade
is and must be "reciprocity." Every transaction of
commerce by which one man voluntarily sells his
produce or property to another is an act of reciprocity,
and is complete in itself. The imposition of a duty
by one country on the produce or manufactures of
another only affects the transaction by rendering it
less profitable both to the seller and to the buyer ;
the variations of supply and demand will cause the
incidence of the tax to fall upon the seller and the
buyer, the producer and the consumer, in varying
degree ; but, in the long run, it will be equally shared
between them.

This may be put in a way which leaves no door
open for dispute or discussion. It must be admitted
that, in principle, the effect must be precisely the
same whatever the amount of the tax or the extent
of the restriction—whether a duty of 10, 50, or 100
per cent. be imposed, there must be a point at which
a duty becomes a prohibition. What is true in this

extreme is equally true at every point and at every stage of the protective process. To whatever degree a country protects its own productions, it protects in precisely the same degree the productions of the countries with which it trades; for to whatever extent it closes its ports on foreign commodities, it prevents foreign countries from importing its own.

If this be true, and it cannot be otherwise, it follows that the more nearly the tariffs of foreign countries approach to the limits of prohibition, the more will the British producer be protected in his own market.

Those, therefore, who desire this kind of reciprocity—viz. the reciprocity of monopoly—must rejoice at every new restriction placed upon British trade abroad, as necessarily involving increased protection to British trade at home.

I am sometimes almost led to think, in reading the speculations of those who are always raising the cry of alarm at the importation of foreign goods, that they are still under the influence of the exploded mercantile theory of the Balance of Trade, according to which the advantage of commerce to a country resides in what it parts with and not in what it obtains—in its exports and not in its imports, the balance being paid in money, which was supposed to be the only wealth.

I am unwilling to believe in the survival of this delusion; but if it still prevails in any quarter, it is so important to dispel it, that I am tempted to quote at

some length the clearest exposition which I know of
the phenomena of international trade.

"All interchange is in substance and effect barter: he
who sells his productions for money, and with that money
buys other goods, really buys those goods with his own produce. And so of nations: their trade is a mere exchange of
exports for imports; and whether money is employed or not,
things are only in their permanent state when the exports
and imports exactly pay for each other.

"When this is the case, equal sums of money are due
from each country to the other; the debts are settled by bills,
and there is no balance to be paid in the precious metals.
The trade is in a state like that which is called in mechanics
a condition of stable equilibrium." *

Mr. Mill goes on to show that a country which
wants more imports than its exports will pay for has
to pay the difference in money; that by this trans-
mission of the precious metals the quantity of the
currency is diminished in such a country and increased
in the countries with which it trades; that prices fall
in the former and rise in the latter; and that the imports are checked and the export trade stimulated until
the equilibrium of prices is restored, and the imports
and exports again balance each other. He adds—

"The equation of international demand under a money
system, as under a barter system, is the law of international
trade. Every country exports and imports the very same
things in the very same quantity under the one system as
under the other. In a barter system the trade gravitates to
the point at which the sum of imports exactly exchanges for
the sum of exports; in a money system it gravitates to the
point at which the sum of the imports and the sum of the

* Mill's "Principles of Pol. Econ.," cap. 21.

exports exchange for the same quantity of money. And since things which are equal to the same are equal to one another, the imports and exports which are equal in money price would, if money were not used, precisely exchange for one another. . . . In international as in ordinary domestic interchanges, money is to commerce what oil is to machinery, or railways to locomotion, a contrivance to diminish friction."

Some apology appears to be necessary for thus reproducing a statement of doctrine which I always have thought had been· thoroughly understood and accepted by all economists, but there would appear to be a widespread belief among certain classes of our countrymen that importing and exporting are two totally distinct processes, with no necessary connection between them ; and that to place our foreign trade in a thoroughly satisfactory condition we should direct all our efforts to exporting as much as possible, and importing nothing in exchange. It cannot, therefore, be too broadly stated, or too often insisted on, that the two processes are as inseparably connected as the ebb and flow of the tide—that without imports there can be no exports, and without exports there can be no imports.

These two factors do not, of course, show the whole extent of our commercial intercourse with foreign countries ; but they are most important elements in it, and their relative value is more easily calculated. We have heard of late a great deal too much about the enormous excess of our imports over our exports, as if this were necessarily a symptom of unsound trade. There can be no greater fallacy.

Even if the values of our imports and exports were strictly accurate, which they are very far from being, they would convey no correct idea of the real conditions of our foreign trade, unless we could be presented with a balance-sheet giving a Dr. and Cr. account of all the items in our dealings with all the countries with which we trade, including capital lent or borrowed, and the interest thereon, both in the form of public loans and private investments, and every particular of international indebtedness.

Without this knowledge it is of little use to talk about our trade accounts ; but upon two points we may feel an absolute certainty—first, that we cannot import without giving a *quid pro quo ;* and, second, that whatever may be the balance, it is only in certain cases, and within very moderate limits, that it is cancelled by a bullion payment.

As has been shown above, a country which does not produce the precious metals can never effect its purchases in gold or silver, except in liquidation of some comparatively trifling balance. And, as a matter of fact, the imports of gold and silver bullion into the United Kingdom have in recent years exceeded the exports. In 1878 the excess amounted to nearly six millions sterling, and the average annual excess in the last five years has been nearly five millions.

So far, then, from seeing anything disquieting in what is called an "adverse balance of trade," it appears to me to be a feature on which we have

K

every reason to congratulate ourselves, showing, as it does, that we are liquidating our debts in the least inconvenient way to ourselves, *i.e.* by means of commodities which we can produce at less cost than other people.

If foreign countries are content to accept £50 worth of British goods in exchange for £90 worth of their own, are we to complain of their generosity? The preachers of the new gospel of reciprocity would apparently answer in the affirmative. " Our policy," they say, " is to induce foreign countries to take more of our goods and give us less of theirs in return." If this is what is meant by reciprocity, I fear it is not a doctrine which is likely to be very popular either with the producing or with the consuming classes in the country; but it would certainly be a better practical illustration of what Lord Bateman calls "our magnanimous but disastrous liberality" than a system of Free Trade.

It may, then, be stated broadly that every Englishman who sells or buys in a foreign country, whatever be the tariff of that country or the tariff of his own, is already in the possession of complete reciprocity; and it must be apparent that the term "reciprocity," if applicable to the object of which we have lately heard so much, must be used in a different and much less accurate sense.

This sense would not be far to seek were it not for my second difficulty.

I might have supposed that a policy of reciprocity

meant, in a rough-and-ready way, the policy of Mr. Huskisson and his successors in negotiating what were called " reciprocity treaties," by which two countries mutually engaged to relax or remove restrictions on each other's trade or navigation, and to extend to each other " most favoured nation " treatment in a conditional or unconditional form.

In a still more general sense—viz. in that of a simultaneous reduction of tariffs—I might have supposed that the commercial policy of Mr. Cobden's Treaty with France in 1860 was in the minds of the modern advocates of " reciprocity ; " but it was at once apparent that their aims were very different from those of Mr. Huskisson and Mr. Cobden.

The kind of reciprocity which Mr. Huskisson and Mr. Cobden had in view, although their methods were different in some essential respects, had this in common, that they both recognized the vital importance, in the cause of Free Trade, of international action.

Sir Robert Peel, probably very wisely, at the time of his great reforms in our commercial system, resolved to proceed independently of the co-operation of foreign countries, and trusted not unnaturally to the effect of sound principles, and to the example of success in provoking the reciprocity which he was at the time unable or unwilling to invite.

I am very far from disputing the wisdom of the course which was then pursued ; on the contrary, I am quite disposed to think that it was the only course which it would at that time have been wise to take ; but it became clear, after twenty years of trial, that great as was its success, the policy of "masterly inactivity" towards other countries had entirely failed in securing their adhesion to the Free Trade cause, and so far defeated the expectations of its authors.

It was under these circumstances that Mr. Cobden was led to consider whether any means could be found of giving a new impulse to tariff reform and international progress.

It was impossible to revert to the discriminating system and the conditional engagements of Mr. Huskisson ; this would have been reaction, and not progress : but there could be no deviation from the strictest rules of sound economic policy, on the occasion of a sweeping reform of our own Customs system, in securing the co-operation of France with a view to simultaneous reductions which were not intended to be in favour of England and France alone, but to be general in their application.

Unfortunately, the sound maxim of Sir Robert Peel at the time of his reforms, that the best way of fighting hostile tariffs was by free imports, developed, by some strange process of reasoning in the minds of certain English economists (to say nothing of politicians, from whom anything may be expected and forgiven), into a notion which found ultimate expression in the maxim, "Take care of your imports, and your exports will take care of themselves."

This school of English Chauvinism has always

strenuously denounced and resisted all attempts to
secure the co-operation of foreign countries in estab-
lishing reciprocity of freedom, as if it were only less
objectionable than reciprocity in monopoly, and has
succeeded in doing two very mischievous things.

1. It has prevented the execution of a commercial
policy which had been eminently successful in promoting freer trade on the continent of Europe, and
which, if completed as it might have been, would
have effectually barred the course of the present
reaction.

2. It is to a great degree responsible, if, indeed,
it has not directly caused, the present blind cry for
reciprocity. By discouraging and discrediting all
attempts to obtain reciprocity of free trade, and by
ignoring the incontestable truth that you cannot have
free trade without reciprocity, the still grosser error
has been generated in a section of the public mind
that it is better to have reciprocity without free trade.
The doctrine that half a trade is as good as a whole
trade has led, logically, to the opinion that no trade is
as good as half a trade.

But in their haste to find rest in a comfortable
abstract doctrine which should at once flatter the
national vanity by asserting our independence of other
countries, and save all further trouble, the advocates
of this rule of policy entirely overlooked their facts.
They forgot that, until the French Treaty, our tariff
was bristling with import duties, many of them protective, and that even now we draw a larger revenue

from customs than any country in the world, except the United States. They forgot that their own condition was absent—that, in the sense of admitting them free, we do not take care of our imports.

I am very far from wishing in the slightest degree to palliate the attempts which are now being made by some foreign Governments—and, I regret to add, by Governments of our own possessions with even less excuse—to pursue still further a protective policy, and to plunder their people at large for the benefit of a privileged class.

On the contrary, I regard these attempts in the present state of Europe as little less than criminal; and I foresee a day of heavy reckoning, when Socialism, which is the direct offspring of Protection, claims its inheritance, and demands a share for the many in the dishonest gains of the few.

But if we were unable to raise even half our present Customs' revenue without having recourse to duties which were (as the phrase goes) incidentally protective, and our choice lay between such duties and direct taxation, I fear that there are some among us whose virtue would hardly be equal to the strain.

In thanking God, then, that he is not as other men, or even as this foreigner, the British Pharisee must not be allowed to deceive himself by a phrase. So long as we continue to raise half our revenue from customs and excise, our fiscal system may be very convenient, but our trade is not free. We may, if we like, rejoice that our wretched climate enables us to levy millions on wine, tea, and tobacco without recourse to excise duties—and the risk of subsidized domestic industries; but no trade can be called free till all fiscal impediments to its freedom are removed.

It is no consolation to the grower of wine in France or of tobacco in America to be told, when he is trying to promote a wider trade in these commodities, that our duties are imposed "for revenue purposes only," and are, therefore, above criticism. He very naturally replies, "It is true you do not grow wine or tobacco, but I do; and, on the other hand, there are many things which you do produce, and which I wish to buy of you, but, to enable me to do so, you must accept payment in the only coin which I have to offer —namely, my wine or my tobacco. The more you take of these, the more shall I be able to take from you in exchange."

The maxim of "free imports" has never yet been tested, and never can be till our own tariff is purged.

This kind of reciprocity is, however, clearly not the object of the present agitation, which aims at the contraction and not at the expansion of our foreign trade, and invites us, in spite of the teaching of our wisest statesmen and of the conclusive evidence of our own experience, to enter upon a course of retaliation and a war of tariffs.

I must, therefore, ask those who are disposed to listen to this appeal how they would set to work.

Reciprocity in their sense means, I suppose, that we should treat other countries as they treat us, whatever the effect upon ourselves—*i.e.* that we should apply to each foreign country a tariff of duties which would correspond, as nearly as might be, with that which it enforces against us.

Let us see where this would lead us.

Our imports may be divided broadly into three classes.

1. Raw products or raw materials.

2. Manufactured and half-manufactured goods.

3. Articles of consumption, as food, drink, or tobacco, subdivided into (so-called)

    a. Necessaries.

    b. Luxuries.

The values of our imports in 1877 in each of these classes were—

1. Raw products or raw materials   ... £130,041,052
2. Manufactured and half-manufactured
    goods   49,089,241
3. Articles of Consumption—
    a. Necessaries   ... £140,954,110 ⎫
    b. Luxuries   ... £36,371,041 ⎭   177,325,151
    Articles not classified   37,954,336

I presume that it can only be in respect of the second of these three classes that any new scheme of taxation could be proposed; for it is improbable that our manufacturing industries would desire to curtail their supply of raw material, or that the people of England will ever again submit to Corn Laws or Sugar Duties, and return to their small loaf and dear grocery, while our so-called luxuries, such as spirits, tobacco, wine, beer, tea, and coffee, are already so heavily taxed that the less we say about them the better.

It is, therefore, only with an eighth part of our import trade that we are, at the most, free to deal, and from this no inconsiderable deduction must, I presume, be made, for I can hardly believe that our manufacturing interest, as a whole, would desire duties on half-manufactured goods, intended for further processes which employ British capital and labour.

If, then, for the purpose of a policy of reciprocal restriction, it were proposed to reimpose duties on this small class of our imports, how could that purpose be attained?

Let us examine the sources of our supplies, and see how far they correspond with the foreign countries upon which we desire or are able to retaliate by restrictions on their trade. And first on the list of offenders stand the United States of America.

What manufactures do we import from them? In value less than £2,000,000 sterling, of which more than half consists of tanned and curried hides! There is little room for reciprocity here, for no one would dream of taxing their raw cotton and bread-stuffs, and we had better leave them to tan and curry their own hides than attempt to do it for them.

Next in the illiberality of their tariffs come Russia and the Peninsula. But here the case is even worse, for we import no manufactured goods worthy of enumeration from any of them, while in the case of Spain and Portugal we already tax their wines not only heavily, but in a way which, in practice, affects them differentially, and derive from them a revenue infinitely greater than that which they raise from our exports to them.

Reciprocity here, therefore, would lead us in a contrary direction altogether from that which is desired.

But France, it will be said, which sends us every year a value of £16,000,000 in silks and woollens, shoes, and gloves, and "articles de Paris" and other finished manufactures—surely here at least we can do to others as we do not wish them to do to us. No doubt we could; but to retaliate on a country which as a rule taxes our imports about 20 per cent. or less, while we leave untouched a country like the United States, which taxes them double, may be good or bad policy, but it is not reciprocity.

Nor could we give effect to such a policy without a further gross departure from the principle of reciprocity, by placing similar taxes on the manufactures of Belgium, Holland, and Switzerland, the tariffs of which are more liberal than those of France; for in these days of railroads and transit trades the antiquated machinery of differential duties and certificates of origin could never be made effectual again.

And what applies to France applies still more to Germany, whose trade must always largely pass through Dutch and Belgian ports, as well as to Russia, whose produce would always find its way through Germany to the sea.

It may also be as well to ask whether we might not get the worst of it in a game at which two can play, and whether we should not injure ourselves more than we should injure France by a war of tariffs ?

The following table gives the total value of the trade between France and England in 1859, the year which preceded Mr. Cobden's treaty, and in 1877, the last year for which the account is complete :—

Exports from France into the United Kingdom.	Exports from the United Kingdom into France.		
In 1859, £16,870,859	British exports ... £4,754,354 Re-exports ... 4,807,602	}	£9,561,956
In 1877, £45,833,324	British exports ... £14,233,242 Re-exports ... 11,430,360	}	£25,663,602

This table shows that in that part of our export trade which consists of British produce and manufactures, the proportionate advance since 1859 has more than kept pace with the progress of the total importations from France, and we have seen that the importations of manufactured goods from France do not greatly exceed the amount of the British exports. Any check which might be imposed on the French trade in silks and woollens would be dearly bought by the corresponding check which a return to the policy of 1859 would place upon our export trade.

"*Ex uno disce omnes !*" It would be tedious to repeat a similar story with respect to other countries on the continent of Europe. I append for reference a list * showing the value of the manufactures which we imported in 1877 from most of the countries with which we trade, from which it will be seen that, even

* Appendix A, p. 148.

if possible, a policy of retaliation would be utterly
futile.

Of India and China, which for commercial purposes must be considered together, it is unnecessary to speak in connection with this subject, for
we levy on one of their products—tea—alone little
less than the whole amount of their joint Customs
Revenue !

I turn to the British Colonies, and take the
Dominion of Canada and the Australian group as
the largest and most important of our customers.

What is the prospect for this kind of reciprocity
here ? We look in vain for a single item in the list
of their exports which we could afford to tax, whatever their treatment of our manufactures may be.
Canadian timber and Australian wool have become
the breath of our industrial life, and must be admitted
free.

Any attempt, then, at a discriminating reciprocity
of restrictions must be abandoned in despair; not
only would it fail in giving effect to its essential
principle, but it would land us in inextricable confusion.   There is only one course left—viz. that of
placing a general import duty of a "moderately"
protective character, say 10 per cent., upon all foreign
manufactures.

But this cannot be intended, for it would be a
simple return to a policy which we have already tried,
and which we have abandoned step by step from a
bitter experience of its disastrous results; and I would

ask what reason there is for supposing that such a course would be more profitable in the future than it has been in the past.

If any one wants a proof, let him look at the history of our foreign trade, in that branch of it alone (if he likes) which consists of British exports.

In 1829, soon after Mr. Huskisson's and Mr. Poulett Thomson's reforms, the declared value of the British and Irish produce exported from the United Kingdom was	£35,842,000
In 1839 it was	53,233,000
In 1849, just after the repeal of the Corn Laws	63,596,000
In 1859, the year before the French Treaty	130,411,000
In 1869, after nine years of the Treaty system, and before the Franco-German war	189,954,000
And in 1877	199,000,000
After having risen in 1872 to the astonishing amount of	256,257,000

And even now, until quite recently, as Mr. Giffen has shown, it is only the value and not the actual quantity of the goods which has sensibly diminished.

Another equally good illustration of the immense progress which our export trade has made is to be found in the proportion of the above value per head of population, which stood as follows :—

In 1829 the value of our exports was £1 10 6 per head.
In 1839   „   „   2 0 8   „
In 1849   „   „   2 5 11   „

In 1859 the value of our exports was £4 11 2 per head.
In 1869   „   „   6   2   7   „
In 1877   „   „   5 18 11   „

I will adduce a few other proofs of the effect of the Free Trade policy on the national prosperity.

The following are ·the figures representing the tonnage of the British merchant navy at various periods :—

	British Empire.	United Kingdom.
1840	3,311,000	2,724,000
1860	5,710,000	4,586,000
1870	7,149,000	5,617,000
1878	8,266,000	6,198,000

The consumption of the following imported and excisable articles per head of the population was—

	1852	1877
Sugar, raw …	28·15 lbs.	54·06 lbs.
Tea …	2·00 „	4·52 „
Tobacco	1·04 „	1·49 „
Spirits	1·10 gals.	1·23 gals.
Malt	1·50 bush.	1·92 bush.

Mr. Caird, in his recent valuable work on the landed interest, states that thirty years ago not more than one-third of the people of England consumed animal food more than once a week. Now nearly all of them eat it in meat or cheese or butter once a day, more than doubling the average consumption per head. He adds that within the last twenty-five years the capital value of the live-stock of the United King-dom has risen from £146,000,000 to £260,000,000 ; and he puts the total gain to the agricultural interest

—landowners, farmers, and labourers—in rent, farm capital, and wages, at £445,000,000 in the period under review.

Agricultural wages have risen from 9s. 7d. to 14s. 6d. since 1850; and it is needless to add that the wages of manufacturing labour have increased in a similar manner.

Among collateral indications of the national prosperity, which has, at all events, coincided with the adoption of our recent fiscal and commercial policy, I may refer to the growth in the assessments of income tax in Great Britain :—

> In 1843 they were £251,013,000
> In 1875 „ 535,708,000

To deposits in savings banks, which were—

> In 1840, £23,471,000, or 17s. 9d. per head of population.
> In 1876, £70,280,000, or 42s. 6d. „ „

And to the decrease in the percentage in pauperism to the population, which was—

> In 1841 ... ... 8·2
> In 1876 ... ... 3·1

And to other facts given in a recent interesting paper on the strength of England in the *Fortnightly Review*, by Mr. Farrer.

Can this be all ? or is there yet some undiscovered policy which I have failed to divine ?

If not, and if further reciprocity of restrictions is unattainable, I have yet one consolation for its advocates. In a still more general sense, but in a sense very distinctly affecting the conditions of our foreign trade, their policy is actually in force.

It will, no doubt, be a source of unmixed satisfaction to them to find that our so-called "revenue duties" cannot fail to produce results as injurious to the exporting industries of the countries affected by them as their protective duties cause to our own trade.

The £20,000,000 which we annually raise in duties on foreign goods may be roughly divided among our different neighbours in the following proportions :—

The United States of America ...	£6,000,000
India and China	3,500,000
France	1,500,000
Spain	1,000,000
Germany	880,000
Portugal	450,000
Greece	320,000
Holland	150,000
Italy	80,000
British possessions	4,000,000
Other foreign countries	2,000,000

And of all these countries there is hardly one which draws as large a revenue from the taxation of British produce. To take only two examples, the United States and France. The total value of British produce exported to the former country in 1877 was £16,300,000; making allowance for the entry of a certain amount of goods duty free, the average rate levied can hardly be put higher than 30 per cent., which would give a total revenue of about £5,000,000; while in the case of France, the duties actually levied on British goods in the same year amounted to a little over £800,000.

What more could the most strenuous advocate of a retaliatory policy desire?

There is one ground upon which protective duties have been urged which appears at first sight rather more plausible than those which have been hitherto discussed. I mean the claim set up by our manufacturers in compensation for restricted hours of labour and exceptional taxation. It is said that if the Legislature chooses to place disabilities on particular industries, the country at large should bear the cost, and not the particular industries.

Now, in the first place, any such disabilities as are here in view are not imposed intentionally by the Legislature. The assumption has always been that cheap labour is not necessarily efficient labour, and that a system which leads to the degradation of the working class, and prevents them from attaining a certain moral, intellectual, and physical standard, directly impairs their productive energy.

But if it can be shown that any restrictions on labour or any special disabilities really diminish the efficiency of the industries which they affect, it should be the object of our reformers to address themselves to the very legitimate task of obtaining relief from unwise or unjust laws, and not to extend their operation to the whole community.

For to what does the claim amount?

Because the cost of production is increased in certain industries by an undue interference with labour, we are asked to raise the cost of living all round to the whole community.

Because an injustice. is done to a section of the people, it is to be extended to all. To enter upon such a course would be to move further in a vicious circle, which could only end in the general impoverishment of the nation.

If the aid of Government is sought to equalize conditions of production at home and abroad, let it at least be invoked to diminish our burdens and not to add to them !

But, after all, what a hollow cry this is about foreign competition ! A country which exports her manufactures to a value of £150,000,000 per annum to rival and neutral markets, is represented to us as on the road to ruin, because she cannot succeed in preventing the importation of £50,000,000 worth of foreign goods !

I have now combated various imaginary propositions, but end as I began, without having discovered one which accounts for the action and language of so many of our countrymen on this matter of reciprocity.

Will you think me very uncharitable if I say that an unworthy suspicion has sometimes crossed my mind that the policy which we are called upon to adopt might more fitly be called by another and a less innocent name ?

Can it be that while the hands are Esau's hands, the voice is the voice of Jacob, inviting us, in the name of reciprocity, to barter our Free Trade birthright for a mess of Protectionist pottage ?

I prefer to believe that the fault is mine, and to seek for further light.

The proposal, therefore, which I have to make to the Committee is that they should offer a prize for the best essay explaining the objects of this much-debated policy, and the means by which it is proposed to carry it into effect.

I shall await the result without impatience, but not without curiosity, for the prize essayist must at least succeed in proving that no bread is better than half a loaf, and that because we cannot sell in the dearest, we ought not to buy in the cheapest market.

I am always,

Dear Mr. Potter,

Yours sincerely,

LOUIS MALLET.

APPENDIX A.

IMPORTS OF MANUFACTURES INTO ENGLAND, 1877.

From				Amount in Value.
Russia	...	...	...	about £108,000
Sweden	...	...	...	„ 1,083,000
Norway	...	...	...	„ 39,000
Denmark	...	...	...	„ 27,000
Germany	...	...	...	„ 2,862,000
Holland	...	...	...	„ 6,830,000
Belgium	...	...	...	„ 5,312,000
France	...	...	...	„ 16,060,400
Portugal	...	...	...	„ 17,000
Spain	...	...	...	„ 18,000
Italy	...	...	...	„ 318,000
Austria	...	...	...	„ 33,000
Turkey	...	...	...	„ 112,000
Egypt	...	...	...	„ 3,000
Persia	...	...	...	„ 13,000
China	...	...	...	„ 180,000
Japan	...	...	...	„ 5,000
United States	...	...	...	„ 1,843,000

APPENDIX B.

Revenue derived by various countries from Customs duties, according to the latest returns available :—

United States	£26,200,000
Great Britain	20,000,000
France	10,250,000
Germany	5,330,000
Russia	5,300,000
Italy	4,240,000
British India	2,700,000
Austria	2,320,000
Portugal	1,850,000
Spain	1,600,000
Sweden	1,200,000
Denmark	1,100,000
Belgium	865,000
Holland	385,000

VII.

A STATEMENT OF BIMETALLIC THEORY.

1. IF the only demand for any two commodities which are required for the same purposes, and serve the same function, is subject to the condition that they shall exchange in a fixed ratio, one to the other, so long as the supply of both continues, they must exchange in that ratio, or not at all.

2. Bimetallism is the application of this principle to gold and silver when used as standard coins of the realm.

3. Such gold and silver coins are only in demand for the purposes of exchange, *e.g.* the purchase of other commodities, the payment of labour, or the liberation of debt. Both gold and silver coins equally serve for any of these functions, and they are only available for such purposes because Governments give them currency as legal tender, and affix to them a stamp, which is accepted as a guarantee of their being of a certain weight and fineness.

4. If, therefore, all Governments agree to establish and enforce a fixed ratio between gold and silver in

the form of coined money, such gold and silver coins, if they exchange at all, must exchange in that ratio.

5. For if, with $15\frac{1}{2}$ or any other number of ounces of silver coins, the same exchanges can be made, or the same debts discharged, as with one ounce of gold coins, or *vice versâ*, that metal will inevitably be preferred which can be obtained at the least cost. If, therefore, the relative value of the two metals varies from that ratio, a double process will be set in motion. On the one hand, any addition to the metallic currency will be made in the metal which can be obtained at the least cost; and on the other, the coins of the dearer metal already in circulation will be melted down, until the price of the bullion has reached the same level as the coin.

6. This process could only terminate in one of two ways. Either the increased demand for the cheaper, and the lessened demand for the dearer metal, would proceed until the latter has been driven and kept out of circulation, thus escaping altogether from the control of Governments, *or* the value of the first will rise and that of the latter fall, until the equilibrium is restored, *i.e.* until (in the case supposed) $15\frac{1}{2}$ oz. of silver coin will exchange again, by the adjustment of supply and demand, exactly for one ounce in gold coin.

7. The first is an extravagant hypothesis, for such a result could only be brought about by the subversion of all the conditions which have hitherto governed the production of the precious metals, or by the adoption of a ratio, such, for instance, as 1 to 1, which would

entirely defeat the purpose of a double standard, and
could therefore never be proposed by its advocates ;
but, even if admitted as a conceivable possibility, it
could not be urged by monometallists as an objection
to the adoption of bimetallism, as it would then directly
lead to the universal use of a monometallic standard in
the monetary systems of the world.

8. For it must be borne in mind that, under a
system of free mintage, the market price of gold and
silver bullion must always be the same as their mint
price, plus or minus the cost of coinage.

So long, therefore, as both gold and silver coins
are in circulation and therefore, *ex hypothesi*, necessarily exchangeable in the ratio of $15\frac{1}{2}$ to 1, so long
must the relative value of the gold and silver bullion
be also in the ratio of $15\frac{1}{2}$ to 1.

9. But the latter alternative is the only one, it is
urged, which deserves practical consideration, and, if
so, it appears to follow that the only possible divergence from the fixed ratio in the value of the two
metals, so long as they are used as coin, would be
within the narrow limits of the cost of coinage and
melting, as well as of the charges of transport from
one market to another.

10. In reply to the objection that this theory rests
upon an inadmissible assumption, viz. an universal
agreement among nations, it is urged that, if universal
agreement is impossible, it is also unnecessary. All
that is needed for the success of the policy is that an
union shall be maintained on a sufficiently large scale

to neutralize the operation of the so-called " Gresham law," and ensure the constant and certain presence of both gold and silver in the currency, so that there could be no cheaper or dearer metal.

11. It can hardly be doubted that an union of the four great States, England, France, including the Latin Union, Germany, and the United States of America, would more than suffice for such a purpose. But, if this is questioned, it must, at least, be admitted that, as such a combination would include all the important States with a gold standard, no increase in the supply of silver could drive out the gold coinage (for where could it be driven ?); while, on the other hand, the expulsion of silver by gold could only arise from such an increase in the supply of the latter as would provide the union with a sufficient basis for a single gold standard. The bimetallic system could, therefore, in this case, only fail from causes which would obviate the main practical evils of monometallism.

VIII.

THE NATIONAL INCOME AND TAXATION.

(Published in 1885.)

There are indications that before long the profound apathy which has prevailed in this country during recent years on the subject of finance and taxation, may be succeeded by a reawakened interest, and receive some degree of public attention.

The foreign policy of the last two Administrations has culminated in an expenditure during the current year of nearly £100,000,000; and although, if peace is preserved, it may be hoped that considerable reductions in this amount may be made in the future, it is now clear that the average expenditure of recent years will be permanently exceeded.

The politicians, however, who are most keenly alive to the moods and dispositions of the electoral body, do not appear to have found it desirable, or, perhaps, possible, to sound the note of retrenchment or economy. On the contrary, leading Liberal candidates have, for the most part in their recent appeals for popular favour, vied with their Tory rivals in admitting the necessity of a large and liberal expenditure for the purposes both of war and peace. So great, indeed, has been the change in the sentiments of the British people in this respect, that the temper of mind for which the phrase "ignorant impatience of taxation " was invented, has probably no meaning, and has become unintelligible to the mind of the present generation.

It must further be observed that this remarkable change of opinion has coincided with an unprecedented growth of the public burdens for the normal requirements of the country. At the period succeeding the Repeal of the Corn Laws, when it was still possible for Mr. Cobden to speak of an annual Imperial Budget of £50,000,000, the local taxes levied in rates did not exceed, according to Mr. Porter, the sum of £7,000,000, making with the Imperial expenditure a total of £57,000,000. The expenditure of the country, both Imperial and Local, at the present time, has reached at least double that amount.

The general answer to criticisms of this description is of course obvious enough. It is said, " Doubtless our expenditure has doubled, but our population has largely increased, and our resources have more than doubled."

In 1841, prior to Sir R. Peel's financial reforms, the population of the United Kingdom was 26,917,591. It is now 36,000,000.

The value of British and Irish exports (the declared value of other branches of our foreign trade was not

recorded) was about £50,000,000. It is now (1883)
£239,799,473.

The estimated national income in 1843 was
£515,000,000. It is now £1,274,000,000.

An income tax of 1d. in the pound produced in
1843 £772,166. It now produces £1,990,000.

The national capital paying probate duty was in
1838 £55,000,000. It is now £140,000,000. '

The deposits in savings banks were, in 1831,
£13,719,000; in 1881, £80,334,000; while the number
of depositors has advanced from 429,000 to 4,140,000.

The number of paupers in 1849 was in England
and Wales 934,000. It is now (1884) 774,310. It is
not always added that, while the number has decreased, the cost has risen from £5,039,703, in 1844-5,
to £8,353,292 in 1883—or from rather more than £5
to nearly £11 per head.

Wages in the leading industries have largely advanced, often doubled, in the same period. The
amount of the national debt has been reduced from
£835,676,000 in 1857, to £746,423,000 in 1884 ; and
so on to the end of the chapter.

These are interesting and consolatory facts; but
they entirely fail to touch the point raised by the
reformers of Mr. Cobden's school.

Their argument was to this effect : The national
taxation is excessive. It is only caused by the burden
of a debt mainly incurred for past wars, and by the
burden of military establishments which, from our
point of view, are unnecessarily large, if the external

policy of the country were conducted on the principle of non-intervention, and of avoiding further extensions of empire. This scale of expenditure is not only, as we think, unnecessary, but also dangerous, when your industries are engaged in competition with the whole world. Therefore, we hold that it ought not to be increased except by such gradual and moderate additions as the requirements of a growing community may render inevitable.

This argument may be right or wrong ; but it is no answer to it to point to an increased population and doubled resources as a justification of a doubled expenditure. This is merely to leave things as they were, and to prevent the increased wealth of the country from bearing its natural fruit in a diminution of the national burdens.

But whatever opinions are held on this question, it is useful to see how the account stands.

The year 1843 must be taken as the starting-point for the comparison, because it was the first year of the income tax. The following data are given in round numbers, representing the general facts of the period under review :—

Date.	Population.	National Income.	Taxation.			Amount of Taxation per head.	Percentage on National Income.
			Imperial.	Local.	Total.		
		£	£	£	£	£ s. d.	
1843	27,000,000	515,000,000	50,000,000	7,000,000	57,000,000	2 2 0	11
1884	36,000,000	1,274,000,000	72,000,000	34,000,000	106,000,000	3 0 0	8

N.B.—The gross public revenue of £87,205,000 includes the receipt of the Post Office, Telegraph Service, Crown Lands, and other sources of revenue which are not of the nature of taxes.

This is a satisfactory result in its general aspect, but an examination of the items suggests less agreeable reflections.

The diminution of the percentage of taxation on income will be found to be entirely due to the important fact, that there has been no increase in the charge for debt, which has thus remained a constant quantity, while the national income has more than doubled. The gain from this cause has been so great, that it has more than counterbalanced the loss from increased expenditure.

It must further be observed, that had it not been for the process which has been in operation, by which a part of the debt has been converted into terminable annuities, and by which the capital of the debt has been reduced from £835,676,254 in 1857, to £746,423,964 in 1884, the annual charge for debt would have been perceptibly reduced. This result is the more remarkable when it is remembered that the period during which this reduction has been effected has been one of what are called minor wars of an almost chronic nature.

Omitting the charge for debt, the results are as follows :—

Date.			Civil List and Civil Charges. £	Military and Naval Charges. £	Total. £
1843	...	...	5,631,061	16,159,070	21,790,091
1884	...	...	18,731,582	28,909,107	47,640,689
	Increase	...	13,100,521	12,750,037	25,850,598

The increase here shown is more than the whole

increase of revenue during the period derived from taxation, and is only met by the extra receipts from other sources, such as the Post Office, etc.

It is also more than in proportion to the increase in the national income, large as this has been, if local taxation be included. Here are the figures in round numbers :—

Date.	Population.	Expenditure—Imperial and Local. £	National Income. £	Per cent.
1843 ...	27,000,000	29,000,000	515,000,000	5·60
1884 ...	36,000,000	82,000,000	1,274,000,000	6·40

In Mr. Gladstone's speech on the national expenditure in the House of Commons, in April, 1883, in a comparison which he makes between the years 1840 and 1882, he minimizes these results by deducting certain items from the account in both periods, in order, as he says, to arrive at a fairer conclusion. The effect is to diminish considerably the apparent increase in the latter year; but with the exception of the special war charges in 1882, these deductions do not appear to affect the complexion of the case. They are as follows :—

1. The cost of collecting taxes.

2. The charges for the reduction of debt.

3. The grants in aid of local taxation.

The first is quite as much a part of the national expenditure as the cost of the army.

The second may be wise or unwise, but is distinctly part of the annual expenditure.

The third, unless it can be shown to be a transfer

of local burdens to the nation at large, is equally an addition to the total annual expenditure.

Still we shall be told that there is nothing in these figures to excite alarm, especially when it is remembered how large a part of the increased expenditure consists of local taxation for professed objects of social improvement, and we are assured in the " Radical programme " " that taxation on equitable principles for objects which the nation approves cannot be on too liberal a scale, and that from this point of view a public opinion may be created, in which taxes ought to be considered as an investment for the general good, and should be cheerfully and, in the main, easily borne."

If these ideas prevail, it cannot be expected that there will be any strong popular feeling against the amount of the national taxation, and public interest, so far as it can be attracted to the subject, will rather be directed to the distribution and incidence of taxation than to its aggregate amount.

Even in this direction it may be doubted whether more than a languid interest can be excited, so long as the current of popular feeling is in favour of increased expenditure. It is true that what is called "readjustment of the incidence of taxation," which forms one of the articles of the Radical programme, has been accepted by Mr. Gladstone in his recent manifesto. We are told, indeed, in the address to the Midlothian electors, that the "balance of taxation as between property and labour should be adjusted when occasion offers with a scrupulousness which was unhappily too

little observed at the time when property had the
absolute command of parliamentary action." No one
can speak on such a subject with so much authority as
Mr. Gladstone ; but if this be so, we shall still find that
it is not so easy to "readjust with scrupulousness"
when taxes are being imposed, as it is when they are
remitted.

If, for instance, it should be discovered that the
rectification of the balance required the remission of
indirect taxes, such as those on tea and tobacco, which
press upon the poor, the adjustment might be made
either by reducing these or by augmenting the taxes
paid exclusively by property ; but while the first would
be the natural course if the public burdens were to be
diminished, the latter would alone be possible at a
time of increasing expenditure. It is needless to say
that to reduce taxes on the poor without raising them
on the rich, would benefit the first and would not injure
the last ; but to raise them on the rich without relieving the poor, would injure the former without benefit
to the latter. Such a prospect is not tempting to a
Chancellor of the Exchequer who desires popularity.

It may be added that the history of taxation in
this and in other countries affords no instance of
"scrupulousness of adjustment" combined with a
lavish and increasing expenditure. On the contrary,
it has usually been found that when Governments
attempt to raise a revenue which bears an undue
proportion to the earnings of the people, as in the
United States of America after the Civil War, and in

M

France and Germany at the present time, the only method is to get the money how and where they can, not only by avoiding unpopular taxes, but also by resorting to popular expedients, among which duties upon foreign trade, into which the protective element often largely enters, invariably find a place.

It is possible, however, that there will be some popular feeling which may find expression in the new House of Commons in favour of transferring to property in some form or other a portion of the taxation now falling on articles largely consumed by the working classes. It becomes, therefore, important to inquire what form such proposals may assume.

The truth is that the remission of the sugar duties and the reduction of the duty on tea, have gone far to knock the bottom out of the argument of those who rest their advocacy of a further remission of indirect taxation on any less comprehensive principle than that of the radical objection to all indirect taxes, as mischievous impediments to trade and grossly wasteful in their collection ; and appeals to the British public on these latter grounds have always failed in securing popular support, owing to the widespread belief or superstition that high taxation on spirits, beer, and even tobacco, are desirable in the interests of morality.

Whether it may be possible, on the plea of the undue pressure of taxation on the working class, to create a public opinion strong enough to complete, at all events, the freedom of the breakfast-table, it is not easy to say ; but the first step is to show that such undue pressure exists, and it is with a view of contributing to this inquiry that the following remarks are offered.

It is obvious that the data for all calculations as to the " Incidence of Taxation " are of a very imperfect kind. For this purpose it is necessary to ascertain both the amount of the national income, and the share of it which falls to the lot of the different classes of the people whose interests it is desired to compare.

We have, therefore, first to ask, What is the national income ?

There appear to be two methods by which it can be computed.

These have been recently described and employed by Mr. Edward Atkinson, of Boston, U.S., in his valuable work on the " Distribution of Products," as follows :—

"Land, labour, and capital" (he says) "are the three factors in production. By the co-operation of these forces an annual product is made. The term annual fits the case, because the year represents the course of the four seasons and the succession of crops. A small part of each year's annual product, commonly called 'quick' or 'active' capital, must be carried over to start the next year's work, as a small part of last year's product had been brought over to start this year's work, one proportion balancing the other. The fixed capital seldom exceeds in value two years' production. It therefore follows that all profits, all wages, all taxes, in fact, all consumption whereby existence is maintained, must be substantially drawn from each year's product. But in order that this product may be distributed and consumed—since no man, economically speaking, lives for himself alone

—the various products of the year must all be exchanged by purchase and sale, and, therefore, must all be reduced to, and measured in, terms of money, except that part of the annual product which is consumed upon the farm by the farmer and his family without being sold. With this exception, the whole product of the year must be substantially converted into terms of money.

"This remainder of the annual product, at whatever sum of money it may be finally valued, when sold for the last time and distributed for final consumption, constitutes the value of the product converted into terms of money, from which sum all money profits, all money wages, and all money taxes must be derived. There can be no other source. . . .

"The total sum of money which represents the value of all that is produced at its point of final consumption is and must be, the final measure of that part of the annual product which is bought and sold.

"On the other hand, by ascertaining what the total sum of taxes, the sum of all wages, and the sum of all profits, may be, we can again approximate to the total value of the annual product.

"No absolute results can be reached by either method, but approximate results can be fairly set off, one against the other."

Mr. Atkinson accordingly proceeds in the first instance to give us the best estimate he can make of the total annual product of the United States, which he puts at about 10,000,000,000 dollars—(an estimate confirmed by Mr. Nimmo, the Chief of the Bureau of Statistics, at Washington)—and then compares it with the results of the estimate made in the Census Department, of the amount of property assessed for taxation. He thus obtains an approximate idea of the profits and savings in the census year, and he arrives at an estimate of the earnings of the nation, in the shape of salaries and wages, by a careful analysis of the occupations of all persons engaged in mental or manual work, and of the rate of wages and salaries actually paid. These data, together with the proceeds of taxation, constitute, according to Mr. Atkinson, the national income, and correspond with the aggregate value of the annual product sufficiently to justify both methods.

On this view of the subject it must be observed that it does not appear how far due allowance has been made for the addition to the value of the annual national product caused by foreign trade.* Probably, however, in the case of the United States, the question is not of so much importance as to vitiate the general result of the estimate, because the proportion of the foreign to the home trade of the States is comparatively small. But in the case of the United Kingdom this element would complicate the question.

There is another consideration to which it is necessary to advert. The national income of the United Kingdom is largely augmented by the sums annually received in the shape of interest and dividends on foreign loans and investments. These form no part of the annual product, but are the interest on a portion of that product in preceding years, which has been saved instead of being consumed or invested in the country. The interest or profits received on this

---

* Ricardo denies that any addition is made to value by foreign trade, but the opinion is open to question.

portion of the savings of the country are an addition
to the value of the annual product in succeeding years,
and in estimating the value of that product for a particular year, with a view of comparing it with the
national income, their amount should be added.

In this country the English capital in foreign
investments has been estimated in 1880 as from
£1,500,000,000 to £2,000,000,000 sterling, and the
interest and profits at about £100,000,000.

If the value of the annual product of the United
Kingdom could be ascertained, the latter sum would
have to be added, but no complete materials for an
official estimate of the aggregate results of English
industry exist, and statisticians have, therefore, had
recourse to the second method, but with an important
difference.

Two estimates of the national income have been
made in recent times, which have been generally
accepted as sufficiently accurate, to justify their use as
a foundation for discussions on questions affecting the
national progress, and the condition of the people, viz.
those of Mr. Dudley Baxter and of Mr. Leone Levi.

In both of them, one of the most important elements in the computation is supplied by the Returns
of the Assessments to the Income Tax, under the
several schedules.

But it seems doubtful whether, in the popular
acceptance of these estimates, it has been generally
understood that very conflicting opinions have been
held, and are apparently still held, by eminent econo-

mists, as to the principle upon which such estimates should be made.

Mr. John Stuart Mill, in the preliminary remarks to the " Principles of Political Economy," .distinctly denies that the National Debt forms a part of the national wealth, or the interest upon it a part of the national income. He says, at p. 9—

" The position of fundowners, or owners of the public debt of the country, is similar to that of mortgagees. They are mortgagees on the general wealth of the country. The cancelling of the debt would be no destruction of wealth, but a transfer of it ; a wrongful abstraction of wealth from certain members of the community for the profit of Government, or of the taxpayers. Funded property, therefore, cannot be counted as part of the national wealth. This is not always borne in mind by the dealers in statistical calculations. For example, in estimates of the gross income of the country, founded on the proceeds of the income tax, income derived from the funds is not always excluded, although the tax-payers are assessed on their whole nominal income, without being permitted to deduct from it the portion levied from them in taxation to form the income of the fundholder. In this calculation, therefore, one portion of the general income of the country is *counted twice over*, and the aggregate amount made to appear greater than it is by about £30,000,000."

There can be no possible mistake as to Mr. Mill's meaning. It is abundantly clear that he considered that the income of the fundholders ought not to be included in the estimate of the national income. But if this view be accepted, it has been well argued by Mr. Macleod that precisely on the same grounds other portions of the national income ought to be excluded, *e.g.* the incomes of all persons paid by the State, civil and military, as well as those of railroads and public companies, indeed the incomes of all persons who are not the original producers as well as the final con- sumers of any portion of the national product.

Mr. Macleod gives us an instance which serves as well as any other to illustrate his meaning—the case of a person with a large establishment of servants and dependents. Such a person with an income, say, of £50,000 per annum, on which sum he pays income tax, and which is justly considered as an item in the income of the nation—may pay £2000 a year to an agent, £500 to a secretary, £300 to a cook, and so on. Each of these sums will justly be liable to income tax, and be included in the account of the national income ; and yet, if the principle asserted by Mr. Mill be sound, the income of the original recipient, which has already paid income tax, without any deduction, for those portions destined to become the incomes of the agent, secretary, and cook, will, to this extent, be counted twice over in the calculation of the national income, the truth being that (with the exception of that part of the annual product which passes at once, without being exchanged, into the consumption of the original producer, as in the case of some farm produce) "every man's income is paid," as Mr. Macleod observes, "out of the income of some one else."

This view raises several curious questions. If the National Debt is part of the national wealth, and the interest on it part of the national income, might it not be contended that the larger the debt, and the higher the rate of interest, the greater would be the national wealth, or the national income?

This would be a startling conclusion; but we will give another instance. The cost of the army, navy, and civil services is about £48,000,000 per annum. Is this sum part of the national income? It is certainly charged with income tax, and forms part of the sum assessed to that impost. It is included in the estimates of the national income. If it be rightly so included, let us suppose that the salaries and pay of all the servants of the State were doubled. Would the national income be increased by such a measure to that extent? And could it be maintained that the national wealth had been increased by such a measure?

This brings us to the core of the subject: the answer seems to be, that as debt represents value for service rendered, it ought to be included in any estimate of national wealth, in the same way that the value of the services rendered by the servants of the State, or by any other class of the community, ought to be so included.

In this sense, and as regards the creditors and the servants of the State, the national wealth and income would be augmented by an addition to the debt or to the cost of the services.

But in estimating the effect of such augmentation upon the sum of the national wealth or well-being, it is necessary to consider the other side of the account, and it will then become clear, that whatever addition is made to the national wealth in one direction, a corresponding reduction may take place in others— the question as to whether or not the aggregate wealth of the community is increased by additions to its debt, or to its services, turning entirely on the balance of advantage or disadvantage which is the result.

Mr. Sidgwick, in his work on the " Principles of Political Economy " (book i. c. 3), discusses this question at length with especial reference to the argument of Mr. Macleod ; but his conclusions, somewhat hesitating as they appear to be, are not satisfactory.

Both he and Mr. Mill seem to have missed the point.

They ask, How can a country be richer because one Englishman lends a portion of its wealth to another ? But this is not the question. The question is this. A. lends a portion of his wealth to B. B. may either use this wealth productively or unproductively. Let us assume that he consumes it unproductively, and destroys it once for all. The country is so much the poorer, and so is B., but A. is still possessed of the debt due to him, consisting of the right either to receive back the capital or the interest. A., at least, is as rich as before ; his wealth remains, and so far as it forms part of the national wealth, the nation is as rich as before ; and this right, or debt due to him, is a part of the national wealth, whether regarded as capital or as income in the form of interest. In any estimate of the national wealth, or of the national income, this debt must, therefore, certainly be included, and the interest on it is as certainly a part of the national income. The loss of wealth or income resulting to the nation from the transaction will be found to consist in the diminution of B.'s share of it, not in that of A. In the case supposed, the country would be poorer and its income less; but the debt held by A., and the interest paid to him, would none the less be part of the national wealth and of the national income.

Let us take the other supposition, viz. that B. employs the sum borrowed productively. Here it is obvious that he might increase his own wealth without diminishing that of A.; and in any estimate of the national wealth, or income, both those of A. and B. would necessarily be included, and the country would be the richer by the transaction; that is, it is richer because one Englishman has lent a portion of its wealth to another.

In both cases the debt, and the interest on it, constitute a part of the national wealth and income, although in the first the country is the poorer, and in the second the richer, by the transaction. In neither is this portion of that wealth or income counted twice over, as Mr. Mill asserts.

Here, then, we find the answer to the question, Is England the richer for her National Debt ?

If the money borrowed and spent has been

expended, whether in war or otherwise, so as to render her richer than she would have been if it had not been so spent—it is idle to say that she would or might have been richer still, in a case which is purely imaginary—viz. one in which the causes of such war, or other expenditure, had been absent. If such war or other objects of expenditure were unnecessary, useless, or unprofitable, then England would be the poorer for them, but not in that portion of her wealth held by the public creditor. This remains, and still forms, part of her wealth. She will be poorer in that part of her wealth held by the debtor, whose share in the national wealth has been *pro tanto* reduced, and which cannot be, and is not, included in the estimate, because it has altogether ceased to exist. England, therefore, is either richer or poorer by reason of her debt according as it has been incurred for purposes which have made her richer or poorer than she would have been without it. The mere fact of debt proves absolutely nothing, and I altogether dissent from Mr. Sidgwick in thinking that "the inference implied in reckoning the funds as part of the country's wealth is, that England, or a railway, is worth more, because it has cost so much—still less that it is worth more because the money had to be borrowed."

The fallacious nature of Mr. Mill's view is suggested by another consideration. It has been observed that wherever, as in the United States of America, the materials exist for such a calculation, there are two methods of estimating the national income. These, if correct, ought to lead to results which approximately correspond, and one method would thus afford the means of testing the other.

In the estimates given by Mr. Atkinson this correspondence is remarkable. The results of both methods are sufficiently alike to justify the presumption that both proceed upon a sound principle.

But it is essential to observe that this correspondence is impossible if Mr. Mill's argument is admitted. In the estimates of the national income afforded by the second method, viz. that of ascertaining, as far as may be, the actual money income and earnings of the different classes of which the nation is composed, Mr. Atkinson includes all money profits and interest, all money wages, and all money taxes. He says, at p. 29—

"The total sum of money which represents the value of all that is produced at its point of final consumption is, and must be, the final measure of that part of the annual product which is bought and sold. Therefore all profits, wages, and taxes constitute a portion of this lump sum. In order to ascertain what the rate of profit, the rate of taxation, or the rate of wages may be, we must ascertain what this lump sum is, and how it is divided. On the other hand, by ascertaining the total sum of taxes, the sum of all wages, and the sum of all profits, we can again approximate the total value of the annual product."

Now it is evident that if the total money value of the annual product is composed of profits, interest, wages, and taxes, the sum of profits, interest, wages, and taxes must constitute the total value of the annual

product.   The two modes of computation are only
two different methods of arriving at the same result.

But Mr. Mill excludes the interest on the National
Debt, which is the income of the fundholder, on the
grounds already stated; and his argument equally
applies, as has been seen, to all taxes and to everything which is of the nature of what Mr. Dudley
Baxter calls "a second-hand income," which, having
been paid by those whose incomes are already included in the estimate, cannot, as it is urged, be again
separately specified, as in that case they would be
included twice.

This appears to be a fundamental error, and if
so, it is a fallacy so serious, that until it has been
thoroughly examined no profitable discussion as to
the incidence of national taxation is possible.

The error seems to be this: let us take the case
of a tax as an illustration.   The sum paid by a taxpayer as a tax constitutes no part of his income.   It
is part of his expenditure.   He does not receive it;
he pays it.   His income on which his income tax
is assessed does not consist of what he pays, but of
what he receives.   In the case of a tax, whether
levied to pay the interest on public debt or to pay
the current expenses of the State, it is not the tax
which is included in the estimate of the taxpayer's
income, but the service received by him as an
equivalent for the tax.   This is his income, and this
is properly included as part of the national income.
The income of the man with, *e.g.*, £50,000 a year

consists not in the money which he pays away, but in whatever he receives in exchange for it. The services of Government, his houses, his servants, his equipages, his library, his meats and wines, his box at the opera, his yacht, the expenses of his public life, his pictures, his entertainments, his travels, and so on —these things constitute his wealth, and so far as they are annually consumed, his income; and these must be included in terms of money in any estimate of the national wealth and income.

On the other hand, the taxes paid become the income of those to whom they are paid—the money in which they are paid being merely an order, so to speak, for so much of the annual product which may either be consumed by the recipient, or again passed on, in exchange for services rendered, to another person, in which case another income is called into existence.

In estimating the national income, therefore, by the second method, it is necessary to include all profits and interest (Schedule A, B, D), all interest on debt (Schedule C), all salaries and pay of Government servants, civil and military (Schedule E), and all earnings in the form of salaries and wages not paying income tax, comprehending the pay of soldiers, sailors, and labourers of all kinds in the service of Government.

It is obvious that unless we include all these general incomes, the total national income cannot be made to correspond with that which results from the use of the first method—viz. that which consists of the "total sum of money which represents the value of all that is produced at its point of final consumption."

This sum can only correspond with the sum of the values of all the services for which it is exchanged.

On the one hand we have a total of the quantities of the material products of the community—food, shelter, clothing, etc.

On the other, we have a total of the quantities of all the services of every member of the community entitled to a share in such products.

On what will the money value or price depend ? On the relation between the total of the objects (whether products or services) to be exchanged, and the total of the instruments of exchange in the different forms of money and credit.

An example may make this clearer.

Suppose a country, entirely self-contained (to give the simplest case), with a population of one million, which, by one year's work, produces a given quantity of the bare requisites of human subsistence, but with no surplus product whatever. Suppose further, to avoid all complications from this cause, that this society is provided with a sufficient currency on a metallic basis (whether of one metal or of two rated metals would in such a country be a matter of absolute indifference) which always bore a constant relation to the demands upon it, so that prices would not be affected by relative changes in its volume.

Here the sum of the earnings will exactly correspond with the sum of the annual product in terms of money.

An invention is now made, by which the productive power of labour is at once doubled. The same population, with the same amount of labour, produces double the quantity of everything, including currency.

In these circumstances, let us suppose, in the first place, that the people in question consume in their own persons this doubled produce. In this case the value of the annual product in terms of money will be double its previous amount.

In the second place, let us suppose that, instead of consuming this surplus product themselves, the population gradually add to their number 500,000 persons, who will be engaged in providing what are called " non-productive" services—such as lawyers, clergy, doctors, public servants, authors, actors, and opera-dancers.

Each of these persons will draw an income from the community as an equivalent for the services which they render, which will be ultimately expressed in the final consumption of the surplus product, which is, by our supposition, one-half of the whole. This exchange of services will add to the general purchasing power of the community in the proportion of one-third. In this second case, therefore, the national income, and the value of the annual product, owing to the creation of new demands on the part of the community, will have been increased threefold, instead of only twice, as in the first case.

N

This national income will thus have been composed not only of the value of the products representing the services of the producers, but also of the value of the services rendered by the " non-producers."

But in both cases alike, the purchasing power of the community, in terms of money, will be the sum of the incomes of all the people ; and this will necessarily be the same as the total value of the annual product for which it is exchanged at the point of final consumption, because the value in money is merely the expression of the relation of the two exchangeable quantities, always excepting (as before observed) that part of the annual product which is neither bought nor sold.

This is a long digression, but it has been necessary to render the estimate of the national income, which must be the foundation of all calculations as to the incidence of taxation, something more than an illusion, and to justify the criticism which it has been necessary to make on Mr. Mill's theory, and the conclusions of Mr. Dudley Baxter and Mr. Leone Levi.

Mr. Baxter, writing in 1867, gives the income of the " Productive Classes " as £479,000,000, that of the " Auxiliary " as £196,000,000, and that of the " Non-Productive " as £138,000,000, with a total national income of £814,000,000. And he adds, " The net income of the United Kingdom—the original earnings, out of which the nation provides food, clothing, and pays all taxes and expenses—may be taken at from £500,000,000 to £600,000,000. The second-hand, or dependent income, which is paid out of the original earnings, and gives a deceptive magnitude to the National Income Roll, is from £200,000,000 to £210,000,000."

Mr. Leone Levi, writing in 1885, states that the "income, apparently amounting to £1,274,000,000, is the gross income of the people, including much which is a simple transfer from hand to hand. The net income of the nation is probably less than £1,000,000,000 per annum."

But if there is any truth in the foregoing remarks, the distinction here made between gross and net income is altogether fallacious. What Mr. Baxter calls the income of the Productive Classes is no more the net income of the country than the income of an opera-dancer. If an attempt be made to ascertain what is really the net income of the country, it will be found that it becomes necessary to whittle away one item after another, until nothing is left but the savings, that part of the income of the year which remains after all the services of the community have been remunerated, and which does not pass at once into final consumption.

The income of the nation, then, is the aggregate of the incomes of all its individual members, and this should correspond, if Mr. Atkinson's view is correct, with the value of the annual product both of labour and exchange, plus the sum derived from foreign investments, in terms of money.

This is the gross income, and it is this which

apparently should serve as the basis for all calculations as to the incidence of taxation upon the different classes into which the nation is divided.

Adopting this principle (which, however, it must be again observed, is at variance with the views of the distinguished authorities to whom reference has been made), the national income of the United Kingdom in 1883–4, the last for which the income tax returns have been published, was £1,289,000,000, and in 1882–3, £1,274,000,000.

Of this sum we have said that the joint amount of Imperial and Local Taxation formed about 8 per cent.

It is a coincidence worthy of remark, that this percentage very nearly corresponds with that of the National, State, County, and Municipal Taxation of the United States of America, on the income of the Union, which, according to Mr. Atkinson, amounted in the last census year to 9,000,000,000 dollars (after deducting domestic consumption), while the total taxation was 700,000,000 dollars.

But it must be remembered, that while, owing to the gigantic efforts made by the United States to pay off debt, the burden of taxation in the Union is steadily and rapidly diminishing by the double process of an increasing income and a diminishing taxation, there is too much reason to fear that the taxation of the United Kingdom will in future more than keep pace with the growth of the national resources.

We have also seen the process by which our statisticians have arrived at their conclusions as to the distribution of the national income between different classes.

The results are exhibited by Mr. Leone Levi in the following table for 1882–3 :—

INCOMES.	1882–3.	Percentage.
1. Gross amount of property and profits assessed to income tax	£613,000,000	47·70
2. Income of Middle and Lower Classes	140,000,000	10·90
3. Earnings of Working Classes	521,000,000	41·40
	1,274,000,000	100·00

What is the incidence of the taxation of the United Kingdom on these three classes ?

It is necessary to say at once that under our present fiscal system no answer can be given to this question which will represent the real facts.

If it were attempted, for instance, to raise the whole revenue of the country by taxes on such articles as beer, spirits, tea, and tobacco, it cannot be supposed that the upper classes would contribute nothing more than the amount of those taxes on the quantities of such articles as they personally consumed ; nor, on the other hand, if the whole revenue were raised by taxes falling directly on the latter classes alone, that the effect would not soon tell upon wages.

It seems only possible to ensure the final payment of a tax by the person on whom it is intended that it should fall, by imposing taxation in such a way as to leave the relative position of producer and consumer, of capital and labour, unchanged. An income tax, equally levied on every man's income and earnings, would fulfil this condition.

But as attempts have recently been made by high authorities, founded on Mr. Levi's figures, to show that the working classes at present bear an undue share of the national burdens, it may be useful, without accepting them as adequate, or as resting on any solid foundation of fact, to take them as a basis for discussion, on the distinct understanding, however, that they are only used as the chosen weapons of the assailants of the existing fiscal system in a political controversy, and with no kind of belief that they help us very much in the discovery of truth.

In order to present as complete a view as possible, let us then endeavour to form some approximate estimate of the amount of taxation borne by each of these classes respectively. We will begin with the working class, as the most important for our purpose, and in some respects the most easy to deal with.

Mr. Leone Levi gives the number of this class as 26,000,000, or 5,600,000 families. It will be convenient to take the latter—the family of 4·67—as the unit in the following calculations.

We have 5,600,000 families with an annual income of £521,000,000. What are the taxes which they pay?

It would seem to be a very outside estimate if we assume that this class pays its full share per head of the indirect taxes (leaving out wine, which is, of course, exclusively borne by the upper classes). On tea and tobacco this certainly is very far from the truth; and if the average is restored by beer and spirits, it is due to the excessive, and not to the necessary, use of them. But, upon this assumption, the whole amount of Imperial taxation which falls upon this class will be about £32,000,000. This practically corresponds with the statement made by Mr. Gladstone in Midlothian last year, that the working class contributes two-fifths of the Imperial taxes, two-fifths of £72,000,000, being £31,000,000.

This amount of taxation will be found to be at the rate of about 6 per cent. The family income, as we have seen, the unit of our calculation, is £83, upon which 6 per cent. is nearly £5.

But the application of another and more practical test leads to the opinion that this is an excessive estimate.

It will probably be thought that for a working man's family of 4·67 persons, an allowance of two gallons of beer, two ounces of tobacco, and half a pound of tea per week, will be sufficiently liberal (in the case of the last, and, perhaps, the most essential article, the allowance here made is nearly double the average consumption).

The taxation on these quantities will be about £3, or on an income of £83, hardly 4 per cent.

It can hardly be doubted that the higher estimate is the result of the taxes on spirits, for which no allowance has been made in the second estimate.

To this must be added the share of local taxation borne by the working class.

As it must be presumed that the statement was made on the best official authority, the estimate given by Mr. Gladstone in his address of November last to the Midlothian electors may be accepted as approximately correct.

Mr. Gladstone stated that it was believed that the working class, or labour, contributed to the local taxation of the country in the proportion of one-fifth.

The amount of local taxation paid in rates was, in 1881–2, £34,000,000.*

A fifth part of this sum is £6,800,000, which, upon an income of £521,000,000, is about 1⅓ per cent.

If this be added to the percentage paid by this class in Imperial taxes, it appears that the wage-earning portion of the community contributes to the national burdens, both Imperial and local, at the rate of 7 per cent. on their income according to the first, and at the rate of only 5 per cent. according to the second, of the above two estimates.

It is less easy to arrive at any clear result in the case of Mr. Leone Levi's second class, owing partly to the difficulty of ascertaining the number of persons who compose it. We know, however, that the income of the family unit must be under £150 per annum (the income tax limit), and as this class probably contains a smaller proportion of families than either the upper or lower classes, we shall not be very far

---

* By the returns since published, it amounted in 1882–3 to nearly £36,300,000 !

wrong in assuming 5,000,000 to be about their number.

This would give a family income of £130, as against £83, in the working class.

The taxation of this class consists of a share in the Customs and Excise, probably some small proportion of Stamps, which it is difficult to estimate—but for which a slight allowance should be made—and local taxes.

We will assume the share of the Customs and Excise to be at the full rate per head, although this is no doubt very excessive, and, in the absence of other data, allow the same percentage on income for local rates as in the upper class, which is obviously excessive. If £500,000 be added for Stamps (death duties, etc.), the result will be—

Indirect Taxes	...	...	...	... £6,000,000
Stamps	...	...	...	... 500,000
Local Taxation	...	...	...	... 5,000,000
				£11,500,000

This would show a rate of taxation on the income of the second class (£140,000,000) of about 8 per cent. ; but it can hardly be doubted that this is too high an estimate.

We now come to the upper or income tax paying class, which will consist of the remaining 5,000,000 persons. This number, with an income of £613,000,000, gives an average income of £122 per head, or of about £570 per family of 4·67 persons.

This class will have to bear the following taxes :—

		1884.
Property and Income Tax	... ...	£10,718,000
Taxes (Land and House)	... ...	2,875,000
Stamps, exclusive of Fees	... ..	11,000,000
Licences	... ...	2,000,000
Shares of Customs and Excise ...	...	6,000,000
Wine	...	1,250,000
Imperial Taxes	...	33,843,000
Local Taxes, probably under-estimated ...		21,200,000
Total	...	£55,043,000

This sum on an income of £613,000,000 shows a percentage of 9 per cent.

This rate of taxation on the upper classes may appear to fail in its application to particular cases. For instance, it is not probable that a man with the average family income of the class (£570) will find that he pays in taxes £51 per annum, but this must be taken as evidence of the large share of taxation borne by property, both in the shape of death duties and of local taxes, and probably also by those who bear the charges on commercial transactions.

So far the results of our inquiry do not support the view that the working classes bear an undue share of the national burdens; but we are here met by the argument, which has recently been revived in connection with this subject, that "equality of taxation as a maxim of politics means equality of sacrifice," and that the first of Adam Smith's well-known canons of taxation, viz. that the subjects of every state should contribute to the support of the government in proportion to the revenue which they enjoy under its protection, is not consistent with this maxim, for that to take £5 from a man with £100 a year imposes a greater sacrifice on him than to take £50 from a man with £1000.

If sacrifice is to be taken, instead of revenue, as a basis of taxation, it will be seen at once that it opens a wide and most unprofitable field of controversy. Nor is it apparent why money, which is taken as the measure of all other values, should be discarded as a measure of sacrifice.

The theory will hardly bear the test of close economical reasoning. Two men perform the same amount of work in a given number of years, and earn the same reward or revenue. The one spends all his earnings year by year; the other saves half of them. At the end of the period the last has double the income of the first. On the principle of equality of sacrifice, it is not apparent why one man should pay more to the State than the other. They have both incurred precisely the same sacrifices in earning the amount of the tax; but on Adam Smith's principle, which is that every man should contribute in proportion to the revenue which he enjoys under the protection of the State, it becomes possible to tax the second man double, which is accordingly done by levying a fixed percentage on his income. The maxim of equality of sacrifice would, if strictly applied, carry us in a direc-

tion very different from that which its advocates
desire.   It is forgotten that capital is merely accumulated labour or its equivalent.

The idea appears to have its origin rather in the
region of sentiment than in that of reason ; and if it is
entertained, it becomes impossible to arrive at any
consistent or intelligible principle of action.   Every
man will form his own notion of what equality of
sacrifice implies.   It might be argued, with apparent
reason, that it would be a less sacrifice for a man with
£100,000 a year to pay £80,000 in taxes than for a
man with £100 a year to pay £10, and yet the first
would pay at the rate of 80 per cent., while the other
would pay at the rate of 10 per cent.

No line or limit is possible.

It is probably from some consciousness of the
hopelessness of adjusting any scale of relative sacrifices that those who have put forward this proposal
have fallen back upon another principle, originally
suggested by Bentham, and adopted by Mr. Mill,
viz. that the "necessaries" of life should be exempted
from taxation, and that a certain minimum income,
supposed to be sufficient for this purpose, should be
left untaxed.

But this principle is scarcely less unsatisfactory
than that of equality of sacrifice.   It is hardly less
difficult to find a measure of what is necessary than
a measure of relative sacrifice.   It is obvious that
what is necessary for one man is quite different from
that which is necessary for another.   The standard of

necessaries varies in every country, and is progressively advancing with advancing civilization. It varies from man to man, and from class to class, and it would be a waste of time to discuss it.

Hence the proposal to cut short all debate by fixing an arbitrary sum assumed "to be ordinarily sufficient to provide" (in Mr. Mill's most elastic language) "a moderately numerous labouring family with the requisites of life and health, and with protection against habitual bodily suffering, but not with any indulgences," an arrangement which, as he justly adds, " would constitute a reason, in addition to others which might be stated, for maintaining indirect taxes on articles of luxury consumed by the poor."

This is an unanswerable argument, but in using it Mr. Mill appears entirely to have forgotten his principle of "equality of sacrifice."

How can this principle be reconciled with such taxes as those on spirits and tobacco, which impose no sacrifice whatever on those who abstain from them because they dislike them, and who thus escape all contribution to £25,000,000 of the national revenue ?

There is not even the pretext of making sacrifice the measure of taxation, its amount being solely dependent on a taste for articles which are a source of pleasure to one man and of pain to another. There is no possible principle on which such taxes as these can be justified, except by those who regard them as penalties on vicious indulgence.

But whatever may be said of Mr. Mill's incon-

sistency on this point, his statement is unassailable
that "the immunity extended to the income required
for necessaries should depend on its being actually
expended for that purpose, and that the poor who, not
having more than enough for necessaries, divert any
part of it to indulgences, should, like other people,
contribute their quota out of those indulgences to the
expenses of the State."

It is, therefore, not a little remarkable, that in
reviving this proposal for the exemption from taxation
of the income required (as it is assumed) for the
necessaries of life, all reference should have been
omitted to the obvious and essential condition with
which Mr. Mill accompanied it.   And yet it would
seem, from Mr. Chamberlain's remarks on the incidence of taxation in his speech at Hull last August,
and also from the language of the Radical programme
on the same subject, that this point has been entirely
overlooked.   .

With the single exception of the duties on tea and
coffee, which only yield between four and five millions
a year, there is no article consumed by the poor the
consumption of which is not largely in excess, even on
the most indulgent estimate, of what is necessary to
provide "the requisites of life and health," and the
argument for exempting the necessaries of life from
taxation becomes curiously out of place when it is
applied to a system from which nearly all taxation on
the actual necessaries of life has been carefully and
anxiously excluded.

In the next place, however possible such a measure might be, if the poor were taxed directly, how is it to be applied in a country where four-fifths of the taxes which they pay are levied on articles of consumption? It is possible that by reducing the tea duty from 6*d.* to 3*d.* per lb. the revenue might be so increased by increased consumption as to be more than doubled—in which case the rate of taxation would be still heavier—while by raising the tax to a prohibitory rate, the poor would be relieved from paying anything in money, the sacrifice exacted from them being the same by diminished enjoyment.

Again, if we speak of necessaries, what can be more necessary than good government, especially for the poorer and more helpless classes? It is to them a vital question. Without the protection of government they would infallibly be reduced to a state of slavery. For a poor man, therefore, payment out of his earnings for government is scarcely less necessary than payment for the bread he eats. If it is said that a man cannot live with less than £50 a year, minus taxes, it is as easy to say that he cannot live on less than £55 a year plus taxes—one limit is as good as another. The whole question turns on what is to be the standard of living. Sound fiscal principles enjoin that this standard should be so fixed as to include taxation.

It may seem unnecessary, after what has been said, to follow this subject farther, but it may be as well to examine from the point of view which has been taken figures given by Mr. Chamberlain in the speech to which reference has already been made.

By omitting local taxation, which is more than a third of the whole amount, Mr. Chamberlain arrived at the conclusion, after deducting £12 per head from the income of all classes for the "necessaries" of life, that the working classes pay at the rate of 13½ per cent. on their incomes, while the upper and middle classes only pay 6 per cent., or less than half.

Mr. Chamberlain's classification is open to serious objection, for he includes in the latter class all those who, without being in the receipt of wages, are nevertheless below the income tax limit; but taking his basis for the purpose of argument, and adding the local taxes in the proportions which have been already given, we find, after the omission of the taxes on spirits and tobacco, which, however legitimate and useful in moderation, cannot be considered as in any sense necessaries of life, leaving the whole of the revenue from beer, much of which is probably drunk in excess, and, above all, allowing to the working class its full share per head of tea and coffee and beer, that the incidence of taxation is, as nearly as possible, 9 per cent. on both of the two classes into which Mr. Chamberlain divides the population, instead of being, as he states, 13½ and 6 per cent. respectively. It should be added, that although the percentage of taxation on working-class incomes which are below the average, such as those of many agricultural labourers, is necessarily higher, this class is especially that which contributes nothing to the rates.

The plea, therefore, for a readjustment of taxation on grounds of fiscal equity appears to be altogether inadmissible, and the fabric of injustice falls to the ground.

On a review of these facts it seems difficult for an impartial person to resist the conclusion, after making every allowance for their loose and general character, and the fallacious nature of all averages, that, whatever may have been the case in former times, " the exclusive control by property of parliamentary action " has not prevented successive finance ministers from gradually relieving our fiscal system from all reproach, of being, at least in intention, either unjust or oppressive to the working classes, and that Mr. Gladstone's apologetic language in the address to the Midlothian electors last September was quite unnecessary and liable to misconstruction.

There is doubtless one very important consideration which must not be left out of sight. All indirect taxes on articles of consumption take out of the pocket of the consumer a much larger sum than ever reaches the exchequer. This it is impossible to estimate, but it cannot be doubted that the burden of all such taxes is considerably greater than the revenue accounts would lead us to suppose.

But in the present stage of popular intelligence and morality, the substitution of direct taxes for those now levied on beer, spirits, and tobacco, would probably be in the highest degree unpopular with those who pay them, and would have this serious drawback, that

o

it would transfer a large part of their burden from the intemperate and self-indulgent to the provident and frugal.

The foregoing calculations have been necessary for popular and controversial purposes. So long as public men and politicians resort to the kind of arguments which have been examined, they must be met with their own weapons ; but, as has been already observed, they are of little value from a scientific point of view.

Without going so far as some economists, in thinking that wherever taxes are first imposed they are so diffused and distributed in the processes of exchange as to render all elaborate attempts at a nice adjustment of them a matter of comparative unimportance, it is undeniable that under no system of taxation can any class escape a share of the burden, and, least of all, the most helpless and improvident class. It is conceivable that if a direct tax were imposed on the working classes they might be unable to recover the whole of it by a rise in the rate of wages. It is not easily conceivable that a tax on capital would not be gradually diffused throughout the community, and ultimately affect wages, and be borne, in a large proportion, by the working class.

In the case of a country which was self-contained, and had no external trade, there would be much to recommend some self-acting system of taxation of this description ; but with international intercourse, and foreign competition, it would be impossible to rely on its operation, and it becomes important, as far as possible, to impose the tax on the final consumer, and not on the producer. Hence the unquestionable advantage of direct taxation.

This brings us to the financial question, which possesses the greatest practical interest at the present time. What is to be the future of indirect taxation ?

Indications are not wanting that some Tory financiers would not be indisposed, if a sufficient popular support could be obtained, to retrace the steps which have been taken by the most enlightened statesmen of both parties, from the days of Huskisson, in the liberation of British trade ; but so far (divided as it is in other directions) the Liberal party has presented an unbroken front in hostility to any such designs. But no minister of any political colour could look, in this country, to protective duties as a fiscal resource, and the question is, what is to be done with regard to the articles of large popular consumption, such as tobacco, spirits, and tea (from which we still derive a great part of our revenue), and sugar, which, until lately, occupied an important place in the same list ?

The augmentation, or reimposition, of taxes of this description, into which the element of protection may be said hardly to enter, can never, it is to be supposed, be popular ; and in the present temper of public men, and of political parties, it may be perhaps safely predicted that, except in the case of some great national emergency, they will be very reluctantly resorted to ; nor was the fate of the unhappy proposals, made by the late and the present Governments last session, in this direction, of a nature to encourage their renewal.

As regards the section of the Liberal party represented by the Radical programme, there can at least be little doubt that, so far from resorting to such measures, it is looking rather, while stoutly maintaining the duties on drink, to the free breakfast-table and freer tobacco. These are excellent objects, but in the present state of our finances how are they to be accomplished?

It may be inferred from the language of the Radical programme, that the writers imagine that some readjustment of taxation can be effected by taxing what they call the luxuries of the rich, such as cigars, wine, and costly teas, at the same rate as the luxuries of the poor—common tobacco, beer and spirits, and cheap tea. They are evidently unaware that the cause of this difference is not the malignant influence of property, paralysing the benevolent wishes of governments, but partly the administrative difficulty, which has been thought insuperable, of applying to these articles *ad valorem* duties, and partly the fact that the object of these taxes is not to act as a sumptuary law, but to obtain money; and that if cigars and wine were taxed as heavily as common tobacco and spirits, the revenue would rapidly dwindle to a sum not worth collecting. In the case of tobacco the question is complicated by the protective element, as if the tax of 5s. per lb. were raised still higher, the manufacture of a detestable article would be artificially stimulated. Mr. Chamberlain speaks of a tax of 1400 per cent. on the poorest kind of tobacco, and of 5 per cent. or 10 per cent. on the highest-priced cigars. How can such taxes be equalized? The highest-priced cigars cost £10 per lb. in retail. It would be necessary to impose a duty of £100 per lb., at least, on these, making the price of each cigar more than £1. What would be the consumption of these, and what the revenue from them? There is no way of equalizing the tobacco tax on rich and poor but by "levelling down." If the Radical reformers will propose a duty of 6*d*. or 4*d*. per lb. on tobacco, so as to bring it nearer to the tax on cigars, they will establish some claim to be the friends of the working class; but largely as such a measure would contribute to the comfort and morality of the labourer, there is little evidence to show that the tobacco duties are generally unpopular. The smokers are a small minority of the people, and although, no doubt, they constitute the bulk of the electors, smoking is still regarded by many almost as a vicious indulgence, and is placed in the same category with alcoholic drinks, and considered as a fit subject for penal legislation.

The same argument is often used with regard to wine and beer. Why, it is said, should the poor man be taxed more heavily on his beer than the rich man on his wine? The answer is twofold. In the first place, the cheaper wines are already taxed far more heavily than beer, and are, indeed, practically prohibited. In the second place, there is no reason for taxing the rich man's wine, as there is not the slightest difficulty in making him pay his full share of taxation by other means.

It may be added that to raise the duties on wine would only tend to diminish a trade which is already dwindling.

It may, therefore, be confidently asserted, that no transfer of burdens from the working classes to the other classes of society can be effected by a readjustment of the existing indirect taxes.

The only resource left, if it were true that the former class bear an undue share of taxation, is to remit part of the existing indirect taxes which specially fall upon it, and to add an equivalent amount to the taxation which exclusively falls upon other classes.

It may be interesting to see the broad results of this form of readjustment.

Let us, therefore, adopt, for the sake of the argument, Mr. Chamberlain's two main positions in his speech at Hull :—

1. That on their taxable incomes the working class pays 13½ per cent., and the upper and middle classes 6 per cent. of imperial taxes.

2. That local taxation should not be considered in estimating the incidence of taxation on the two classes.

It will be found that, in order to restore the equilibrium on both classes, it will be necessary, on Mr. Chamberlain's premises, to remit about £12,000,000 of the indirect taxes, and add this amount to the taxation now levied on the upper and middle classes.

These are the figures on Mr. Chamberlain's estimate :—

	Taxable Income.	Present Taxation.	Per Cent.	Future Taxation.	Per Cent.
	£	£		£	
Upper and Middle Classes	639,000,000	38,000,000	6	50,000,000	7·80
Working Classes	203,000,000	27,000,000	13½	15,000,000	7·34

Such a measure would enable the Radical Chancellor of the Exchequer to remit the whole of the tea, coffee, and miscellaneous duties, and two-thirds of the tobacco duties. In what form the £12,000,000 should be added to the taxes on the upper and middle classes is a much more difficult problem. The method indicated by Mr. Chamberlain is some scheme of graduated taxation—of taxation which increases in proportion to the amount of the property taxed. Mr. Chamberlain appears to think that this might assume the form either of an income tax, a death tax, or a house tax.

The principle of progressive taxation, which has been a favourite idea with the schools of continental socialism, is one which it is impossible to discuss within the limits of this paper. Nor, indeed, is it necessary. The question has been so thoroughly dealt with in past controversies, that there is little new to be said about it. Even Mr. Mill, who favours some scheme of limiting inheritances, observes that such a tax, as applied to incomes, "is a tax on industry and economy, and imposes a penalty on people for having worker harder and saved more than their neighbours. It is partial taxation, which is a mild form of robbery." If the subject has not attracted much attention on the part of English economists, it is because, fortunately, this country has, until lately, enjoyed a comparative immunity from the economic heresies which have sometimes threatened the foundations of society on the Continent ; but it is needless to say that the system in question is altogether at variance with the four rules of taxation laid down by Adam Smith.

In some form or other, graduated taxation, in the sense of unequal taxation, is inevitable in all highly taxed countries, and exists in practice with us. The income tax and the death duties are instances. But there are solid objections to its adoption in a form so liable to abuse as that of a progressive increase in the percentage of taxation on income or on property. The aim of governments should always be to encourage the motives which promote industry and economy ; and there can be no more disastrous folly than to regard wealth, as the commercial classes were regarded in the Middle Ages, merely as a fit subject of fiscal rapacity.

The precedents cited by Mr. Chamberlain in favour of his proposals are of a very ominous kind. He appeals to the example of Mr. Pitt at the height of the French war, of the United States at the close of their death-struggle with the South, and of Prince Bismarck in still more recent times. It is something new for English financiers to borrow their ideas of taxation from the desperate expedients of the governments of countries wasted by war and the crushing burdens of military expenditure.

But whether recourse be had to this, or to less questionable means of readjusting taxation, the task of imposing £12,000,000 more on the class which already pays the income tax (for it would be impossible to extract much more from the lower middle class) will be found no easy one.

The situation is serious enough without these exaggerations.

Fortunately, as we have seen, while so large a part of the taxes paid by the working classes affect articles which cannot be considered as necessaries of life, there can be no pretext for the argument that such a gigantic transference of existing burdens from one class to another is required in the interests of fiscal equity, or of policy; but, nevertheless, they are so full of anomalies, so unequal in their incidence on individuals, and in some cases so exorbitant in amount, and wasteful in collection, that it is impossible to regard their permanence, as a part of our fiscal system, with any degree of satisfaction.

Again, if the estimates of the national income on which our calculations have proceeded are approximately correct (and this, it must be remembered, entirely depends on the soundness of a view which is opposed to that of Mr. Mill, as well as of Mr. Dudley Baxter and Mr. Leone Levi), there is not at present reason to fear that, as compared with that of other countries, the taxation of the United Kingdom is disproportionately large; but it is indisputable that it is larger than it need be and than it ought to be, and that its tendency to a progressive increase, in the face of a falling trade and diminished rentals, is a very serious danger.

The preceding calculations have been made on the accounts of the year 1884, and it may safely be predicted that when the financial confusion of the present year has disappeared, and the normal budget of the future emerges from it, we shall find that the figures which have been taken are largely exceeded, and that while some branches of revenue, owing to the prevailing depression, have diminished or remained stationary, the expenditure has considerably increased.

With this prospect before us, and bearing in mind the precarious nature of the foundations on which the bulk of our taxation, as it affects five-sixths of our population, at present rests, the time has surely arrived when the financial policy of the country should receive more attention than has of late years been given to it, and not be wholly neglected by our younger politicians.

Let us, at least, look the facts fairly in the face. Out of the £72,000,000 which are annually taken from the British taxpayer in imperial taxation alone, £36,000,000 are already paid by not more than one-

seventh of the people. If, as is possible, some attempt
is made in the present Parliament to give effect to the
first instalment of the Radical programme by abolish-
ing the duties on tea and coffee, it is not likely that
it will be accompanied by any proposal to supply their
place by taxes which fall directly on the class which
now principally pays them. The remission of the tea
duty would then mean an addition of something like
another £4,000,000 to the £36,000,000 already reached.
The recent additions to the charges for the services,
and for national defence, together with the general
growth of expenditure since 1884, will probably be
found to have raised the total imperial outlay considerably above the figures of £72,000,000 taken for
that year. This increased charge will also have fallen
on the same small section of the people. Simultaneously with this steady growth of national liabilities and
of Imperial taxation on a limited class, the growth of
local burdens will proceed at a still more rapid rate, if
the future is to be measured by the past, and if the
cherished designs of what is called State Socialism
should be only partially realized. The last most
unhealthy symptom is to a great extent concealed by
the heavy borrowing on the part of local authorities,
for objects which could not have been attained if their
cost had been thrown upon the rates. More than
£50,000,000 have been raised by loan during the last
four years for local (municipal) purposes, and the
amount of local indebtedness of all kinds at the
present time is estimated at £160,000,000, the interest

on which cannot be much less than £6,000,000 per annum. Three-fifths, at least, of this large and rapidly increasing burden falls upon the same small class, representing what Mr. Gladstone calls "property." The growth of this branch of taxation may be seen from the valuable work on "Local Taxation" by Messrs. Wright and Hobhouse, which shows that while, between the years 1867-8 and 1879-80, the burden on the taxpayer only increased 9.6 per cent., that of the ratepayer advanced 56.4 per cent.

Even if, therefore, the remission of the tax on tea, on grounds of general policy, should be allowed to pass without some such attempt, fiscal equity will certainly require (if the tobacco duties should ever be reduced) that some form of direct taxation should be substituted for them, which would provide for a reasonable contribution from the working classes towards the national revenues.

This is a question to which the financiers of the rising generation cannot too soon direct their attention, if the present scale of expenditure is to be maintained and increased, for it is impossible to regard without anxiety any one of the three resources, on which alone reliance can now be placed, for any Imperial taxation falling on at least 30,000,000 people.

It can hardly be doubted that a considerable part of the beer, and certainly of the spirits, consumed at present, is in excess of the legitimate requirements of the population, and it is at least probable that, with the advance of intelligence and morality, the revenue derived from those sources may tend to decline, while, for the reasons already given, a large reduction of the tobacco duties is a reform on many grounds so desirable, that if it ever became the subject of a popular demand it might be difficult to resist it. This state of things imparts an element of great insecurity to the finance of the future.

No one but the most determined optimist can suppose that the growth of taxation, if continued at its present rate, will not in a very few years outstrip the growth of the national earnings, and that the people of this country will not be subjected to a severe strain.

This may be borne again, as it has been borne before, during periods of public excitement, when great efforts are required to sustain the national honour or existence, or even for some temporary object of national ambition; but if such a state of tension were to become the normal condition of English life, and the people of this country were to be perpetually liable to still further demands upon them, for still heavier sacrifices, in the event of any of the sudden emergencies to which they are now constantly exposed, it could not fail to be a source of grave peril to the stability of whatever form of government conducts its administration. Democracies which cannot secure the material prosperity of a people have no better chance of permanence than other forms of government.

One thing, at least, is certain. Whatever may be

the effect on our political institutions, we shall not solve the social problem, nor succeed in raising the general condition of the people to any adequate level.

It was a profound remark of Mountstuart Elphinstone, that "most mistakes in politics arise from the ignorance of the plain maxim, that it is impossible for the same thing to be and not to be."

In other words, it is impossible for a country with a national debt of £750,000,000, and a military and naval expenditure of £30,000,000, to secure for the working class of its people the same standard of living, as in countries with equal or greater natural resources, and without war debts and war establishments.

Of all the dreams in which modern Radicals indulge, there is none so idle as that any country, and least of all an old and thickly peopled country such as England, with a limited territory, can be a great military power, rivalling in its schemes of aggrandizement and influence the fighting organizations of Europe, subjugating and ruling, and aspiring to civilize, vast continents of subject-races, and at the same time accomplish the very different task—requiring all its energies, all its available wealth, and its highest ability —of "raising the condition of its people," and securing to the children of toil their due share in the reward of labour.

So long as England is content to form a part of a political system, such as that which now prevails on the continent of Europe, and which is little better than an armed camp, all hope of effectual social progress must be set aside.

This is clearly perceived by observers on the other side of the Atlantic.

In his recent work on the " Distribution of Products," Mr. Atkinson, of Boston, writes (p. 73)—

"In the grand competition of the world, which now turns on a cent a bushel, or a quarter of a cent a yard, or a fraction of a penny on a pound of iron or steel, no nation which bears the burden of standing armies, like those of Germany, France, Italy, Austria, and Russia, can hope to enter into successful competition with England or the United States, where the whole English-speaking people take advantage of their position, and serve the nations of the world with goods at low cost, in which all who have joined in the work have made higher wages than can be earned in any of the countries named. The commerce of the army-burdened nations with others will be destroyed by their own restrictions. Nations can only be ruined by their own burdens—then what may come? Their own resources will not suffice to sustain their armies, but with the burden of their armies upon them they cannot engage in competition with England or America; their product will be small and insufficient, their wages very low in their rate, barely capable of buying enough to sustain life, if even for that, while their cost of production as a whole must be very high.

"It is difficult to foresee the course of events. These armies are as impossible to be disarmed, as they are incapable of being sustained, without revolution and destructive war? What will be the end?"

He adds the significant warning, "While other nations prepare for war, we prepare for work."

There is this fatal and incurable weakness in the scheme of financial reform of the modern Radicals.

They assume that the class to which they incessantly appeal may be reconciled to a progressively increasing expenditure by a "readjustment" of taxation.

Doubtless the sum now raised from tea and tobacco might be added to a revised income or property tax or death tax on a graduated scale, and there might be little difficulty in reconciling those who now pay the one and would be altogether exempt from the other to such a transfer of their burdens ; but if it is imagined that a sum of £70,000,000, on the very moderate estimate already given, rapidly advancing year by year, as it undoubtedly would (if half the measures of "social co-operation," discussed so lightly by this school of politicians, were adopted), to a much larger sum, can be raised by any "adjustments" on what is called the "property" of about 5,000,000 persons without a disastrous recoil on the interests of the working classes—there can be no greater mistake.

Such a scale of taxation, however adjusted, would infallibly retard the growth of the national wealth, and place our commerce and industry at a further disadvantage, in competition with the increasing rivalry of younger and freer communities, while if the naked principle of graduation be introduced into our fiscal system, its uncertainty and infinite liability to abuse would dangerously impair the sense of security which is essential to prosperous enterprise.*

---

* I am aware that Mr. Giffen, in his essay on "The Reduction of the National Debt," has expressed the opinion that an annual revenue of £220,000,000 might be raised without diminishing our prosperity. I can only regret my entire inability to agree with so eminent a statist and so able a writer.

It may be thought by some that the extraordinary rapidity with which our wealth and resources have increased during the last forty years will be continued in the period now before us, but very little reflection will show that there is no solid foundation for such an opinion.

The concurrence of causes which led to those extraordinary results is known to every one. The adoption of the free trade policy at a time when our manufacturing supremacy gave us an undisputed start in the race of competition, the increased supplies of gold between 1850–60, the rapid development of the railway systems of the world, the substitution of steam and iron for sails and wood, the invention of the telegraph, the multiplication of the instruments of credit—all these causes combined to give to the period in question an abnormal and exceptional character.

Such a combination of propitious circumstances can hardly occur again, and no sober estimate of our future progress can proceed on such a conjecture.

Yet it is upon this slender and irrational hope that all the speculations and all the programmes of politicians of all parties are now founded.

It is not sufficiently remarked how new is the growth of this temper of mind among our leading statesmen.

In the budgets of Mr. Gladstone which preceded 1874, there is evidence that diminished expenditure was ever present to his mind, as among the most

P

important of his financial resources. His memorable proposal in that year to abolish the income tax could hardly have sprung from anything but the opinion that large remissions of taxation were then still possible, and the first act of his successor, Sir Stafford Northcote (now Lord Iddesleigh), by which the whole of the sugar duties were swept away (a beneficent measure, for which he has never received sufficient credit), affords a no less striking proof of the entire absence of any sort of belief that we were entering upon a course of largely increasing expenditure. Both these ministers, representing the two great official parties, evidently at that time still shared the views of the free trade school of financiers, that the time had come when the people of this country might begin to reap the fruits of their increased prosperity in a diminution of their fiscal burdens.

Then came the " parting of the waters."

We had succeeded in obtaining a somewhat reluctant neutrality in the American and Franco-German wars ; but the reopening of the Eastern question in 1876 presented an irresistible temptation to enter once more upon a policy of active intervention. What followed is well known. A wave of " Imperialism " passed over the land and swept all before it. The cry of Russian aggression revived again the passions and the fears, the prejudices and the jealousies, which had been dormant since the Crimean war. Poets in easy circumstances wrote of the " canker of peace," and a country in which 26,000,000 people live on a shilling a day was told that it was becoming rich and selfish. The nobler elements of the national character were invoked, and a successful effort made to extirpate, once for all, the pernicious doctrine of "non-intervention" as unworthy of English traditions.

It was forgotten that among them there are traditions of generations decimated by pauperism and crime, of unnecessary suffering and remediable wrong; and those who could not forget these aspects of the nation's life were denounced as the mean and unmanly advocates of "peace at any price."

So deeply had this spirit entered into the heart of the articulate classes which control the course of policy, that even the succeeding Government—some of whose members, at least, came into power partly on a supposed reaction against it, after a brief lucid interval thought itself compelled to yield to the popular temper, and plunge still deeper into Imperial adventures.

Under the influence of these generous emotions we have renounced our insular advantages, and become a continental power. We have undertaken to defend the frontiers of Asia Minor and the northern limits of Afghanistan. We have made ourselves practically responsible for the government and defence of Egypt. We have entangled ourselves in infinite liabilities in Southern Africa, and are preparing on the dark continent an empire vaster far than any which we have founded in Hindostan. We have annexed New Guinea and Burmah, and sown the seeds of another

British India in North Borneo; we have resumed our place in the political system of Europe, and identified ourselves with its rivalries, its ambitions, its alliances, its military aggressions, its social dangers, and the economic convulsions with which it is threatened.

Probably no country, in so short a space of time, has incurred prospective responsibilities of so grave a nature, with such immense complacency.

All this has been done deliberately by both parties in the State, and apparently with the general acquiescence of the people. It is not surprising, therefore, that little has been heard of finance.

The day of payment has not yet arrived. We have been drawing bills on futurity which it will take some time to mature; and meanwhile governments will change, and, after all, future generations must deal with their own problems.

The modern statecraft of "opportunism" scoffs at the claims of posterity.

But can we count on so long a respite? It seems now to be a recognized part of our political creed that, by some unhappy fatality, England is exposed to the undying hostility of a great military power with irreconcilable interests, with which no friendly relations are possible, and whose frontier is rapidly becoming conterminous with her own. Hence the constant risk, and ultimate certainty, of an internecine war, which may add fifty or a hundred millions to our debt, throw the finances of India into desperate confusion, and which, even if attended with the most brilliant success, would leave us nearly where we were before —unless, indeed, saddled with still greater liabilities.

If this is the prospect before us, and these the conditions of our future national life, there is no very evident limit to the demands which may be made on the national resources. Ireland, Egypt, and India— all have to be heavily reckoned with in future budgets; and the only chance of lightening the strain will be to throw over internal reforms, and revert to a scale of domestic expenditure more suitable to a country struggling with financial difficulties.

At least, then, let us not delude the working classes by dangling before their eyes the prospect of better times and lightened taxation. Let us not deceive ourselves or them, by thinking that we can at once gratify an Imperial ambition, and raise the standard of life of our labouring population to the level of that enjoyed by other people of our own race, and speaking our own tongue.

It will be the standard of the past, and not of the future,—of the old, and not of the new world.

The men who laid the foundation of the Free Trade policy shared no such illusions. They knew that in the present state of continental Europe, no hope of the healthy growth of free institutions, or of the material prosperity of the people, could possibly exist; they thought that, being more than strong enough to defend ourselves, our military efforts might be confined to purposes of self-defence, and that by concentrating our energies on the arts of peaceful progress, by husbanding our resources, by cultivating commercial relations with all countries in an international spirit of cordial co-operation, instead of insular self-complacency —above all, by identifying ourselves as far as possible with communities whose objects are the same as our own—a combination might in time be formed which might be strong enough to resist the contact of barbarism, and withstand the possible rivalry of decaying empires. They may, perhaps, be excused if they also thought that, until some greater progress had been made in the work of governing ourselves, our inherited burden of governing remote and alien races, whom we can neither conciliate nor comprehend, was sufficient for our strength, without fresh additions.

In the light of recent history this political forecast certainly seems strangely sanguine, but it was, at least, consistent and logical, and it had its root in sound reason and common sense.

But if the hopes of those who thought that it might have been England's destiny to-lead the way towards this great deliverance can hardly now be fulfilled, the progress of humanity will not be long arrested by the default of a particular people, and it may be, if the fatal seed of civil discord is not already sown, that the children of our own race may still be guided by other hands into the land of promise.

This, at least, is the vision of a not distant future, even now discernible, as it is portrayed by one who is no dreamer of dreams, but a cool interpreter of facts.*

* Address by E. Atkinson at Ann Arbour Meeting of American Association for Advancement of Science, 1885.

" Venture, then, to imagine one hundred million English-speaking people living in comfort and welfare on our national domain, even then making use for the necessary purposes of subsistence of only one acre in eight or ten of our whole area ; free from national debt, paying their national taxes under a well-devised and intelligent system, meeting their competitors in the commerce of the world with vast quantities of every kind of produce, and of manufactured articles which will have been produced by the application of the best machinery to the greatest natural resources to be found in any similar area of the earth's surface. The working people will then, as they do now, constitute more than ninety in every hundred of the population, gaining a constantly increasing product with less effort or labour in each decade as the decades pass.

"Can the standing armies of Europe be sustained when the full economic effect and the moral influence of this nation is thus exerted ?

" Of a truth the swords shall be beaten into ploughshares, and the spears into pruning-hooks.

" In our far Southern land, upon the heights around Chattanooga, were many ramparts before which thousands rendered up their lives in order that liberty might be established over all our domain.

" Even from death unto life sprang forth the new industry of the new South ; those very ramparts are now the walls of the reservoirs which supply the free men of that city with living water.

" So may it be in all lands when men learn to serve each other in beneficent commerce, and when all the nations of the earth shall have become interdependent."

PART II.

THE LAW OF VALUE AND THE THEORY OF THE UNEARNED INCREMENT.

CONTENTS.

—◦✦◦—

CHAPTER I.

THE "SHATTERED SCIENCE."

PAGE

Difficulties of Free Traders in defending their views—Want of freshness in their arguments—Failure of Cobden's predictions—
Principle of nationality—Intellectual reaction against Free Trade
doctrines—Traced to the narrow conception of that phrase
presented by the English economists—Connection between the
principles of private property and free exchange recognized by
the French school (Bastiat) and "Manchesterthum," not by
Ricardo-Mill school—In England the two movements, the
abstract scientific movement represented by the last two names,
and the practical movement represented by Cobden and Free-
traders, have never run upon parallel lines—Yet they are often
confounded—Distinction turns on the different conceptions of
value held by schools founded by Condillac and Adam Smith
respectively—Ideas of the latter reproduced by Ricardo and
restated by J. S. Mill—"Cost of Production" theory—Many of
the most powerful arguments of the Socialists drawn from
this source—Views of Mill and Condillac as to the importance
of conception of value—Definitions of value by A. Smith,
Ricardo, Condillac—Consequences of these differences seen in
various views taken by (1) Ricardian school, (2) Socialists, (3)
Free-traders, and (4) school of Mill and Cairnes, respecting
natural monopolies and land—Reconstruction, not deletion,
required in English Political Economy—Ideas of historical and
inductive school of Political Economy appear to be inconsistent
with maintenance of the Free Trade system   225

CHAPTER II.

VALUE.

PAGE

Charge against Ricardo-Mill school that they confound utility with
value, attributing to raw materials and natural forces inherent
value—The plus-value due to the co-operation of nature became
therefore gratuitous gift of nature, whose appropriation, if not
condemned as it is by the Socialists, could only be justified on
ground of necessity—English economists illogical in confining their view to case of land—Confusion arose according to
Bastiat from idea that labour is cause of value ; but to explain
rent the Ricardo-Mill school were driven to adopt theory of two
or three different laws of value governing different classes of
commodities—Limitation of Ricardo's inquiry to the class of
commodities upon which "competition operates without
restraint," and which is "governed by cost of production,"
makes it of small practical importance—Jevons' Preface gave
cost-theory its death-blow—Demonstration that in the case of
all other commodities exchange value is not determined by cost
of production—To what, then, is due the margin of difference
between cost and price?—De Quincey on value and cost of
production—Two elements indispensable to exchange value,
one affirmative and one negative—Utility and Difficulty of
Attainment (U. and D.)—Method of operation of the two
principles explained—Conflict between pain and pleasure—
Cost and reward of cost—Ratio between U. and D. represents
maximum of U. and minimum of D.—Object of economics is
"à satisfaire à nos besoins avec la moindre somme de travail
possible"—But in usual case of exchange, viz. that of two
different commodities or services, there will be four causes of
value, two affirmative and two negative—Illustration of shoemaker and hatter showing operation—Value (final utility)
always in inverse ratio to utility (total utility)—Exchange
value rises *pari passu* with scarcity, or difficulty of attainment
—"Cost of Production" theory an inversion of cause and effect
—"Une chose ne vaut pas parcequ'elle coûte mais elle coûte
parcequ'elle vaut"—Concluding remarks and definitions ... 245

APPENDIX A.

Difference between Ricardo and Bastiat alluded to at beginning of
chapter more fully explained 263

APPENDIX B.

PAGE

Effect of Cost of Production theory on the attitude of the Ricardo-Mill school towards Free Trade 267

CHAPTER III.

NATURAL MONOPOLIES.

Statement of case against property in land—Founded on distinctions analyzed in last chapter—Natural monopolies and artificial monopolies—All property monopoly—There can be no property in that which is " gratuitous "—Positions that land is both limited and common to all are inconsistent—Mill's attack on private ownership of land quoted, and shown to be based theoretically on the fundamental error of making labour the cause of value—Consequence of the error traced—Position of "Manchesterthum" stated—Process described by which free exchange of values and law of competition operate for the benefit of society—Distinction attempted to be drawn between right of property in produce of labour, and right of property in land declared to be unsound—Capital and wages (as Jevons showed) are under the same law as rent—The farmer—The labourer—Non-agricultural values—Element of natural monopoly enters into all surplus profit, or, unearned increment in all—Instance,. Madame Patti and landlord—Leading to the second challenge made in Mill's attack, whether the institution of private property in land can be shown to be "conducive to the general interest"—This to be considered in Chapter IV. ... 272

APPENDIX.

Mr. Herbert Spencer on Property in Land 294

CHAPTER IV.

THE UNEARNED INCREMENT.

The doctrine now to be dealt with exclusively in its relation to the land—Wherever population increases in a limited area, exchange value of land against labour must become greater and greater—Appropriation by community would be an attempt to

circumvent this law, but would be worse than useless, for it
would neutralize the process by which demand is adjusted to
supply—Statement of argument in favour of the State—Answer
suggested by illustrations—What is rent?—Ricardo's and De
Quincey's definitions—Limitation of land, not its various
degrees of productiveness, the essential condition of rent—
De Quincey anticipated the use made by Socialists of the
theory in the unqualified form given it by Ricardo, that
rent arises from the progressive cultivation of inferior soils—
But facts do not warrant these gloomy anticipations—
Carey—Counteracting agencies, agricultural improvements,
better means of communication, Free Trade, by which rent is
kept in check—Ricardo's discussion altogether theoretic, not
founded upon actual facts—If taken, however, as basis for
argument, how would appropriation of rent by State work?
—Table (Ricardo) showing how law of rent operates—"Loi
d'airain"—Unearned Increment theory assumes that this will
always operate—If it does not, charges of Socialists fall to the
ground—If it does, their proposals would only aggravate the
evil—If supply cannot be increased, the only way of checking
progressive pauperization is to limit the demand—Private
ownership does this by placing control of supply and demand
in the same hands—If State becomes responsible for supply
by becoming landlord, it must also control demand and regulate
population—This would involve the sacrifice of personal
freedom and personal responsibility—Equilibrium between
demand and supply would therefore be destroyed—Results of
collective ownership sketched—If numbers of community
remain the same (which the law of population forbids), each
would have a slice of the unearned increment—But the same
result might be attained as it is by the working classes if they
were capable of arresting their progressive increase—General
bearings of the adoption of the theory—Mill's omission to
show how State proprietorship of land would benefit the people
—Impossibility of vesting the ownership of land in the
community at large—There cannot be collective property in
that which, in Mill's language, is common to all—To vest it in
a government would insure inequality and injustice in distribution—Appropriation of economic rent in relief of taxation considered—This arrangement would benefit the richer at the
expense of the poorer members, and would also be a most
dangerous weapon to place in the hands of a government—
Special taxation of ground rents—Interference of this kind
with a mutual-monopoly is like the creation of artificial

PAGE

monopolies, a form of the doctrine of protection—Proposals such as these for dealing with the unearned increment absolutely inconsistent with the policy of Free Trade, which holds that all man can do in utilizing the gifts of nature, limited as they are, is to expose them to the greatest possible competition by freedom of exchange—Protection and Socialism mean privilege and compulsion, as opposed to equal rights and freedom   298

APPENDIX A.

Tables exemplifying the fallacy of the theory of the Unearned Increment   335

APPENDIX B.

Further illustration of the working of the theory   ... 340

APPENDIX C.

The rate of wages—Law of diminishing returns—Mill's stationary state   346

APPENDIX D.

Capital and labour 353

.

CHAPTER I.

THE "SHATTERED SCIENCE."

THOSE who in recent years have been called upon to take a part in the defence of the Free Trade policy (to use that expression in its more special sense) against the attacks of its avowed or disguised opponents in this country, must often have felt the difficulty of imparting to their advocacy the fire and freshness which are required to rouse and stimulate public opinion. It is hardly possible to kindle enthusiasm by appeals to principles which most people have accepted, and to facts with which every one is familiar. As Mr. Bagehot has said, to the modern Englishman Free Trade is an accepted axiom of tedious orthodoxy, and to many minds even a heresy or a paradox is often less unattractive than a truth which has become a commonplace. Then it too often happens that when the well-worn arguments have been exhumed and revived, and the old statistics brought down to date and adapted to present purposes, nothing can prevent a feeling of flatness and languor on the part of the reader, only exceeded by the sense of weariness which attends his attempts to discover in the

Q

fallacies of the Fair Traders something more than the exploded sophistries of Protection.

Free Traders have laboured under other disadvantages. They have been constantly reminded of the failure of the confident predictions by Mr. Cobden and others as to the speedy adoption of the Free Trade policy by other countries, which, although only partially true (for no one acquainted with the facts can deny or doubt that in Europe, at all events, considerable progress has been made), has nevertheless produced a certain feeling of discouragement, and contributed to the natural disposition of every generation to think itself wiser than its predecessor.

These are, however, transient and unimportant phenomena, and afford no reason for apprehension as to the maintenance of the Free Trade policy.

A more serious danger consists in the movement during recent years in favour of the principle of nationality, and in the check given to commercial and fiscal reform by wars, and by military preparations on a scale of unprecedented magnitude, with their inevitable accompaniment of heavy taxation and accumulating debt.

In view, indeed, of the present condition of Europe, the wonder rather is that a Free Trade policy should have so far held its ground.

The essential principle of this policy is that the world, and not the nation, should be the economic unit. Its aim and tendency is to counteract distinctions of race, climate, and institutions, by diffusing among the different nations common material interests. It is a policy of international union, concord, and peace, as opposed to one of separation, rivalry, and war.

The whole current of popular sentiment during the period which we are considering has been running in the opposite direction both in Europe and America.

National unity, national greatness, obtained if necessary by force, has been an object to which all the claims of international intercourse and progress have been unscrupulously sacrificed, and in justifying the course which has been pursued, it has been necessary to combat and depreciate ideas which suggested that the interests of humanity, and especially those of the working classes, would be better served by the co-operation of nations in the arts of peace.

This cause is perhaps of itself sufficient to account for the arrested progress of Free Trade, as well as for the indifference, if not distaste, with which its doctrines are so commonly regarded by the general public ; but hardly for the kind of reaction, the existence of which it is difficult to deny, against the intellectual movement which brought about the Free Trade policy. But I think it probable, especially with reference to this last consideration, that while it is unnecessary to seek for other causes for the partial prevalence of reactionary ideas upon this question with the general public, deeper and subtler agencies have been concurrently at work, which have been slowly undermining the foundations of the intellectual movement which brought about the

Free Trade policy, and have lent their aid to the formation and diffusion of a popular opinion favourable to arbitrary and artificial methods of social regeneration.

I suspect that this cause will be found in the radical difference which may be traced between the conceptions of Free Trade held by the English school of economists, who trace their descent from Adam Smith, and that of Free Exchange as understood by the French school from the time of Condillac. The former, without any very logical inquiry, have confined their meaning to the free exchange of the products of industry or labour, while the latter have always considered free exchange as nothing more than one of the incidents of private property. To their minds it was idle to speak of the free exchange of the products of labour, if the labour itself was not also free, and if profits were to be subject to exceptional and arbitrary taxation. It is at least remarkable that both in England and Germany, in which the term "Free Trade" is used to designate the policy, it may be questioned whether the institution of private property is even now so secure as in France, where the expression "Free Exchange" has been adopted; and that while Mill in England, who probably claimed to be considered as a Free Trader, is the author of the most serious attack yet made in this country upon the institution of property, Thiers, who wrote one of the best books in its defence ("La Propriété"), was the most uncompromising champion of Protection.

There is nothing more remarkable than the failure of English economists of the Ricardo-Mill school to recognize the connection between the principles of private property and free exchange, which are in fact one and the same, and it probably accounts for the lukewarmness of some of them, and especially of Mill, in the cause of free trade.

But the connection was always present to the mind of Bastiat, who more than any English writer represents what is called in Germany "Manchesterthum." In a letter to Mr. Wilson, the President of the Anti-Corn Law League, he writes, in 1849, as follows :—

"You have not been able to demonstrate the right of exchange without discussing and consolidating, as you went along, the right of property ;* and perhaps England owes to your teaching that she is not at the present hour infested, like the Continent, by the false communistic doctrines which, as well as protection, are nothing but the negation in different forms of the right of property.

"You have been unable to demonstrate the right of exchange without throwing a vivid light on the attributions of governments and the natural limits of law. These attributions once understood and these limits fixed, the

* It is necessary here to remark, to put a stop decisively to all verbal cavils as to the sense in which the words "*right* of exchange" and "*right* of property" are used, that they are always used and intended precisely in the sense explained by Professor Cairnes in a note to his essay on "Political Economy and Land" (leaving on one side his distinction between landed property, and property in the products of industry from which I absolutely dissent), to the following effect : "To guard against misapprehension, it may be as well to state that I do not recognize in this argument any 'natural right' to property in anything, even in that which our hands have just made. If it is right that it should belong to us, it is not, if we go to the root of the matter, because we have made it (or, I should add, acquired it by exchange), but because it is expedient that property so acquired should belong to him who so acquires it. The distinction is all-important."

governed will no longer expect from governments prosperity, well-being, absolute happiness, but equal justice for all ; while governments no longer dissipating the public wealth as fast as it is formed, circumscribed in their sphere of action, and no longer repressing individual energy, will themselves be relieved of the immense responsibility which the chimerical hopes of the people throw upon them, and will no longer be driven from power at every inevitable deception."

Mr. Bagehot has told us that Adam Smith fulfilled two functions. " On the one hand, he prepared the way for, although he did not found, the abstract science of Political Economy ; and, on the other, he was the beginner of a great practical movement, and thus became the legitimate progenitor of Ricardo and Mill, as well as of Cobden and the Anti-Corn Law League."

But it should have been added that the two movements, the one in the department of abstract thought, and the other in the practical world of politics, have never run upon parallel lines. Nevertheless they have been confounded by German economists in the common designation of " Manchesterthum." No clear idea can ever be formed as to the course of economic speculation and opinion in the last fifty years of the present century until these two movements are carefully discriminated from each other, and yet I have been unable to discover that this has been done by any of the economists with whose works I am acquainted except Bastiat. Even M. de Laveleye appears to have confounded them together ; and Mr. Macleod and Jevons, although the distinction may easily be gathered from their writings, have failed to indicate it directly.

This distinction will be found to turn upon a radically different conception of the causes which determine the ratio of exchange in the case of natural and of artificial monopolies respectively.

In order to comprehend the nature of this divergence, it is necessary to go back to the works of Condillac and Adam Smith, who have been justly regarded as the founders of the French and English schools respectively. In them we shall easily discover its germs.

But although to Adam Smith, from the want of clearness and consistency in his language on the subject of value, must be traced much of the confusion which has since arisen, I think that Ricardo must be held in the main responsible for the doctrine which has led to the controversy which has unsettled the foundations of the science.

It may even, I think, be doubted whether, rightly interpreted, Adam Smith's view essentially differed from that of Condillac.

But however this may be, it is unquestionable that the doctrine of Ricardo derived much of its authority from the assumed support of Adam Smith, and that in spite of the contemporary protests of Malthus, Bailey, Whately, and others, as well as of the trenchant condemnation of Bentham, who dismissed Ricardo's work as a confusion between cost and value, and notwithstanding the more recent criticisms of Macleod and Jevons, its acceptance by Mill has made it the distinctive feature of the English school of Political Economy.

I shall always consider this fact the most remarkable instance in my experience of the influence of authority.

The three great names in English Political Economy, which has always been essentially insular in character, are Adam Smith, Ricardo, and J. S. Mill. It began with Smith, it was constructed into a science by Ricardo, and after infinite discussions by James Mill, Senior, Torrens, McCulloch, and others, was at last presented in a form so attractive in literary style, and so suitable for popular purposes, by John S. Mill, as to have practically superseded all that had gone before, and to have held its ground against all that has come after. As Mr. Bagehot has told us, "to many students" (he might have added, to the whole of the general public) "his work is the Alpha and Omega of Political Economy;" and yet he adds, "taking his own treatise as a standard, what he added was not a ninth of what was due to Ricardo, and that for much of what is new in his book he was rather the Sécretaire de la Rédaction, expressing and formulating the current views of a certain world, than producing by original thought from his own brain."

It is thus that the general conception of value, formed by Smith, and reproduced in a more precise and scientific form by Ricardo, was finally engrafted in the work destined more than any other to mould

and stamp opinion, and that the so-called law of cost
of production has been ingrained in the minds of at
least two generations of Englishmen.

It would have seemed strange to Adam Smith,
who spoke of the "absurdity" of expecting the complete freedom of trade in England, that his teaching
should have caused, more than anything else, the
adoption of Free Trade as the cardinal principle of
English commercial policy; it would probably have
surprised Ricardo still more to have been told that
some of his doctrines would have been among the
most serious obstacles to its general acceptance. Yet,
although this has perhaps not been sufficiently recognized in England, no one can have read the controversies between the Free Traders and Socialists on
the Continent, without being convinced that Ricardo
and his followers have supplied the latter with their
most powerful arguments, and interposed the greatest
difficulties in the way of those who have endeavoured
to defend the theory of private property and free
exchange. Vidal, Considérant, Proudhon, Karl Marx,
and Lassalle have drawn their deadliest weapons from
Ricardo's armoury; and we have lately seen, from Mr.
Henry George's * constant appeals to his authority,
what was apparent enough to Ricardo's most ardent
disciple, De Quincey, even in 1844, † how readily his
doctrines lend themselves to attacks upon the social
order.

L* See also Mr. Shaw's treatment of the theory of rent and the law of diminishing returns in the recently published volume of "Fabian Essays."—ED.

† Refer here to p. 309 of Chap. IV.

What is Free Trade, or rather Free Exchange ? It is the free exchange of values. "The question of value," as has been well said, "is that into which every problem of the science ultimately resolves itself. The appeal comes back to that tribunal, and for that tribunal no sufficent code of laws has been yet matured which makes it equal to the calls upon its arbitration."

Its fundamental importance is admitted by all writers of all schools, but there is a wide difference of opinion as to the extent of its controlling operation, as well as to the nature of the law itself.

By the writers of the French school and their English representatives, Archbishop Whately and Mr. Macleod, the operation of the law has been considered as co-extensive with the boundaries of the science itself, and Political Economy has been called " Catallactics," or the Science of Exchange.

Mr. Mill has formally expressed his dissent from this view ("Principles," vol. i. p. 513)—

"It is nevertheless evident that of the two great departments of Political Economy, the production of wealth and its distribution, the consideration of value has to do with the latter alone ; and with that only so far as competition, and not usage or custom, is the distributing agency. The conditions and laws of production would be the same as they are, if the arrangements of society did not depend on exchange, or did not admit of it. Even in the present system of industrial life, in which employments are minutely subdivided, and all concerned in production depend for their remuneration on the price of a particular commodity, exchange is not the fundamental law of the distribution of the produce, no more than roads or carriages are the essential

laws of motion, but merely a part of the machinery for effecting it. To confound these ideas, seems to me not only a
logical, but a practical blunder."

In opposition to this opinion of Mill, that value
is only called into existence by exchange, Condillac
asserts—" Le Commerce et le Gouvernement," p. 20).

"Il ne faudrait pas dire avec les écrivains économistes
que [la valeur] consiste dans le rapport d'échange entre telle
chose et telle autre ; ce serait supposer avec eux l'échange
avant la valeur ; ce qui renverserait l'ordre des idées. En
effet, je ne ferais point d'échange avec vous, si je ne jugeais
pas que la chose que vous me cédez a une valeur. . . . Les
écrivains économistes, pour me servir d'un proverbe, ont donc
mis la charrue avant les bœufs."

It may be doubted whether the logical blunder is
on the side of Condillac; but even Mill goes on to
say, in words which are hardly reconcilable with the
preceding sentence, that in an economic society—

"the question. of value is *fundamental*. Almost every
speculation respecting the economical interests of a society
thus constituted implies some theory of value ; the smallest
error on that subject infects with corresponding error all our
other conclusions ; and anything vague or misty in our conception of it creates confusion and uncertainty in everything
else."

Then follows what can only be called an astound-
ing passage (p. 515)—

"Happily there is nothing in the laws of value which
remains for the present, or any future, writer to clear up. The
theory of the subject is complete."

Who, in reading this sentence, could suppose that
not only had the two men, who have been called the

founders of two different schools of Political Economy, Adam Smith and Condillac, formed conceptions of the law of exchange value essentially opposed to each other, but that these two conceptions had divided the world of science ever since, and that so far from there being any agreement on this fundamental question, Bastiat was engaged, at the very moment when it was written, in refuting Ricardo, and that it was as true then as it now is, after another forty years of ineffec- tual controversy, that the state of the science can only be described as one of complete anarchy.

I have said that the conceptions of the law which governs exchange value, formed by Adam Smith and Condillac respectively, were radically opposed. I will give their own words.

Smith says ("Wealth of Nations," bk. v. ch. i.)—

"The value of any commodity to the person who possesses it, and who means not to use or consume it himself, but to exchange it for other commodities, is equal to the quantity of labour which it enables him to purchase or command. Labour, therefore, is the real measure of the exchangeable value of all commodities. The real price of everything, what everything costs to the man who wants to acquire it, is the toil and trouble of acquiring it. What everything is really worth to the man who has acquired it, and who wants to dispose of it, or exchange it for something else, is the toil and trouble which it can save to himself, and which it can impose on other people. What is bought with money or with goods, is purchased by labour as much as what we acquire by the toil of our own body. That money or those goods indeed save us this toil. They contain the value of a certain quantity of labour which we exchange for what is supposed at the time to contain the value of an equal quantity. Labour was the first price, the original purchase-money, that was paid for all things. It was not by gold or silver, but by labour, that all the wealth of the world was originally purchased ; and its value to those who possess it, and who want to exchange it for some new productions, is precisely equal to the quantity of labour which it can enable them to purchase or command."

There is a strange mixture of truth and error in this statement; but there can, I think, be little doubt that the pervading conception is that labour is the cause of value, and that the exchangeable value of commodities is regulated by the quantity of labour employed in their production.

Ricardo, in his comments on this famous passage, observes (ch. i. sect. 1)—

"That this is really the foundation of the exchangeable value of all things, *excepting those which cannot be increased by human industry*, is a doctrine of the utmost importance in Political Economy ; for from no source do so many errors, and so much difference of opinion in that science proceed, as from the vague ideas which are attached to the word 'value.'

" If the quantity of labour realized in commodities regulate their exchangeable value, every increase of the quantity of labour must augment the value of that commodity on which it is exercised, as every diminution must lower it."

Let us now hear Condillac ("Le Commerce et le Gouvernement," p. 14)—*

"Une chose n'a pas une valeur parce qu'elle coûte, mais elle coûte parce qu'elle a une valeur."

We have here two statements directly opposite to

* Œuvres Complètes, tome iv.

each other. The one is indeed the converse of the other.

According to Adam Smith, labour is the cause of value ; and according to Condillac, value is the cause of labour. What was to Smith the cause, was to Condillac the effect ; and what to Condillac was the effect, was to Smith the cause.

We have still to inquire what, according to Condillac, is the cause ·of value — labour or cost being in his view the effect. This is his statement (pp. 10, 11) :—

> " On dit qu'une chose est utile lorsqu'elle sert à quelques-uns de nos besoins, et qu'elle est inutile lorsqu'elle ne sert à aucun, ou que nous n'en pouvons rien faire. Son utilité est donc fondée sur le besoin que nous en avons.
>
> " D'après cette utilité nous l'estimons plus ou moins : c'est à dire que nous jugeons qu'elle est plus ou moins propre aux usages auxquelles nous voulons l'employer. Or cette estime est ce que nous appelons valeur. Dire qu'une chose vaut, c'est dire qu'elle est, ou que nous l'estimons, bonne a quelque usage.
>
> " La valeur des choses est donc *fondée sur leur utilité,* ou ce qui revient encore au même, sur l'usage que nous en pouvons faire. . . .
>
> " Dans l'abondance on sent moins le besoin . . . on le sent davantage dans la rareté . . . or puisque la valeur est fondée sur le besoin, il est naturel qu'un besoin plus senti donne aux choses une plus grande valeur, et *vice versâ.* La valeur des choses croît, donc, dans la rareté, et diminue dans l'abondance. Elle peut même dans l'abondance, diminuer au point de devenir nulle."

This will be seen to be nothing more nor less than the doctrine of final utility as explained by

Jevons, which has re-emerged after a hundred years of controversy.

A few words will indicate the bearing of the differences between the different schools of Political Economy on the subject-matter of these chapters. We shall observe, in the chapter on Value, that Ricardo and his followers divided commodities into two classes—the one in which competition was assumed to operate freely, and the value of which was supposed to be regulated by cost; the other consisting of monopolies whether natural or artificial, the value of which was determined by supply and demand, irrespective of cost. From this point of view, it was inevitable that whenever in the latter category the exchange value exceeded the cost, the notion should arise that the surplus value was "unearned," and was due to a privilege possessed by the proprietor of exploiting the gifts of nature, or, as Ricardo puts it in the case of rent, that it is something paid to the landlord for the "use of the original and indestructible powers of the soil."

The idea has its origin in the radical error of this school of economists, in attributing value to labour, instead of attributing labour to value, and it will accordingly be seen that it rests upon a totally false foundation, the result of a most defective analysis of "cost." Those who desire to satisfy themselves on this point have only to read Jevons' remarkable preface to the "Theory of Political Economy," in which the error of the Ricardian school is conclusively shown. It need only be observed here that wages do not enter into cost of production any more than rent ; that both are the effect and not the cause of value, and both are governed by precisely the same law.

But while regarding the so-called surplus value derived from monopolies as a privilege, the Ricardian school nevertheless held this privilege to be necessary in the interests of society, and therefore to be sanctioned by science. They therefore accepted the principles of private property and free exchange as applicable to both classes of commodities without distinction.

Mill and his contemporaries have formally dissented from this conclusion.

They split up commodities into three classes. 1. Absolute monopolies. 2. Those on which competition freely operates. 3. Land.

The first they set aside as of no practical importance, and thus get rid of an inconvenient objection to their theory.

The second they assume to include everything of practical importance except land.

The third, land.

Here they observe that the cost of production varies according to quality of soil, situation, etc., and conclude that the difference between the cost on the worse soil and the better is "unearned increment." This surplus value they attribute not to nature, but to the labour and efforts of the community at large. They therefore condemn private property and free exchange in the case of land, and decide in favour of collective appropriation, in the name of science and on the plea of social expediency.

This is a totally new departure in the history of English Political Economy, which marks an adhesion to the Socialist school and a renunciation of Free Trade principles in the case of land on the part of the disciples of Mill.

The problem for solution is how to deal with natural monopolies, and in considering it the following questions immediately arise :—

1. What are natural monopolies ?

2. Can they possess and acquire value in exchange ?

3. If so, ought such value to be the subject of private property and free exchange ?

These questions receive widely different answers from the four different schools which are in presence.

(*a*) The Economists grouped round Ricardo hold that all commodities are natural monopolies, upon which from the nature of things competition cannot freely operate; that they can only acquire exchange value by the human agency of appropriation; that such appropriation is unjust, but necessary to society, and therefore to be sanctioned by science.

(*b*) The Socialist schools hold essentially that all property is a natural monopoly; that it is unjust, and ought, in the interests of society and in the name of science, to be disallowed.

(*c*) The Free Trade school ("Manchesterthum") holds with the Socialists that all property is mono-

R

poly, as Jevons has said; that it is just, that it is
essential to society and sanctioned by science, if
accompanied by its attribute, Free Exchange.

(*d*) The school of Mill and Cairnes distinguishes
land from other commodities, and agrees with the
Socialist schools in the treatment of land, while accepting the view of the Ricardo school as regards all
commodities, on which, as they think, competition
operates without restraint.

In the presence of such vital differences of doctrine
as these, well may Jevons call Political Economy a
"shattered science."

I have so far spoken from the point of view of
those who agree with Jevons that it is not "deletion,"
but reconstruction and reform, which is required in
English Political Economy; who accept its methods, but
dispute some of its essential doctrines; who complain,
not that it is too abstract, but that its abstract conceptions are wrong, and who believe that the truth
lies rather with Condillac or Bastiat than with Adam
Smith and Ricardo.

Before passing to a more detailed consideration
of the theory of value, I may say a word upon
another school, composed of those who discard what
they describe as the deductive or *à priori* method
altogether, and seek to build up some comprehensive science of sociology by inductive and empirical
methods.

No rational economist, indeed, pretends that the
" so-called " science covers the whole ground of human

life and motives. Very far from it. What is said, and said, I think, with unanswered cogency, is this— that there are certain universal characteristics of human nature, as human nature now exists, which furnish data for certain deductions. That some portion of the human race, and especially the least civilized and least progressive, do not possess these characteristics, does not affect the question, even if it were proved. It is enough for the purpose that they should be so general as to be universal among all people deserving to be called civilized.

The most striking characteristics of the school I have mentioned, which has drawn much of its inspiration from Germany, appear to be the substitution of the national for the cosmopolitan, or international idea ; and of constraint, or State control, for individual action and personal freedom. It is obvious that these principles are in direct opposition to those on which the Free Trade system is founded, and it was inevitable that they should soon have been found in open hostility to " Manchesterthum," or even to " Smithianismus,"— names by which the doctrines of the League and of Adam Smith and Ricardo have respectively been designated by the German professors.

It cannot be doubted that the views of this school have exercised a considerable influence upon many minds in this country—ably represented as it has been by Mr. Cliffe Leslie and Professor Ingram—but it may be questioned whether they can ever be made widely acceptable, in a popular sense, either to the practical nature of Englishmen or the logical faculty of the French. However this may be, it is obvious that they cannot coexist with the maintenance of a Free Trade system, and that their acceptance would involve a period of purely empirical legislation, and a series of reactionary economical experiments, which could not fail seriously to retard the progress of civilization.

CHAPTER II.

WHAT is the charge brought by certain economists against Ricardo, Mill, and other writers who may be classed as belonging to their school?

According to Bastiat it is this: that they confound utility with value. They attribute to the raw materials and forces of nature an inherent value, independent of all human service or agency; in other words, they consider that whatever is the product of the co-operation of man and nature, owes its value partly to the former and partly to the latter.

From this view the natural inference flowed, that the portion of value, or "plus-value" due to the co-operation of nature, was a gratuitous gift of nature, which, according to some, such as Ricardo (and Adam Smith before him), Buchanan, McCulloch, Scrope, Senior (to these Bastiat adds the following French and Italian writers—Scialoja, Florez Estrada, J. B. Say, Blanqui, J. Garnier), could only be justified as the subject of private appropriation on the ground of necessity or social expediency; according to the Socialists, on condition of compensation, in the form of "Le droit au travail ;" and which, according to the Communists, ought not to be allowed as private property at all, but to be regarded as the common inheritance and common property of the community. It should, however, be observed that the English economists in question have usually confined their view to the case of the rent of land, while some of the most eminent of the Socialist and Communist writers have with more logic, or perhaps greater courage, extended the scope of their inquiry to the share due to natural agencies in other than agricultural industries, and have passed a similar condemnation on the profits of capital, and sometimes on the inequalities in the wages of labour.

This confusion arose, according to Bastiat, from the idea which pervades Adam Smith's writings, and infects more or less those of the school which Ricardo is said to have founded, that labour is the cause, or the principal cause, of value. In considering the case of land, the phenomenon of rent soon presented itself, and it became impossible then not to admit that in this case, at all events, one of the constituent parts of the value of its products in the market went to the proprietors of rent-paying soils, and not to the cultivator as wages or profits. These writers were therefore driven to adopt the theory formulated by Ricardo, and repeated with some qualifications by Mill, that there were two or even three different laws of value, governing different classes of commodities, viz.—

1. Commodities susceptible of indefinite multipli-

cation, upon which competition operates without restraint.

2. Commodities which can only be increased in quantity at an increasing cost.

3. Commodities which cannot be increased at all.

(Ricardo places the two first in one class and subdivides it, but the result is the same.)

These classes are governed by different laws of value.

1. With regard to the first (those which can be increased at will by human labour without assignable limit—it is "cost of production which must ultimately regulate price, and not (as has often been said) the proportion between supply and demand." * (Then follows the distinction between *natural* and market price.) In this class minimum cost determines value.

2. With regard to the second class (those which can be increased at will, but not by equal cost of production), such as corn and minerals, the prices will be regulated by the cost of obtaining the last quantity produced, *i.e.* the quantity produced at the greatest cost (Mill, bk. iii. ch. v. 1). In this class maximum cost determines value.

3. With regard to the third (absolute monopolies), "their value is wholly independent of the quantity of labour originally necessary to produce them," and is exclusively governed by the law of Supply and Demand.

* Ricardo's works by McCulloch, p. 232; cf. Mill, bk. iii. ch. iii.

It is to be remarked that even here, on the threshold of his inquiry, Ricardo stumbles, and his voice has an uncertain sound. He probably felt, as every one must, that there are very few articles of which it can be said with certainty that they can be produced, to any extent required, by human labour at an equal cost of production ; and this thought betrays itself in the passage which follows, in which he says (after admitting that all monopolies are subject to the law of supply and demand), " But the prices of commodities which are subject to competition, and whose quantity may be increased *in any moderate degree*, will ultimately depend, *not* on the state of supply and demand, but on the increased or diminished cost of production " (p. 234). This is a very loose foundation on which to erect a law which is to be the regulating principle of a system of economics, and yet it is to the class of commodities the value of which is, according to Ricardo, governed by cost of production, that his work is almost entirely confined (except as regards his theory of rent), though, as Mr. Macleod has observed, this " express limitation of his inquiry is quite overlooked by some of his ardent disciples."

This limitation must always be kept in view in an estimate of Ricardo's work ; for whether we agree or not that cost of production is the law of value for such a class of commodities as he describes, we should certainly admit that in their case the value will coincide with cost of production (if it is not determined by it). But it is impossible not to feel that any general theory of value, which has exclusive reference to a class of commodities so limited as to fall strictly within Ricardo's limits, can only have the interest attaching to an abstract question, and is of small practical importance. This has been seen by most economists of repute during recent years, and even Bagehot and Cairnes, who still cling, in a fashion, to the "Cost Theory," have so whittled away its applicability and so contracted the sphere of its operation, that there is really little left to dispute over of practical importance for those who are unconvinced by Bastiat, Macleod, and Jevons. The last of these, I think, gave it a death-blow in his preface to the second edition of his "Theory of Political Economy."

This narrows our inquiry—for all are now agreed that, as regards all commodities the supply of which cannot be indefinitely increased at an equal cost, and upon which competition does not operate with unrestricted freedom, the law, or ratio, or as Mill prefers, the equation, of supply and demand, and not cost of production, will determine the exchange value or ratio of exchange. I say this because it seems to me that to include, as Ricardo does,* as a subdivision of his second class, such articles as corn and minerals, because their value is determined by the cost of the last, or most costly portion produced, is a palpable

* I hardly think that this is the case as regards Ricardo, but the remark is substantially true. Mill says ("Political Economy," pp. 557, 558), "The value of an article (meaning natural value) is determined by the cost of that portion of the supply which is produced and brought to market at the greatest expense." He is here speaking of this class of commodities.

blunder. Even Ricardo himself and Mill admit that
rent does not form part of cost, but that, on the contrary, cost is the cause and not the effect of rent.
Rent is the result of an enhancement in the price of
agricultural produce, or generally of land, which is
caused by the pressure of demand upon a limited
supply. It follows, irresistibly, that it is the ratio of
demand and supply which determines the cost of the
last, or most costly portion produced, and not the cost
which determines <u>such</u> value.

In other words, the admission of Mill and Ricardo,
that rent is the effect and not the cause of the price or
value of agricultural products, is fatal to their contention, that such price or value is determined by the
cost of production of that portion of the supply which
is "brought to market by the greatest expense." This
may be proved by a very simple test.* Suppose that
the price of corn on the best soil (A.) is 40s. a quarter,
the pressure of demand on supply raises it to 45s. ;
but it will not pay to cultivate the next best soil (B.)
unless the price rises to 50s. per quarter. No additional
supply will therefore take place—the price of corn will
remain at 45s., which does not represent the cost of
any of the corn in the market, and cannot therefore
be caused by the cost of its production. The cost of
production will still be 40s., but the value will be 45s.

---

* It may perhaps be said in reply that although it may not pay to cultivate the
next best soil (although it is improbable that there would be so much difference
between the two soils), it *will* pay to expend more capital on soil A at 45s., and
that there can be no point at which no additional supply can take place. I do not
know how far this may be true in practice, but in theory the margin of a fraction
of a penny would be enough to prove the law.

per quarter, and this value must be caused by the ratio or equation of supply and demand.*

We then see that, even according to believers in the Cost Theory, it is only to that class of commodities which can be indefinitely multiplied, and upon which competition operates without restraint, that it can possibly apply. Those who have read Mill, Cairnes, Bagehot, and Jevons (it is unnecessary to speak of Mr. Macleod) will, I think, agree with me that this class must be a very small one, even if it exist at all.

It follows that in the case of all other commodities exchange value is not determined by cost of production, and that things produced by equal quantities of labour will not necessarily exchange for each other, but that there may be, and often or generally even is a certain margin of difference, more or less, great or small, between cost and price, or cost of production and exchange value—which is due to what? On the

---

* The absurdity of the theory that Cost of Production regulates value in the case of land, which is the same thing as that of the products of the land, may be shown by the following table. There are, of course, infinite gradations of soil before that which pays no rent, and which is supposed to govern the whole series. We will suppose that there are ten such grades.

Soil.	Cost.	Rent.	Value.	
1	10	90	100	The value of all
2	20	80	100	the series in
3	30	70	100	this bracket is
4	40	60	100	governed by
5	50	50	100	" supply and
6	60	40	100	demand," and
7	70	30	100	
8	80	20	100	that of the
9	90	10	100	
10	100	Nil.	100	last by cost of production.

answer to this question very important consequences will be found to depend.

I think that the fallacy which lies at the root of all the speculations of the advocates of the Cost of Production Theory is revealed by De Quincey.*

Following Ricardo, he sees that Utility must be an element of value. This he calls U., or affirmative value, in contrast to D., or Difficulty of Attainment, negative value. So far well; but instead of seeing that cost of production is merely one manifestation or form of Difficulty of Attainment, which it unquestionably is, he again runs off on the false scent laid by Ricardo, and creates a new antithesis between Cost Price (as he calls it) and Monopoly Price, or Scarcity Price—terms which he properly condemns, but which he confounds by some extraordinary blunder with U., or affirmative value, thus making Difficulty of Attainment caused by scarcity identical with Utility (p. 51).

His explanation of this position on pp. 60, 61, is one of the most extraordinary instances of the straits to which a logician is reduced when he starts on false premises which I ever recollect meeting with.

He says (p. 17) that there are two modes of value in exchange : 1. Intrinsic Utility ; 2. Difficulty of At-

---

* "Logic of Political Economy," p. 60. The remark has been made to me that the "treatment of De Quincey is more serious and respectful than modern economists would approve." I may, therefore, say that Sir L. Mallet obviously selected him for comment as being Ricardo's most ardent and brilliant champion and interpreter. "The best defence," as he said, that can be made for Ricardo's position " was probably that offered by De Quincey, always excepting his extraordinary views on the subject of protection, which it is hardly conceivable that Ricardo shared, and which are absolutely irreconcilable with any possible justification of economic rent."—ED.

tainment ; and that these two must concur. Leaving aside the term "intrinsic," which is an absurdity, we may agree so far, these two expressions corresponding with Demand and Supply, Reward and Cost, and being, as De Quincey well expresses it, affirmative and negative value respectively.

The two modes of value are now quite apparent. The one affirmative, which corresponds with Demand, or Utility the cause of Demand, or, in other words, with the reward of Cost ; this is called U. The other negative, which is composed of two elements, according to Ricardo—labour and scarcity (these being really the same), called D. At this stage (p. 44) De Quincey, quite forgetting that he has included scarcity in D. (Difficulty of Attainment), the negative form, as part of the resistance to the possession of a commodity and to the act of its reproduction (which it undeniably is), by an extraordinary piece of legerdemain, actually makes scarcity suddenly figure as the incident which brings into play "the latent affirmative principle of utility, which accordingly regulates the exchange value of all articles on which competition does not freely operate."

I never saw so audacious a piece of "surreptitious logic."

That what is loosely called Monopoly, or Scarcity Value, by Ricardo, is just as much negative value, *i.e.* resistance to man's efforts, as cost of production, no one can for a moment deny, and to suppose that the affirmative principle, Demand caused by Utility, alone governs the exchange of monopolized articles, and not of articles subject to competition, is the height of illogical absurdity.

It is satisfactory to find that De Quincey, the fanatical champion of the Ricardian law, is "hoist by his own petard."

May not the case be this : All are agreed that Exchange Value must be composed of two elements—the one affirmative, which represents Utility; the other negative, which represents Difficulty of Attainment. These De Quincey called the two modes of Exchange Value, U. and D.

It is clear that neither of these alone can cause or determine Exchange Value.

The utility of a thing, such as the air, may be indefinitely great, but as it is attainable by all, without cost or effort, it is absolutely without Value in Exchange.

The difficulty of attainment may be the highest possible, but unless the object possesses utility, it will be without the smallest Exchange Value.

Therefore the two *must* co-exist and concur. Each is equally indispensable to the common idea of Value in Exchange. The one we call the positive or affirmative principle, the other the negative.

How do these two principles, then, in concurrence or opposition, operate in causing Exchange Value ?

This is the problem. The difficulty is one which De Quincey's logical acumen detected, although he failed in solving it.

It is that up to a certain point the two principles

appear to operate in the same direction, and after this has been reached, in opposition to each other. This confusion arises from the double character of the kind of Exchange Value, which is usually considered, viz. that of two different commodities or services. The essence of Exchange Value lies in the conflict between pain and pleasure, cost and the reward of cost. In a state of isolation a man who makes an effort to satisfy a want effects an act of exchange. He exchanges his labour for the object or satisfaction which it procures him. Here there is no common action between " Utility and Difficulty of Attainment." The two principles which we may also call by the names usually employed, Demand and Supply, are in direct conflict. The man weighs the force of the two motives in the scale—the desire on the one hand and the effort on the other—and the utility of the trans-action is measured by the excess of the first over the second. It is the balance of satisfaction remaining after making the effort. The ratio between U. and D. will always represent the maximum of U. and the minimum of D.* But where two or more men ex-change commodities with each other, there are two complete values, each composed of the affirmative and negative conditions, which have to be measured against each other. There are thus four causes of value, two affirmative and two negative, which operate

---

* The value or final utility will be the equation of U. and D. The greater the utility and the smaller the Difficulty of Attainment, the greater will be the utility (total).

in determining the exchange value of those commodities and services.   How is the balance to be
struck ?

A. is a shoemaker, and B. a hatter.

A. wants a hat.   He has two motives operating in
his mind, pleasure and pain ; (1) desire for the hat, and
(2) the trouble or cost of getting it ; an affirmative
and a negative motive.   These he will compare,
weigh against each other, and decide on the balance.
The determining principle will be that of obtaining
the maximum of the first with the minimum of the
second—to buy in the cheapest and to sell in the
dearest market.   But what is the cheapest market ?
Here comes in cost of production.   If the hatter wants
more than cost and ordinary profit, it is thought that
the shoemaker will make the hat himself.   This is not
so, for this consideration leaves out of account the
effect of division of labour, which enables a hatter to
make a hat cheaper than a shoemaker can make one ;
but in this simple case it may be urged that if the
shoemaker made the hat, the hatter would be compelled to make a pair of shoes, and then they would
both be, in this particular, again on a level.

I will therefore proceed on the extreme assumption that the shoemaker would not give the hatter for
a hat more than it would cost him in labour to make
the hat himself.   This is the measure of its final
utility to him.   Beyond this point it is not useful, for
he can get another hat for the same or less labour.
Its affirmative value stops at this point, but it is not

the less operative as far as it goes. Cost, which is merely one form of negative value, can only fix the limit of Difficulty of Attainment, which must necessarily be the maximum limit of utility or the measure of final utility. But it cannot fix the minimum of utility or any degree of utility between maximum and minimum. The concurrence of the affirmative element of value is essential to exchange value, and it can never therefore be exclusively regulated by cost or one form of negative value alone.

We have merely to reverse the cases of the two men, A. and B., to form a complete idea of the transaction, which may be thus summed up.

In striking the balance of motives, each undergoes the same mental process, each is guided by the same fundamental economic law of obtaining the greatest result with the least effort. As Courcelle Seneuil says, the object of economics is "à satisfaire à nos besoins avec la moindre somme de travail possible." This Jevons calls the best possible statement of the problem of economics. Herein lies naturally the explanation of the central principle of the science, the Law of Value.

Each will therefore compare the minimum cost at which he can buy with the maximum price at which he can get. The first will represent the minimum of the negative, and the second the maximum of the affirmative. What will be the Exchange Value of the hat and the shoes ? To the hatter the hat will represent the minimum of cost, and the shoes the maximum of

S

utility; to the shoemaker the hat will represent the maximum of utility (U.), and the shoes the minimum of cost (D.).

From a subjective point of view the affirmative and negative forms of the respective values are transposed, but both elements are co-present and co-operative, as they always are and must be. It is an extraordinary blunder on the part of so acute and subtle a man as De Quincey not to have seen that the fact of the coincidence of the two apparently conflicting forces (the affirmative and the negative) is the result of the same principle operating on both. That principle, or, to speak more correctly, that cause, is scarcity. It is scarcity which causes final utility, and it is scarcity which causes Difficulty of Attainment. Value in exchange increases in direct ratio to scarcity, and diminishes in direct ratio to abundance. Value in exchange is therefore always in the inverse ratio of total utility, or, more concisely, final utility is in inverse ratio to total utility. The conflict which De Quincey observes is between utility in the sense of total utility, or what Adam Smith calls value in use, and value in exchange, which is final utility, and which increases as total utility decreases, and increases *pari passu* with Difficulty of Attainment. When we speak of the two elements in modes of Exchange Value—Utility and Difficulty of Attainment—we use the term Utility in the sense of final utility, as distinguished from total utility or value in use. Utility in the former case is concrete utility for the purpose of exchange, not for the abstract purpose of satisfying a want. The greater the value in exchange, or final utility, the less the pleasure or reward. Exchange Value is, in this form, in the inverse ratio of quantity of utility. The greater the total utility, the less the final utility. The same object may be worth anything or nothing according as it is scarce or abundant. Thus Exchange Value rises *pari passu* with scarcity, or difficulty of attainment; and when De Quincey speaks of his two modes, he should have made it clear that they are practically convertible terms. The final utility of an object must always be identical with its difficulty of attainment, and *vice versâ*. If final utility were greater than difficulty of attainment, supply would increase and reduce final utility to the old level. If it were less, supply would diminish until final utility were raised. If difficulty of attainment were greater than final utility, supply would cease until the reduced amount had increased the final utility to an equation; and if it were less, it would increase to the same point.

It is vital to remember that the two causes of Exchange Value, U. and D., are absolutely interdependent. They must rise or fall together, always in the same ratio. The truth is that they both arise from scarcity, but the scarcity may be produced by an increased demand or by a diminished supply. A sovereign is worth a hat. If the supply of sovereigns is doubled, the hat will be relatively scarce, and become worth two sovereigns. If the supply of hats is less by half, the hat will be relatively scarce in the same degree, and be worth still a sovereign ; in both cases it will have doubled in exchange value, although from opposite causes, and the effect on its exchange value will be the same, because in both cases its final utility, its difficulty of attainment, are, as they always must be, in exact equation.

We see thus the absurdity of the doctrine that cost of production can regulate exchange value, even where competition operates freely. It is. a complete confusion and inversion of cause and effect. It is not because things are made by the same quantity of labour that they will exchange for each other. It is because they exchange for each other that they are made by the same quantity of labour. "Une chose ne vaut pas parcequ'elle coûte, mais elle coûte parcequ'elle vaut" (Condillac).

Possessing utility, as Ricardo says, exchange value (this he does not say) must depend, not on cost, but on *degree of utility* or *quantity of utility*. As this diminishes exchange value will rise, and it will fall as quantity increases.

But scarcity may arise either from increased demand (which is the affirmative cause of value), or from decreased supply (which is the negative cause). The effect on exchange value will be precisely the same, whichever cause is in operation.

This (the exchange value) will always be at the point of equation between supply and demand.

But it is asked, What is the cause of this equation?

Cairnes and others say, "It is all very well to talk about relation between supply and demand regulating value, but what is the cause of the relation? There must be an antecedent cause."

To this question the Ricardo-Mill school, of which Cairnes is the most determined adherent, say in reply, Where competition operates without restraint (a purely abstract hypothesis), cost of production; where it does not, even they are compelled to fall back on what Mill calls, I suppose by some accidental lapse into logic, the "anterior law" of supply and demand. This is a very lame answer, for it gives a wrong cause in one case and none in the other.

Bastiat says, "Equivalence of services in both cases." And he is undoubtedly right; but the term is liable to the criticism that it is perhaps not so precise as it is possible to make it, although in defining what is in its essence the most subtle and variable of all the ideas which can be clothed in language, it is impossible to avoid expressions which are sufficiently general to cover a variety of different cases of value.

Jevons says, "Final utility." This is good, because it really denotes cost of production, or rather difficulty of attainment (which includes the former as one of its forms), as well as utility. It therefore expresses in one term both affirmative and negative value, the word "final" determining the negative limit, for if the D. were greater than the U. or less, the utility would not be final.

Perhaps a better definition might be Cost of Attainment—this also includes both the affirmative and negative causes of value; or better still, as more sharply in contradistinction to the one-sided and erroneous term "Cost of Production," Cost of Consumption.

APPENDIX A.

BROADLY, I think it may be said that the difference between Ricardo and Bastiat may be summed up as follows :—

That Ricardo and his school reluctantly admit (and only specifically in the case of land) that a commodity can derive exchange value, except from labour or human agency. Wherever an extra value or plus value arises such as rent, it is attributed by this school to nature.

Bastiat, on the other hand, refuses to allow that nature can ever add anything to value. All that nature gives is gratuitous, and all value is attributable to human agency, which he calls "service;" but he admits, with his adversaries, that the value of land, "ou plûtot du capital engagé dans le sol, a deux eléméns. Elle dépend non seulment du travail qui y a été consacré, mais encore de la puissance qui est dans la société de rémunerer ce travail ; de la demande aussi bien que de l'offre."

I have described the difference between Ricardo and Bastiat in a letter to M. de Laveleye as follows :—

"Both admit that nature and man co-operate in the work of production, but Ricardo adds that the value of the product is due partly to man and partly to nature, while Bastiat strenuously insists that it is due exclusively to man, that the share of nature is gratuitous and remains gratuitous—'à travers toutes les transactions humaines.'"

Ricardo's view justifies the charges of the socialists against private property, for it admits that man can appropriate the

forces of nature and obtain remuneration for them ; Bastiat
denies this with the greatest emphasis (" Harmonies Economiques," p. 266).

"On a commencé par confondre l'utilité avec la Valeur
Puis comme la nature co-opère à la création de l'utilité, on en
a conclu qu'elle concourait a la création de la valeur, et on a
dit : cette portion de valeur, n'étant le fruit de travail de
personne, appartient à tout le monde [that is to say, to no one,
for it would cease to exist]. Enfin, remarquant que la valeur
ne se cède jamais sans rémunération, on a ajouté : celui-là vole
qui se fait rétribuer pour une valeur qui est de création
naturelle, qui est indépendante de tout travail humain, qui est
inhérente aux choses, et qui est par destination providentielle,
une de leurs qualités intrinséques."

Bastiat's distinction between utility and value appears to
me incontestable, always remembering his distinction between
" utilités onéreuses " and " utilités gratuites."

If nature were suddenly spontaneously to provide for man
all that he requires, utilities would be enormously increased,
while value would absolutely disappear and cease to exist.

The confusion in the minds of those who attack Bastiat
is, I think, in their conception of the gratuitousness of natural
gifts. What is meant by "gratuitous"? Cairnes says that a
gratuitous gift of nature, limited in extent, was to Bastiat an
"inconceivable idea." Of course it was, and ought to be to
any one ; but why? Because a gift of nature so limited can
only be a gift at all if it is given to a limited number. It
may be gratuitous to them, but it cannot be gratuitous to the
whole human race.

The only mode by which such gifts can be equitably
made available as far as possible, and to as large a number
of people as possible, is by the institution of private property.
In the case of land, the object is that its products should
be rendered as cheap, *i.e.* its utility rendered as great and
its value as little, as possible. It is only through the agency
of private property that the share contributed by nature to
the work of production (whatever it may be) is diffused and
distributed to as wide a circle as possible. It is this function,

viz. the best distribution of the gifts of nature, the adaptation of supply to demand, which constitutes the service rendered by the proprietor, and it is the greatest which can be rendered to society, for society would dissolve without it.

It is this service which receives and deserves remuneration. It is not a question between A. and B. A. has as good or as bad a right as B. It is a question between A. and the whole human race. Does the possession of the land by A. increase or diminish the share which falls to the lot of each member of the human race? The answer can hardly be doubtful. Were it not for the existence of private property, the inherent and intrinsic qualities of the soil might indeed be gratuitous to all. They would also be worthless.

It is this function of distributing in the most equitable manner, as far as they will go, the gifts of nature, the function of adapting supply to demand by restraining the undue pressure of the latter on the former, which constitutes the value of the land or of the product of the land, over and above cost (plus value), and not the co-operation of nature, as is taught by the Ricardian school. It is this which constitutes what Bastiat called a service on the part of the proprietor of the soil, and it is perhaps the greatest service which can be rendered to society.

It seems to me the superficial aspect which this service bears has greatly contributed to obscure its real character. The old economists who admit that the monopoly (as they call it) is useful to society, nevertheless always disparage the functions of the landlord or so-called monopolist. Say speaks of this function as a " fonction commode à la vérité," and others speak in still more uncomplimentary terms. It is forgotten that it is of no sort of consequence whatever to the man or to the society receiving a service, whether or not the man or class rendering it is remunerated in proportion to his labour, or his sacrifices, or his merits of any kind. The only important question for the recipient of a service, is whether or not he can obtain what he requires more cheaply, or as cheaply, *i.e.* with as little exertion or sacrifice on his part, from any one else, or by any other arrangement of society.

If not, then the service is worth the price he pays for it, and it is his highest interest to maintain a social system which gives him what he requires at the least possible cost. If one man gets what he wants with the least possible effort on his part, how can it possibly injure him that another man should get what he wants with a still smaller effort?

It is not the labour incurred, but the labour saved, which concerns the recipient of a service.

APPENDIX B.

FREE Traders consider that Free Trade means the free exchange of values, and they include in this term all values whatsoever, whether of articles subject to the freest competition, or of those which are the subject of monopoly, whether natural or artificial. They claim this perfect freedom of exchange for all values on the ground that they are all derived from one and the same source, viz. human service, and that the free exchange of values is and must be the exchange of equivalent services.

The English school, on the contrary, divide value into two classes, and while accepting the doctrine of Free Trade in its application to those values which can be indefinitely increased in quantity (they do not always add, as Cairnes does, and as they ought logically to do, at a uniform cost) by human efforts, including, therefore, all those which are subject to artificial monopoly, deny its application altogether to values which are attributable to the effect of natural monopoly. They do so upon this ground—that the value of the first class is caused by human labour or effort or sacrifice, and that the value of the second is due not to man but to nature; that it is a gift of nature to the whole human race, and that it is therefore a value which cannot be justly appropriated or exchanged by an individual.

The vital importance of this divergence of opinion between the two schools will become at once apparent, if we recall the nature of the values which fall within the two divisions then created by the English school. In the first will be found all those which are governed by what is popularly called "cost of production," in the second all those which are governed by demand and supply.

But there is a third class of value which consists of commodities which, although susceptible of practically indefinite multiplication, cannot be produced in increasing quantities at a uniform cost. The law of value, according to Mill, in the case of those commodities, is the cost of production of that portion of the supply which is obtained at the greatest cost, and which, by reason of what Jevons calls the law of indifference, must govern the value of the whole.

We have thus three categories which comprehend all that can be made the subject of property or exchange.

1. Those commodities the value of which is governed by "cost of production."

2. Those commodities the value of which is governed by the cost of production of the most costly portion.

3. Those commodities which are governed by demand and supply.

According to the Free Trade school the values which are called into existence in each and all of these three classes are derived from the same source, human service, and are proper subjects of private property and free exchange.

According to the English school, those only of the first class, and of that portion of the second class the value of which is governed by "cost of production," can justly be either appropriated or exchanged, except by the community as a whole, in the name of the whole human race.

It is important to form a clear conception of the limitations which this latter doctrine places on the operation of Free Trade. It will be strictly confined to the sphere within which it is possible to create artificial monopolies. Wherever a natural monopoly exists, wherever any part of the value possessed by any commodity is the result of a natural monopoly, such additional value is, according to the view of the English school, an illegitimate subject of private appropriation, *and therefore of Free Exchange.* It is what Mr. Mill calls "an unearned increment;" it is something which no man has made, which was intended as the inheritance of the whole human race, which whoever appropriates keeps others out of its possession.

What, then, in this view is left to the operation of the law of Free Exchange?

In the first place, all foreign trade (and yet it is precisely in connection with foreign trade that Free Trade is advocated) must, in Mill's own showing, be excluded. In the chapters on International Trade, in his " Principles," it is clearly admitted that all values which are the subject of international exchange are determined not by cost of production, but by demand and supply, into which the element of value due to natural monopoly constantly and largely enters.

This opinion Mr. Bagehot shares. In his essay on Cost of Production, on p. 184 of the " Economic Studies," he confines its operation to "articles which human industry can indefinitely multiply for the hope of profit and within a nation in an economical sense, *i.e.* a group of producers between whom labour and capital freely circulate."

He then goes on to explain more fully what is a nation in an economic sense, and proves conclusively that it often means a single district such as Birmingham, owing to the length of time required to bring together the different kinds of skill in their proper proportions suitable for particular trades. A new place, he says, cannot have this combination for a long time, and an old place for a long time will be superior in this cardinal advantage. This is a conservative force ; but, on the other hand, motive power, wind, water, coal, is an element of cost, which tends to make trade move from one place to another.

But it is equally an element which gives one place a partial monopoly, and causes "the unearned increment." It equally interferes with and frustrates the so-called law of cost of production.

He goes on to show that in facilities for obtaining the raw material of industry, for borrowing capital, and advertising, certain places have special advantages—in other words, monopolies—which still further limit the operation of the law of free competition, and render the law of cost of production (if it be a law at all) little more than an abstraction.

If these limitations on what is called the law of cost are admitted even by those who are the chosen representatives of the English school, what becomes of a system of Free Exchange which is confined to that of those commodities which are covered by its operation? Manifestly there is no longer any ground for considering Free Trade, any more than the law of cost, as anything but an abstraction.

And yet to show that Mr. Bagehot has in no way over-stated the extreme narrowness of the area within which cost of production or unlimited competition can possibly operate, let us hear the view of another of the latest and most eminent writers of the English school. Professor Cairnes, in his work on "Some Leading Principles of Political Economy," examines at much length the received theory of the law of cost, and points out with much ingenuity the defective nature of Mill's statement of the doctrine. He urges with abundant reason that "there are not within the range of economic speculation two ideas more profoundly opposed than those of cost and the reward of cost—the sacrifice incurred by man in productive industry, and the return made by nature to man upon that sacrifice; that all industrial progress consists in altering the proportion between these two things—in increasing the remuneration in proportion to the cost, and diminishing the cost in relation to the remuneration. Cost and remuneration are thus economic antitheses to each other, so completely so that a small cost and a large remuneration are exactly equivalent expressions" ("Leading Principles," p. 49).

Having established, I think, this proposition with un-answerable cogency, Professor Cairnes proceeds to reconstruct, after his own fashion, the doctrine of the law of cost, which in the received form he has thus completely demolished, but in doing so he makes admissions which entirely confirm Mr. Bagehot's views.

He says (p. 72), "What has appeared is a tendency in commodities to exchange in proportion to their costs of production, *only so far as there exists free competition among their producers ;* the exchange, therefore, would only take place in proportion to cost, within the limits of the field of free competition, and a commodity produced within this field, but exchanged against one produced from beyond it, would not in such case exchange in proportion to cost of production. . . . In order that this should happen, effective competition should be established among producers over the whole field of industry—a condition which I need hardly say is very far yet from being anywhere fulfilled. The true conception of the law of cost is, then, not of a law governing universally the values of any class of commodities, but that of one governing the values of certain commodities in certain exchanges ;" that is to say, according to Professor Cairnes, in exchanges between producers in the same competing groups —a conclusion identical with that of Mr. Bagehot.

CHAPTER III.

NATURAL MONOPOLIES.

WITHOUT having recourse to Mill's Jacobinical declamation (quoted by Cairnes with the rapt admiration of a fervent disciple), the case against landed
property may be stated very clearly and simply.
It is this—that the cost of the products of the soil,
owing to the progressive appeal to inferior qualities,
will always command a price determined by their
maximum cost of production; *i.e.* that the price, for
instance, of corn will be that of the corn produced at
the highest cost; whereas, owing to the effect of what
is assumed to be unlimited competition, the price of
all, or almost all, other commodities, such as manufactures, will be determined by the minimum cost of
production.   In the case of land, therefore, the proprietors of the soils which render at a cost less than
the maximum will gain the difference.   To them the
return will not be determined by cost of production,
and this difference is the unearned increment.

The last chapter will have shown how much
foundation there is in the facts of value for these
distinctions.   In the view of the Free Trade school,
monopoly is inevitable wherever exchange value arises;

Nomenclature. The word thus loses all significance

it enters alike into capital, wages, and rent; and the differences between rent and other kinds of value, which the Ricardian school treated in such a manner as to convey the impression that they constituted differences in principle and in kind, are really merely differences in degree, accidental or temporary, and not such as to afford a foundation for special and exceptional legislation.

"There are some things," says Mill, "which, if allowed to be articles of commerce at all, cannot be prevented from being monopolized articles. . . . Now, land is one of these natural monopolies."

It is very important, in view of the consequences drawn from this fact, to determine in what sense the term "natural monopoly" can properly be used, and to show that the two positions taken by Mill and Cairnes, viz. that land is both limited and common to all, are inconsistent.

Bastiat observes ("Harmonies," p. 180), "Les personnes qui assimilent le monopole artificiel et ce qu'elles appellent le monopole naturel parceque l'un et l'autre ont cela de commun qu'ils accroissent la valeur du travail, ces personnes, dis-je, sont bien aveugles et bien superficielles."

I would add what appears to me to be the complement of this remark. Those who assimilate natural monopolies (gifts of nature limited in quantity) to those gifts of nature which are common to all mankind (if, indeed, there are any which are at all times common) because they have this in common,

T

that they are gifts of nature, are very blind and superficial.

The first are not gratuitous in the sense in which the second are, and the confusion which Cairnes and Mill have fallen into on this subject has arisen from the use of the word "gratuitous" to convey two different meanings. It is nothing more than a verbal quibble.

Gifts of nature limited in quantity cannot in the nature of things be gratuitous to everybody. They may be gratuitous to a certain number;* but this is a

---

* A. on the sea-shore picks up a diamond, which he sells to B. for a large sum of money. Bastiat says that the diamond is a gratuitous gift of nature, and is gratuitous (for nature exacts nothing in return), the value in exchange being derived not from nature, but from the human service rendered by A. to B. in sparing him the trouble of finding the diamond, which it would have cost him more to do. Cairnes says that the diamond is gratuitous to A. but not to B., and that A. has no right to a value derived from a gratuitous gift of nature.

Both these views proceed from the mistaken notion that value can proceed from anything but the combined though opposing elements of utility and difficulty of attainment, and from the equally mistaken notion that anything which has both of these qualities and thus has value can ever be gratuitous. Nothing can be gratuitous or common to all for the purposes of common service of which the supply does not exceed all possible demands, and in regard to which there can be no difficulty of attainment or cost. Because a particular diamond is obtained gratuitously by a particular man, to speak of it as a gratuitous gift of nature to the whole human race is an abuse of language; the question is not whether this particular diamond is a gratuitous gift, but whether diamonds are gratuitous. It might as well be said that if A. found a banknote in the street for which he could not find an owner, that it was a gratuitous gift which ought not to be allowed to acquire value in exchange.

It may, of course, be possible that a particular man may by a fortunate accident acquire a diamond, and that to him it may be called a gratuitous gift; but the value of the diamond is determined in no sense by the effort of this acquisition, but by the condition of demand and supply with respect to diamonds in general. No one could be injured by paying this fortunate person the price which it would cost to procure a similar diamond, and to attempt to eliminate altogether the element of chance, or luck, or fortune, from human life is as futile as it is unreasonable.

It is also necessary to guard against as grave an error, viz. the notion of intrinsic value in anything. The diamond might be gratuitously acquired by A.,

law of nature, not a social fact. It injures no one, and nobody would benefit by the non-existence of these gifts. The attempt to make them gratuitous by making them common property (as Mill does in dealing with the unearned increment) is a foolish and delusive enterprise, which can only end by making them valueless.

If, then, these are not gratuitous, in the sense of being common, they constitute values, and values constitute, or ought to constitute, property.

"Toute propriété est une valeur. Toute valeur est une propriété; ce qui n'a pas de valeur est gratuit. Ce qui est gratuit est commun;" because exchange is an attribute of property. A man cannot exchange what he does not possess. Nothing can therefore have value in exchange which is not property. There can be no property or value in that which is gratuitous. Nothing can be gratuitous which possesses both the necessary conditions of value, Utility and Difficulty of Attainment. Therefore, so-called "gifts of nature" which are both useful and limited in extent can never be gratuitous at all.

But not only such gifts of nature. Nothing (*i.e.* no "utility") of which the supply is limited can ever be gratuitous to the whole race. If all property is a value, and that which is not a value is gratuitous, and that which is gratuitous is common, that which has a value cannot be common. If all property is

but it might also be absolutely worthless if he did not desire it, and he could not exchange it for something else. It might in that case have no exchange value whatever.

monopoly, and also a value, all that has value must be a monopoly ; ergo, land, if, as Mill says, it has exchange value, *cannot be common to all*, or a gratuitous gift of nature to the whole human race.

Natural monopolies (or advantages, as they should rather be called) can only be made more available to society by increasing their supply. This can only be done by recognizing them as values, *i.e.* as property. It is only by passing through the stage of *values* that they can become utilities. To make them common by arbitrary and artificial methods, such as their nationalization, is simply to destroy their value, and thereby strike at the root of the motives, which are perpetually operating to discover and utilize them. The first course in benefiting the individual tends gradually but surely to extend the benefits of gifts to the community at large in more or less degree ; the second can only end in sacrificing the interests of both.

"Le monopole artificiel est une spoliation véritable. Il produit des maux qui n'existeraient pas sans lui. Il inflige des privations à une portion considerable de la société, souvent a l'égard des objets les plus nécessaires.

"Les avantages naturels ne font aucun mal a l'humanité. Tout au plus pourrait—on dire qu'ils constatent un mal pré-existant et qui ne leur est point imputable. Il est fâcheux peut-être que le tokay ne soit pas aussi abondant et à aussi bas prix que la piquette. Mais ce n'est pas là un fait social. Il nous a été imposé par la nature. Il y a donc entre l'avantage naturel et le monopole artificiel cette différence profonde : l'un est la conséquence d'une rareté pré-existant inévitable ; l'autre est la cause d'une rareté factice, contre nature."

"Dans le premier cas ce n'est pas l'absence de concurrence

qui fait la rareté, c'est la rareté qui explique l'absence de concurrence. L'humanité serait puérile si elle se tourmentait se révolutionnait, parcequ'il n'y a dans le monde qu'une Jenny Lind, un Clos Vougeot et un Régent.

"Dans le second cas c'est tout le contraire. Ce n'est pas à cause d'une rareté providentielle que la concurrence est impossible, mais c'est parceque la force a étouffé la concurrence qu'il s'est produit parmi les hommes une rareté qui ne devait pas être."

If a natural monopoly is disallowed, the only effect must be to create an artificial monopoly.

What are the grounds of abstract principle and social justice on which Mr. Mill rests his claim on behalf of the State ? These are stated with much emphasis in an essay on "The Right of Property in Land," published in his "Dissertations and Discussions" (vol. iv. p. 288).* He says—

"Rights of property are of several kinds. There is the

---

* It will be seen from the following quotations (from "Dissertations and Discussions," vol. iv.), which complete Mill's case against private property in land, that the reasons he gives are inconsistent, as well as being contrary to the facts as to the causes of value in exchange :—

"The land is the original inheritance of all mankind" (p. 243). "While leaving the owner the full enjoyment of whatever value he adds to the land by his own exertions and expenditure," there is no reason for "allowing him to appropriate an increase of value to which he has contributed nothing, but which accrues to him from the general growth of society ; that is to say, not from his own labour or expenditure, but from that of other people—of the community at large "(p. 244).

By the proposals of the Land Tenure Reform Association "the increase of wealth which now flows into the coffers of private persons from the mere progress of society, and not from their own merits or sacrifices, will be gradually and in an increasing proportion diverted from them to the nation as a whole, from whose collective exertions and sacrifices it really proceeds" (p. 244).

"Land—and by land I mean the whole material of the earth, underground as well as above—not having been made by man, but being the gift of nature to the whole human race " (p. 255).

"The land is not of man's creation ; and for a person to appropriate to himself a mere gift of nature, not made to him in particular, but which belonged as much to all others till he took possession of it, is, *primâ facie*, an injustice to all the rest " (p. 289).—ED.

property which a person has in things that he himself has made . . . in what one has received as a recompense for making something for somebody else, or for doing any service to somebody else, among which services must be reckoned that of lending to him what one has made or honestly come by. There is property in what has been freely given to one . . . by the person who made or honestly came by it. . . . *All these are rights to things which are the produce of labour*, etc.

"But there is another kind of property which does not come under any of these descriptions, nor depend upon this principle. This is the ownership which persons are allowed to exercise over things not made by themselves, nor made at all. Such is property in land. . . . The land is not of man's creation ; and for a person to appropriate to himself a mere gift of nature, not made to him in particular, but which belonged as much to all others until he took possession of it, is, *primâ facie*, an injustice to all the rest." And further, "to make such an institution just, it must be shown to be conducive to the general interest, in which this disinherited portion of the community has its part."

He then proceeds to argue that the institution cannot be shown to be conducive to the general interest, and passes sentence accordingly.

These remarks of Mr. Mill really go to the root of the whole difference between the so-called English school of economists (Ricardo and Mill) and the Free Trade school represented by Bastiat, Macleod, etc. They deserve, therefore, very careful examination.

It is enough, as a practical answer, to say that those who defend private property in land are quite willing to rest their case on the social expediency of the institution. They fully accept the challenge that it must be shown to be conducive to the general interest, and they assert, in opposition to Mill, that it is so conducive in the highest possible degree. I shall endeavour to show this in the following chapter.

But although, for practical purposes, this argument appears sufficient in reply to Mr. Mill's, it is necessary to point out that he is quite as wrong on points of theory and principles as on those of social expediency. To many minds, and mine is among them, there is something peculiarly repugnant in any conclusion which fails to satisfy the requirements of sound theory as well as of policy.

The fundamental error which pervades and vitiates all Mr. Mill's speculations on this subject, is his conception of the law of value. The fatal mistake of making labour the cause of value crops up here again. In the passage already quoted, he says, " All these are rights to things which are *the produce of labour,*" evidently implying that it is because they are the produce of labour that they are proper subjects of property. But it cannot be proclaimed too loudly that labour neither causes nor determines value. That it does not cause value hardly requires stating, and the sense in which it alone could have been supposed to determine value is so limited and so much of an abstraction, that the hold which the doctrine has obtained on the minds of eminent economists is surprising.*

* The truth appears to me to be this—that in the case of all commodities there is a constant tendency of value to cost of production ; this is the result of competition, which for ever tracks and undermines, if it cannot always destroy, monopolies. In certain cases where competition operates without restraint, the value of commodities will therefore coincide with their cost of production, or may be said, in popular parlance, to be determined by it ; but this is really not the case. Cost

The practical result of the notion that "cost of production" regulates or is the law of value in the case of all commodities which, as it is said, human industry can indefinitely multiply, and on which competition operates without restraint (whatever these may be), while "supply and demand" is the law of value in the case of all commodities which are in any degree the subject of monopoly, has been a fatal stumbling-block in the progress of the science, and is obviously the cause of the distinction made by Mill between property in the produce of labour, and property in that "which no man has made." When once the idea that value is due to labour has taken possession of the mind, it is difficult to avoid the feeling that property which is due to causes independent of the action of the proprietor, or at all events incommensurate with it, is illegitimate; and yet nothing can be more false. It is clear that two men may devote exactly the same amount of labour to the production of a commodity, and that, from causes altogether beyond their control, the result may be in the case of the first of the greatest value, and in that of the second worthless. It is the demand (the consumer) who causes the value, and in all social arrangements, in all legislation, it is to the consumer that exclusive regard should

of production is itself eternally fluctuating, according to the fluctuations in the ratio of supply and demand. Indeed, what is cost of production except an element of supply? A diminished cost means an increased supply.

It may be said that if, after all, it is a question of logomachy, there cannot be a very essential difference between the two principles; but this is a mistake. It is the idea that commodities are governed by different laws of value which has led Mill and the Socialists to attack private property in land.

† This is so obvious that it must be assumed to have been recognised by the other side — they not being tautologists.

be had. The interest of the consumer is always that
of the community at large, and the only proper meaning of the tèrm " right of property " is the right to
whatever it is in the interest of society to recognize as
property. If by any scheme of socialism the general
welfare of the community could be raised to a higher
level than by the institution of private property and
free exchange, no one would have the right to claim
for his own advantage the benefit of those institutions,
for no one can have a right to injure his fellow-
creatures. But it is because the Free Trade school
believes that private property and free exchange are
infinitely more favourable to the general interest than
any system of collective property which has ever been
proposed, that they insist upon their recognition.

Contrary to Mr. Mill and to all other socialist
writers, " Manchesterthum " asserts that the distinction which he attempts to draw between right of
property in the produce of labour and right of property in land, is false; that it reposes upon the
erroneous idea that value is due to labour and to the
co-operation of nature; that it is in the interest of
society that all values should be the subject of private
property—those values which are under the control of
competition (as even Mill allows), and *still more, not
less*, than those which are the result to any degree of
natural monopoly; for this very sufficient reason, that
a natural monopoly is the result of scarcity, and that
where supply is limited, it is necessary strictly to
limit the demand; that this can best be done, and

only be done effectually, by vesting their property in individuals, who act as "forestallers and regrators," and thereby perform to society an invaluable service.*

Let us observe the process by which the free exchange of values and the law of competition operate for the benefit of society.

Political Economy deals with man in a social state. It is concerned to show by what arrangements communities may secure the conditions most favourable to the largest production and the best distribution of wealth.   Exchange is the main source of wealth; without it, it is clear that each person would only produce what was necessary for his own wants; there would be no division of labour, no production on a large scale, and no advance for society beyond the earliest stage of civilization.   But property must precede exchange—hence the necessity of property; and freedom of exchange is the surest method of giving to it the largest efficiency.   Hence the two fundamental principles of an economical society—private property and free exchange.   But property in and exchange of what?   Of values?   Value cannot exist without exchange.   As Bastiat says, "La valeur est le rapport entre deux services échangés."   It may, indeed, be said that the idea of value would exist in the mind of Robinson Crusoe if he compared the results of his labours with his desires; but this is really a potential exchange, an exchange in germ, and falls still within Bastiat's definition.

* This point is worked out in the next chapter.

Man, then, in a social state, is incessantly occupied in creating and discovering values for the purpose of exchange.   If these values are not recognized as property they cannot be exchanged, and will certainly, therefore, not be created.   In order to stimulate to the utmost the production of wealth (which is the general name for values) it is essential that values, when created, should be recognized as property, and made freely exchangeable.   Yes, says Mill, but there are two kinds of value and of property; property in that which a man himself has made, and property in that which no man has made.   Is it desirable, *i.e.* would it promote the production or distribution of wealth, that the first kind alone should be recognized ?   Shall no value be recognized in property, to the creation of which natural forces have contributed ?   The answer is that natural forces do not any more than human labour cause value.*

---

* Mill and Cairnes, and generally the school of so-called English economy, has made *fausse route* altogether in their theory of value, and hence all the confusion and error which infects modern speculations on property in land, and threatens to inundate us with all kinds of experiments in the direction of State socialism.   Cairnes' extraordinary inability even to understand the essential difference between "labour" and "service," which Bastiat has so unanswerably pointed out, is the best proof of what I say.

The moment that it is clearly apprehended that property in values of all kinds, whether earned or unearned by the producer or possessor, is important to society, not in the interest of the proprietor, but in that of the consumer or public at large, all this "échafaudage" of dangerous folly falls to the ground.

Nowhere has the law of value been more admirably presented in its true outlines than in the magnificent parable of the labourers in the vineyard.   They received every man a penny, those who had worked only one hour and those who had borne the heat and burden of the day.   "Take that thine is, and go thy way.   Didst thou not agree with me for a penny ?   Is thine eye evil, because I am good ?   And the first shall be last, and the last first : for many are called, but

The difficulty which has led Mill and others to deny the right of individuals to property in that which they have not created, in what they call the gratuitous gifts of nature, is caused by precisely the same error as that which has led them to attribute value to the results of labour. The value of a commodity, whether produced by man or nature, is not due to human labour or to nature, but to the fact that its possession satisfies a human want, and that men are ready to give their labour or their property (from whatever source derived) in order to obtain it. It is the *service* for which they pay, and it is this which causes and determines its value.

It is remarkable that Mill, with his trained intellect and great capacity, had not sufficient subtlety of intelligence to perceive this. The question is not, What did it cost the producer? but, What is the article worth to the consumer? The question is not what it costs you, but what labour it saves me. You say that part of the value is caused by a gratuitous gift of nature which an individual has no right to appropriate. Can any arrangement be made by human law by which this surplus value, this unearned increment, can be transferred from the individual to the public with any advantage to the latter? *

few are chosen." It would be well if the modern socialist would lay this divine lesson to heart.

* This gift of nature, if it is so called, in no way causes the value of the object, whatever it may be (say land of unusual fertility). The cause of its value is that there is so great a demand for its produce, that the price rises to a point which causes rent. It is the demand which causes value, not the fact that the object has been made with or without labour.

If rent be appropriated by the State, will the consumer get his food, or his clothing, or his lodging cheaper? If not—if, on the contrary, these things will be less cheap—it is mere folly to complain of a state of things which, in benefiting the general public, benefits a particular class especially. If the poor are poor because the rich are rich, there is just ground for reform; but if the poor would be poorer, if the rich were not rich (which is the truth), no one except those who are animated by a fanatical and unreasoning passion for equality can desire to encroach upon a fund which, in making the few rich, indirectly improves the lot of all.

Mill and Cairnes, misled by their totally false conception of "value," persist in speaking of natural forces, gifts of nature if you like, which are local and limited, as *gratuitous;* Cairnes even goes so far as to express surprise with the utmost *naïveté* that Bastiat was unable to conceive a gift of nature limited in extent and at the same time gratuitous. Bastiat was far too good an economist not to see that a gift of nature limited in extent might possess value,* and that whatever possesses value cannot be gratuitous.

To call it so because it is gratuitous to the individual is a mere quibble. Nothing can make it gratuitous to the community at large unless the supply be unlimited, which is contrary to the supposition. The

---

* Although such value would not be *caused* either by the fact of its being a gift of nature or by its being limited in extent. It might be both, and yet, if there were no demand, or an insufficient demand, be worthless.

only question is, Shall this value belong to the individual or to the State? Bastiat contended, with a logic which Mill and Cairnes would have done better to imitate than to neglect, that this value would be more useful to the community at large if distributed through the individual than if so distributed by the State, and for this reason, that it would prevent an undue pressure of demand on a supply necessarily limited, by the double process of checking the growth of population, and at the same time stimulating the discovery and creation of new values.   Value is opposed to utility.   As the sum of utilities increases, the sum of values relatively diminishes.   The constant aspiration of society is to *increase utilities* and substitute them for values (steam, electricity, etc., for human labour or horse-power); but while this is the goal to which human effort for ever unconsciously tends, and must tend in the nature of things (for it is in obedience to the law that men will always try to satisfy their wants with the least possible effort), it is important to observe that the effort of every individual is to create *values* in order to command a larger share of the labour and services of others.   Individual effort is thus for ever working in an opposite direction to the universal aspiration of society.   The function of the individual as a producer is to create as much value as possible.   If it were not so, there could be no sufficient motive for his exertion, and in serving his own immediate interests he promotes the ultimate interest of society.

For, in a system of freedom, the individual is constantly tracked in his efforts to create values and benefit himself by the great law of competition, that is, by the efforts of others to rival and share and eclipse his profits. There is thus an unceasing process by which values are reduced or destroyed, neutralizing, in the interests of society, the efforts of the individual to increase and create them in his own. All this process State socialism would arrest and vitiate ; and thus, in stupid impatience and false philanthropy, the beneficial mechanism which controls and overrules in the common interest the isolated actions of the individual, is thrown out of gear and paralyzed.

Professor Jevons has observed (preface, p. 55) that capital, fixed and free, as well as wages, are under the same law as rent. The element of natural monopoly enters into both.

Much of the confusion which has attended this subject has arisen from the peculiar form which the present arrangement of landed property between landlord, tenant, and labourer in England has taken. Rent, in the sense in which the term is represented to our minds, would not exist at all if every man cultivated his own land. In such a case it is evident that the portion of the produce which now constitutes rent would be simply a part of the profits, and it would be more difficult than ever to separate that portion which could be considered as unearned increment. Yet the real net profit derived from land would be precisely the same as at present. The relation of

landlord and tenant would give place to a kind of
partnership, a sleeping and a managing partner, or
partners would probably divide the profits between
them in any proportion agreed upon, in precisely the
same way as is now done constantly in commercial
and manufacturing undertakings.   In these last it
constantly happens that the man who has founded the
enterprise (corresponding with the man who first takes
up and settles on the land), when he discovers that the
profits are sufficient to yield more than he wants,
hands over to a partner or manager a certain share,
retaining only that portion which is due to the capital
which he leaves in the concern.   If the partner have
no capital, he will of course have a smaller share in
the profits.   In this case he would perhaps be rather
in the position of a paid manager, corresponding
with the bailiff or land agent in agriculture; but if
he were a capitalist, as in the case of a tenant farmer,
he would get his share of profits upon his capital in
addition to whatever was necessary to remunerate his
labours of direction.   The original founder, become
at last merely a sleeping partner, neither toils nor
spins, but draws a revenue from the joint property
precisely as the landlord draws a revenue from the soil.

I entertain much doubt whether if the land had
been divided in England as it is in France, and the
bulk of the proprietors had been themselves the
cultivators, we should ever have heard of the theory
of the "unearned increment;" and yet it would have
existed quite as much in one case as in another, so

long as the produce of each property was greater than the cost of its production.

When pressed home the arguments of Mill come to this, that whenever the exchange value of any article, or of anything which constitutes property, exceeds its cost of production (including the market rates of interest and profit), the excess value is "un-earned increment."

"Economic rent," called by Mill "unearned increment," is in fact nothing more nor less than the monopoly profit derived either from land, capital, or labour, over and above the present market rate of profit. This is what the French call the "plus-value." The distribution of the aggregate returns to any employment of labour and capital—in short, to any agency of man—will take place according to the conditions of demand and supply between these three elements, or component parts of the return to their joint operation, and will be determined in exchange of each against the other.

This value will depend on the conditions of the demand and supply of each. If land is abundant rela-tively to the other two, rent will be low, profits and wages high; if capital is relatively abundant, profits will be low, and rent and labour dear; if labour is relatively abundant, wages will be low, and rent and profits high.

There is nothing in this monopoly profit, when derived from land, which differs from similar profits derived from capital and labour applied to any other purpose than the utilization of land.

U

Let us take the other two great Ricardian divisions of industry with which the landlord shares the produce of the soil, represented by the capitalist (the farmer) and the labourer. The two first, the landlord and the farmer, bring their capital into the concern; the first is the sleeping, and the second is the managing partner. The produce is divided between them after paying wages, in whatever proportion they agree upon; and if the landlord is allowed to appropriate too large a share of the "unearned increment," it is the farmer's fault. The latter calculates that he will be able to get the market rate of interest, and profit from his capital; the former, the market rate of interest. If from any causes the value of the produce is increased so as to pay more than enough to provide this, the additional value will go to the tenant during his lease and to the landlord afterwards. This potential value is probably taken into account both by landlord and tenant in making their bargain. And the advantage will probably lie either with one or the other, according to the conditions of the land-market at the time, *i.e.* whether there are more landlords seeking farmers than farmers seeking landlords, or *vice versâ*. As regards unearned increment, therefore, landlord and farmer seem to be on the same footing.

Is the case different with the labourer? It may be said that the "loi d'airain" of Lassalle will always prevent him from obtaining more than the means of subsistence. But is this true? Are there not causes always in the long run operating on the labour market, equally independent of human control, which tend to raise as well as depress the price of labour ; and without indulging in hypothesis removed from actual facts, have we not seen that price increased by money 50 per cent. in our time in England, by the movement of the agricultural population towards the great cities, and the comparative scarcity of hands in agricultural districts ? What is this but the unearned increment ? Is it due in any sense to the exertion, or foresight, or abstinence of the labourer, and not to the general progress of the community to which he belongs, quite as much as the "unearned increment" of the landlord or the tenant ?

So much for the "unearned increment" as between the three recipients of the produce of the soil. How far does it exist in non-agricultural values ?

As regards these, it is evident that certain countries and certain localities, partly from natural advantages and partly from propinquity to markets, possess a partial monopoly. The pressure of demand upon supply raises the price of the articles which they produce to a point which leaves a margin varying in degree (as in the case of land) between the smallest price and the cost of production in the favoured localities. There can only be one price in the same market, and this surplus profit is quite as much "unearned increment" as rent.

A final example will perhaps confirm the conclusion at which we have arrived, that as an abstract question the contention of Mr. Mill, Mr. Cairnes, Mr. George, and others that there is a distinction between land, for example, and the products of man's labour, has no foundation.

A man may possess 100,000 acres of land in uninhabited country, but it will possess no value whatever.

Madame Patti receives £100 for singing a single night at a private concert, but if there was no one to attend the concert her voice would possess no value whatever.

But the distinction between the two cases is said to be that the first is the possession of an external gift of nature, to which one man has as good a right as another; while the second is a personal possession, which, if not allowed as property to Madame Patti, cannot be acquired by any one else.

But the answer in both cases is the same. Society owes nothing to the proprietor of the acres or to Madame Patti irrespective of the services they render. If the right of property is denied both, the first will not occupy the land and Madame Patti will decline to sing. The question, therefore, becomes, Is it in the interest of society that the land should be occupied, and that Madame Patti should be induced to sing? If it is, the further question arises, whether the interests of society will be promoted by allowing property in both the land and the voice.

To this second question, Mr. Mill, and those who think with him, answer unhesitatingly, " No," in the case of land; " Yes," in the case of Madame Patti.

But I have now come back to the question whether the institution of private property in land can be shown to be conducive to the general interest. This I purpose to consider in the following chapter.

APPENDIX.

Mr. Herbert Spencer on Property in Land.

"But there is no reason to suspect that while private possession of things produced by labour will grow even more definite and sacred than at present, the inhabited area which cannot be produced by labour will eventually be distinguished as something which may not be privately possessed.

"As the individual, primitively owner of himself, partially or wholly loses ownership of himself during the militant *régime*, but gradually resumes it as the industrial *régime* develops; so, possibly, the commercial proprietorship of land, partially or wholly merged in the ownership of dominant men during evolution of the militant type, will be resumed as the industrial type becomes fully evolved" ("Political Institutions," ch. xv.).

It is extraordinary that Mr. Spencer in this passage should have overlooked the essential difference between property in land and property in men. It is no doubt within the competence of society to determine what shall be the limits of private property, but the important thing is to ascertain the principles on which those limits are determined. Now whatever principle may be right or wrong (and I suppose that Mr. Spencer would concede that the interests of society generally should be the object to be kept in view), there can be no doubt that the principle which excludes property in human beings is the same as that which includes property in land, viz. the principle that the general interests of society are promoted by freedom. It is unnecessary to say that slavery is inconsistent with freedom; but it is necessary to insist on what is almost always forgotten by those who

declaim against private property in land, that this also is
an essential condition of freedom. Whoever holds the land
holds that which, being limited in extent, at least in every
particular community, imposes on the possessor the duty and
the necessity of restricting an undue pressure on the soil by
the increasing wants of the population. If the family is the
unit, this is effected by the personal responsibility of the
head and by the exercise of parental authority, as regards
the cultivating class ; and as regards the consumers of the
produce, or the community at large, by a gradual augmentation of price and ultimately of rent. When the limits of
production have been reached, any additional population
must migrate to other lands, or perish, unless they can be
supported by charity. If they perish, the responsibility must
rest with those who call into life beings for whom there is no
means of support, and this is as it should be.

But the moment the unit is extended so as to include
a whole community, this personal responsibility, and with
it personal liberty, is destroyed. In a village in a primitive
society the evil is scarcely felt—the conditions approximate
too closely to those of family life ; but in a large community,
to vest the property of the soil in the State, *i.e.* the Government, centralized and removed from all personal contact with
individuals, is to throw upon it the paramount obligation
either to regulate marriages, and, indeed, all sexual intercourse, or to provide food for the people (so long as this
can be done) by progressive inroads upon the accumulated
capital of the country, or the annual " produit net " by which
it is maintained and increased.

The first course I cannot better describe than in the words
of Bastiat : " Ce serait créer le plus faillible, le plus universel,
le plus immédiat, le plus inquisitorial, le plus insupportable,
le plus actuel, le plus intime, et disons fort heureusement, le
plus impossible, de tous les despotismes que jamais cervelle
de pacha ou de mufti ait pu concevoir."

The second course could only lead to the gradual pauperization and ultimate bankruptcy of the country which
had the folly to enter upon it.

I have said that in determining the limit of private property and its corollary free exchange, the general interests of society should be the guide of legislation. I assume further, because I suppose that the proposition will command the assent of Mr. Spencer, that the general interests of society would not be served by a mere increase, however large, of the gross products of labour (although I must own to a suspicion that this notion underlies most of the socialist theories), but by such arrangements as tend to afford the largest possible return to labour, over and above its cost ; in short, that civilization depends on the increase of the net, and not of the gross, products of human industry.

Applying this principle to the case before us, I believe I may adduce the evidence of a sufficient experience to prove that slavery, in the form of compulsory labour, is less productive than free labour ; and if this be so, we may conclude, even setting aside all considerations of morality and humanity, that the general interests of society, so far as the productiveness of industry goes, will be better promoted by free labour, private property in one's self, than by slavery, or private property in others. And here I must observe that Mr. Spencer appears to have fallen into some confusion of thought. He begins by insisting on what he, in common with Mr. Mill and other writers, conceive to be a radical distinction between property in land and property in the products of labour, and by a very confident statement that "there is reason to suspect that the private possession of things produced by labour will grow even more definite and sacred than at present." He then suggests an analogy between private property in human beings and private property in land, and argues that as the first has been abolished in civilized countries, the second will share the same fate. But private property in human beings has not been abolished ; it is the contrary process which has taken place. The destruction of slavery asserted the right of every man to private property in himself. What it did was to prohibit the right of one man to property in another. It was simply the restitution of a right of private property from a wrongful to a rightful owner. In order to render

This is really lamentable quibbling

Mr. Spencer's analogy applicable, the destruction of slavery should have taken the form of transferring the right of private ownership of men from individuals to the community, which would indeed not have abolished slavery at all. It was, in short, not the abolition of private ownership of men, but the abolition of all ownership of men by other men, whether collective or private. A falser analogy than that which Mr. Spencer has attempted to establish it is impossible to conceive.

of [illegible] or [illegible]
and "justice".

CHAPTER IV.

THE UNEARNED INCREMENT.

IT has been seen that the "unearned increment" is a phrase by which Mill denoted value in exchange derived from the possession of a natural monopoly ; and that both Mill and Cairnes, as well as Mr. Henry George, have endeavoured to draw a broad distinction between land (by which is meant, according to Mill, the "whole material of the earth, underground as well as above") and "things which are the products of labour."

The distinction rests on the alleged ground that land is "a thing which no man has made," and which is "the inheritance of all mankind," or "a gift of nature to the whole human race," while the products of labour are the creation of men.

The fallacious character of this distinction has been shown in preceding chapters, but even if it be admitted for the sake of argument, or if it could be sustained, the objection to the doctrine of the unearned increment would remain the same, and it will now therefore be convenient to confine the arguments strictly within this limit, and to deal exclusively with the doctrine in its application to the land.*

The fallacy, as we have already seen, which lies at the bottom of the theory, is the result of the old confusion between value in exchange and value in use, the distinction between which Adam Smith pointed out long ago in the fourth chapter of the first book of the "Wealth of Nations."

He observes that things which have the greatest value in use have frequently little or no value in exchange, and that things which have the greatest value in exchange have often little or no value in use ;

* It is needless to remark that there can be no such thing as value (in exchange) without exchange, and that there can be *no* exchange without property—for men cannot exchange what they have not got. Wherever, therefore, private property and free exchange cease to exist, value disappears, and with it the science of Political Economy as it has been hitherto understood. Mill himself admitted that "value is the question into which every problem of the science ultimately resolves itself." The Communists find no difficulty in accepting this result, and look to some reorganization of society in which neither property, exchange, nor value would exist, and in which the distribution of commodities would be made by some arbitrary and despotic power among its members, instead of by a self-acting process. Are the followers of Mill, Cairnes, Walker, etc., prepared for this? And yet I think it can be shown that it is involved in the unearned increment theory. Here is a value, says Mill, which is not due to man's own exertions, and therefore unearned. But no value is due to any man's exertions. It is due solely to the presence of two elements in the object—utility and difficulty of attainment. All authorities agree in this, and Mill himself admits it. No value, therefore, is earned ; and if property is to be disallowed in all unearned value, there can be no property, and no exchange, and no exchange value, and the whole fabric falls at once to the ground. If any part of the value of any commodity is held to be due to a man's exertions, and he is to be entitled to nothing more, the argument of the Communists, that he is entitled to the same reward for his exertions, whatever the exchange value may be, appears unanswerable. If it is desired to advance a single step in the examination of this problem, we must get rid at once and for ever of the idea suggested by the phrase "unearned increment." That such a misleading and inapplicable phrase should have been invented, or used by Mill, is no doubt both strange and deplorable; but as he himself avowed that his object was to excite the political passions of his audiences (see "Dissertations and Discussions," vol. iv. p. 283), it is not surprising that he neglected to appeal to their reason.

he should have added, to complete his thought, that these two kinds of value are necessarily in inverse ratio to each other. Mr. Jevons has described them more accurately as total and final utility.

It requires little reflection to perceive that anything, say land, of which the quantity is limited, must become less valuable in use as the demand for it increases (one hundred acres of land must be more useful to ten men than to one hundred), and it must equally become more valuable in exchange. Divide the land into ten equal portions among ten men, and leave them to deal with it as they please: it will soon be seen that, as their numbers increase, the idle and improvident will be bought out at ever-increasing prices by the industrious and frugal. Forbid all exchange, in the vain hope of arresting this inevitable result: still it will be found that each family, as it increases from generation to generation, will have to work harder for the same return until the point has been reached when no additional labour will enable it to subsist. The exchange value of the land against labour must become greater and greater.

This is a condition of human life *whenever population increases in a limited area*, from which there is no escape and no appeal. It is one of those laws which men must obey, or perish.*

* Rent, say what we will, is in the nature of a storm-signal, warning a community that demand is pressing on supply, and that, unless either demand is checked or supply increased, the condition of that community must progressively become worse.

It is sometimes asked, Why, if this be so, is rent always highest in the richest countries and cities?

The appropriation of the unearned increment by the community at large would be an attempt to circumvent this inexorable law. It is thought that by preventing private property in land a progressive rise in its exchange value might be arrested as its value in use diminishes. The attempt is futile, but it is also mischievous, for it neutralizes the beneficent process by which an undue pressure of demand upon supply can best be averted.

The argument in favour of the appropriation by the State of economic rent appears to be this : Land and houses paying ground-rents are, *ex hypothesi,* limited quantities, and therefore natural monopolies. Is it just or expedient that certain members of a community should be allowed the benefit of such monopolies ? Is not the proper policy that of allow-

For the same reason that the common necessaries of life are always dearer in such countries.

That country is the richest in which the aggregate of values is largest, and each particular value smallest ; *e.g.* in which the aggregate value of the wheat or iron is greatest, and their value per quarter or ton the lowest.

Rent may be low from a large supply of land, or from a small demand for it. Two countries may have exactly the same quantity of land of the same quality. In one there may be no rent, in the other high rent. Which will be the richer ? Clearly the second ; but why ? Certainly not because rent is high—in this respect it will be the poorer—but because, owing to the existence of a larger aggregate of other values in the community, the supply of which has increased, while that of land has not, the total wealth of the country is greater, although in respect of land it is poorer. No country can be the richer because land and houses are dear—on the contrary, they must *pro tanto* be poorer; but whenever land and houses are dear, it is a proof that a country is rich in spite of this drawback, owing to the greater efficiency of labour in the production of other values. An increase of value is a sign of poverty, and increased aggregate of values is a sign of wealth.

Applying this principle to the case in point—will the transfer of economic rent from private proprietors to the community increase the value of land and houses per acre or per house, or will it increase the aggregate values which go to make up the wealth of the community ? There can be no doubt that the effect would be to increase the first and diminish the second.

ing the use of them to private persons on condition
of their paying rent to the community, whereby every
member of it would participate in the benefit, instead
of that benefit being appropriated by a limited number ?

The answer is this : If the appropriation of economic rent by the community would be a benefit to
it, certainly the latter policy would be wise and right ;
but could it be so ?

An illustration will suggest the answer to be given
to this question.

Let us assume that a ship's crew of a hundred men
are cast on an uninhabited island with an area of ten
thousand acres. They divide the land between them
in equal shares, taking a hundred acres each. So far
nature's gift of the land has been acquired by no effort
beyond the trouble of appropriation, and may perhaps
be called gratuitous. Whatever small value it may
at that stage possess, probably the condition of the
proprietors would be infinitely worse than that of a
day labourer in a civilized country.

We will now suppose that another ship's company
of a hundred men was cast upon the island. They will
find all the land appropriated, and unless they resort
to force, must either work for hire or subsist on charity.
We will assume that the first inhabitants are capable
of holding their own, and of dealing at their discretion
with the problem. How should they proceed in the
interests of the society ? The new-comers would say,
with Mill and Cairnes, to the proprietors of the soil,
" You have no right to claim a value which you have

not earned by your own labour. The land of this island is a thing which no man has made, which exists in limited quantity, which was the original inheritance of all mankind, and the appropriation of which keeps others out of its possession. As one man only can cultivate the same plot of land at a time, and you are the first comers, you have a right to whatever repays the actual cost of production ; but if there is any surplus value, any economic rent, this is due not to your labour, but to your appropriation of a natural gift of God to the whole human race, and we demand an equal share as the representatives for the time being of collective humanity."

The original occupants would reply, "We know and care nothing about abstract rights ; we think that they would not stand the test of a close examination. But we know this—we are in possession of a certain property, which we have acquired without either force or fraud, and the conservation of which is indispensable to the progress and civilization of our community. If we admit you to a share in our surplus or net product, without receiving from you any equivalent service in return, not only shall we as a class be so much the poorer, but the fund to which we look, and on which we alone can rely for all that we require beyond a bare subsistence and for accumulating capital, will at once disappear. We and our children shall remain as we began, little better than savages; and if the same principle is applied, as it must be, to all future comers, whether by increase of population among ourselves or by fresh immigration, there will never be the slightest hope of our emerging from that condition. If by any services you can render us you can give us an equivalent for the share which you demand, and thus add to the total wealth of the community, we are quite ready to exchange services freely with you; more than this we altogether decline to do. We will support you by charity till the next ship passes our way, and then request you to seek some other place of rest, where your presence may not be incompatible with the well-being of others."

Who can deny the justice and wisdom of this policy? To do so would be to condemn the human race to hopeless sterility in all that can be called civilization. Societies of men would be nothing more than aggregations of semi-savages, living always up to the extreme margin of subsistence, and periodically kept within necessary limits by famine and starvation.

Or take another case as an illustration. The community of a hundred men whom we have assumed to have become possessors of the island, divide the soil equally between them, each man taking a hundred acres. After a few years fifty of these men, by skill, industry, and frugality, have accumulated capital; the other fifty, by stupidity, idleness, and improvidence, have been compelled to subsist by mortgaging their land to their more prudent fellow-citizens, who after a time become possessed of it altogether, while the original proprietors, who equally participated in the gratuitous gift of nature, are reduced to the state of day labourers, working for wages on the land they previously possessed.

After a generation or two, their children would present themselves to the descendants of the frugal fifty who had become the proprietors of the whole island, and also, with Mill and Cairnes in their hands, would say, "The land is a thing which no man has made, which exists in limited quantity, which was the original inheritance of the whole race, the appropriation of which keeps others out of its possession. To all which it produces in the shape of surplus value beyond the cost of production, to all economic rent, we have the same right as you. We demand our share in the name of the community, as representing for the time collective humanity."

The landlords would reply, "We deny your right altogether. Your fathers had their equal share of land with us; they sold it freely to us, receiving in exchange full equivalent. Pay back the sums which they received, with the accumulated value which the land has acquired from the capital and labour we have spent on it, and then we will discuss the question of right; but in any case, in the interests of the community, we refuse to adopt a policy which, by absorbing all the net product of the soil, will strike at the root of all progressive civilization."

Again, who can deny the justice and the wisdom of this rejoinder?

Rent is a symptom of scarcity. It is the proof of the limitation of available land. This is an evil,

X

caused by the pressure of the population on the soil, of demand and supply. It is an unerring sign that the former is in excess of the latter.

What is Mr. Mill's remedy for this evil of scarcity? To increase the supply or diminish the demand? By no means. It is, without adding to the supply, and indeed while impairing the motives which might lead to an increased supply, to increase the demand; and this remedy is proposed not by a novice or sciolist, but by the most eminent economical authority of his day, and a trained statesman.

What is rent?

Ricardo, and with him substantially Mill, Cairnes, and the school to which they belong, define it thus: "Rent is that portion of the produce of the soil which is paid to the landlord for the use of the original and indestructible powers of the soil. It is often," he says, "confounded with the interest and profit of capital, and is applied to whatever is annually paid by the farmer to the landlord." *

---

* This confusion is inevitable so long as one word is used to describe two different things, but it is clear that the word "rent" is just as applicable to the latter source of the landlord's income as to the former. Rent is the hire of land, and in Greek the same word is used for the hire of land and the hire of a chattel.

The truth is that rent consists of two elements—one which is due to the capital expended on the land by the landlord as interest or profit, and the other to its monopoly value. It is this last which Ricardo calls "rent," and which Mr. Mill calls the "unearned increment," and the French economists "le plus value," or "produit net."

Fontenay ("Revenu Foncier") contends that rent of land is in all cases nothing else than interest and profit, whether this profit be monopoly profit or not. He is so far right, that the same monopoly profit, plus value, or unearned increment, which it has pleased Ricardo to call rent, will be found, on a careful analysis, in almost every other branch of industry and in wages (see Jevons, preface to 2nd edit. of "Theory of Political Economy").

De Quincey, Ricardo's most ardent disciple, improves on Ricardo's definition thus: "Rent is that portion of the produce from the soil (*or from any agency of production*) which is paid to the landlord for the use of its differential powers, as measured by comparison with those of similar agencies operating on the same market." *

It will be seen that in all these statements of the theory the whole question is made to turn upon the existence of differences in the return of capital invested in land, owing either to different qualities of soil, or accessibility to the common market.

But this, although true as far as it goes, is a very imperfect account of rent. If there were no differences whatever in the soil under cultivation, and if every field was equally accessible to the common market—if, in short, the return to capital invested in the lands were precisely the same in every case—rent might still rise, as long as available land was limited in extent.

It is the limitation of land, and not its various degrees of productiveness, which is the essential condition of economic rent.

Supposing that the area of available land under cultivation is limited in extent, it is obvious that, even if it were all of the same value, rent would arise if,

---

* Ricardo would probably say that there will always be some soil which will repay the cost of cultivation, but nothing more; and this I suppose is true, but this explanation hardly applies, or applies much less to land used for other than agricultural purposes. Certainly ground values must often arise on building land which are due to the pressure of demand on supply, irrespective of differences in the nature or situation of the land.

owing to its being a natural monopoly, the profit arising from its cultivation exceeded that which could be derived from other employment of capital. If, under the actual conditions of supply and demand, the profit to be derived from every part of the land was 20 per cent., while the market rate of profit in other employment of capital was only 10 per cent., men would pay anything under 10 per cent. extra to the owner of land for the use of it.

Ricardo's definition of rent, or rather his theory of rent, about which so much has been said, is thus defective and misleading. Rent would arise, or might arise, if there were no graduation of soils (as De Quincey expresses it), no difference in the qualities of soil in the world. It is true that, as those differences usually exist, wherever they do exist, and the worst soil under cultivation pays no rent, rent will always correspond with the differences in the cost of production on the different soils, *i.e.* the measure of rent will be the difference between the cost of production (including freight and interest) on the worst soil under cultivation, and that on all superior soils ; but this is a different thing from saying, with De Quincey, that "rent is that portion of the produce of the soil which is paid to the landlord for the use of its differential powers."

Now, the importance of these definitions is derived from the deductions which are made from them. It is not too much to say that in the unqualified form given them by Ricardo they have been the foundation of all the most serious attacks made by the Socialists on private property in land.

For if it be true that rent arises from the progressive cultivation of inferior soils, as Ricardo appears to hold, there seems little hope of anything but progressive scarcity for the mass of the people (see table, p. 313).

De Quincey puts this very forcibly :—

"The tendencies of a natural law like that of rent, or rather," as he says, "the cause of rent, degraduation of soils" (this, we have seen, is the effect, not the cause of rent)—"these tendencies it is always right to expose. . . . But it was not right to keep studiously out of sight that eternal counter-movement which tends by an equivalent agency to redress the disturbed balance. . . . Our own social system seems to harbour within itself the germ of our ruin. Either we must destroy rent, and that which causes rent, or rent will destroy us, unless in the one sole cause where this destroying agency can be headed back uniformly as it touches the point of danger—that point where it would enter into combination with evil co-agencies."

Again—

"And it happens (though certainly with no intentional sanction from so upright a man as David Ricardo) that in no instance has the policy of gloomy disorganizing Jacobinism, fitfully reviving from age to age, received any essential aid from science, excepting in this one painful corollary from Ricardo's triad of chapters on rent, wages, and profits. . . .

"Here is a man (they argue) not hostile to social institutions, not thinking of them in connection with any question of elementary justice, who reveals as a mere sequel, as an indirect consequence, as a collateral effect of one ordinary arrangement of landed property, that it does and must encroach steadily, by perpetual stages, upon other landed claims through all varieties of kind and of degree.

"The evil (they allege) is in the nature of an eclipse; it travels by digits over the face of the planet. A shadow of death steals gradually over the whole disc of what once had offered a luminous field of promise. And that which was meant for the auspicious guarantee of indefinite expansion to human generations, viz. the indefinite expansibility of food and clothing from the land, becomes the main counteraction to these purposes of Providence, and the most injurious monument of social misarrangement. The class of landlords, they urge, is the merest realization of a scriptural idea, *Unjust men reaping where they have not sown!*" (De Quincey, "Logic of Political Economy," pp. 190, 194).

But it will be observed that the whole of this dismal superstructure of progressive misery and injustice rests upon the assumption that every successive demand upon the land entails an increased cost of production by a resort to inferior soils. It is well known that Mr. Carey not only denies this, but has adduced a very respectable body of evidence to prove that historically, and as a matter of fact, the reverse is the truth, viz. that the worst lands are and must be cultivated first. Without going the whole length to which Mr. Carey invites us, it is, I think, abundantly clear that so far in the world's progress, and probably for centuries to come, the two processes are at work side by side : on the one hand, the process by which, as population advances, the pressure on the soils compels a resort to inferior lands or to a less profitable outlay on those already in cultivation, by which rent will rise while profits and wages diminish the first absolutely, the second in real value (see Ricardo's table,* quoted by De Quincey, p. 186); and, on the other hand, the process by which, whether from the discovery of new and better soils, agricultural improvements, mechanical or chemical, improved communications with markets both national and foreign by the service of locomotion, the increased efficiency of labour due to the growth of capital, and the diminishing interest on capital which occurs in most progressive communities, and perhaps, above all, by the annihilation of the barriers to international intercourse and free exchange caused by barbarous tariffs, rent is perpetually checked, destroyed, or diminished. Who can deny that this last process, is continually operating, and so far with no symptom of abatement, but, on the contrary, with a growing force, and that until, if ever, the time arrives when the cultivable area of the world and the productive powers of the soil have finally and irremediably reached their extreme limit, it cannot cease to be generated by the operation of the first process? Every successive rise in price, and therefore in rent, must directly stimulate new and increased efforts to increase and cheapen supply and destroy rent.†

Ricardo's theory depends entirely on the truth of his premises, and his premises, although admirable in an academical discussion, are altogether theoretic, and have little foundation in the actual facts of the present

* See p. 313.

condition of the world. Whether he intended the dissertation as anything more than an abstract argument may well be doubted, but it is not very creditable to Mill and other subsequent writers that they have not pointed out more clearly the nature and the limits of his theory. Even De Quincey, who saw these clearly enough, although writing in 1844, two years before the Repeal of the Corn Laws, and Mill, I believe, shortly afterwards, never even referred to this great economical factor in the problem of rent as it affected the people of England, for whom they were writing.

Ricardo's attitude on this question was perhaps not surprising, although not honourable to him ; but that during the heat of such a controversy two eminent writers should have omitted all reference to the bearing of the Corn Laws on the rent question in England, is indeed surprising, more so perhaps in the case of Mill than in that of De Quincey, who was a keen party man on the Tory side, and doubtless thought those laws a necessary institution for the protection of what he called "our noblest class."

If, however, Ricardo's theory be accepted as a basis of discussion, how would the appropriation of the rent of land by the State operate ?

At p. 127 in the chapter on profits there is a table, quoted by De Quincey, which shows the division of 180 quarters of corn at progressive stages of price between rent, profits, and wages. From this it appears that in wheat, *i.e.* in kind, rent will rise, while profits and wages will fall; but the table is incomplete and misleading.* It leaves the impression that rent is swallowing up profits and wages, and explains nothing. The truth is that the reason why wages in kind diminish, is that there is less wheat to divide, and "Ex nihilo nihil fit." It will be found that wages receive exactly the same *proportion* of the total produce at every stage, and that if on a decreasing quantity they receive *more*, they would soon absorb the whole, and there would be no net product at all; in other words, the whole produce of the soil would be swallowed up in the cost of cultivation.

The process appears to be this. It is obvious that

* 180 quarters of corn, which is divided in the following proportions between landlords, farmers, and labourers, with the stated variations in the value of corn :—

Price per Quarter.	Rent in Wheat.	Profit in Wheat.	Wages in Wheat.	Total.
£ s. d.				
4 0 0	None	120 qrs.	60 qrs.	
4 4 8	10 qrs.	111·7 qrs.	58·3 ,,	
4 10 0	20 ,,	103·4 ,,	56·6 ,,	180
4 16 0	30 ,,	95 ,,	55 ,,	
5 2 10	40 ,,	86·7 ,,	53·3 ,,	

And under the same circumstances, *money*, rent, wages, and profit, would be as follows :—

Price per Quarter.	Rent.	Profit.	Wages.	Total.
£ s. d.	£ s. d.	£ s. d.	£	£ s. d.
4 0 0	None	480 0 0	240	720 0 0
4 4 8	42 7 6	473 0 0	247	762 0 0
4 10 0	90 0 0	465 0 9	255	810 0 0
4 16 0	144 0 0	456 0 0	264	864 0 0
5 2 10	205 13 4	445 15 0	274	925 13 4

at a certain point profits will cease to be sufficient, accumulation will cease, wages will be stationary, and rent will absorb the whole produce of the land, after paying wages; but out of this rent must come, of course, the wages of the farmer, as well as those of the labourer. It is only his profits, or the profits on capital, which will cease. Neither landlord nor tenant can therefore invest capital in the soil, and production will cease to advance. This must arrest the progress of population, which will therefore also be stationary, and the produce of the soil will be divided between landlord and labourer, the latter subsisting on the minimum, and the bulk going to the landlord. Now, if this prospect revolts any one, let him reflect that it affords the only chance for the survival of civilization, in the state of things supposed—a state of things happily (although neither Ricardo nor Mill have made this clear) very far removed from actual fact.

Were it not for the operation of this law of rent in such circumstances, no check would be placed on the growth of population, the whole produce of the soil would be absorbed in the mere subsistence of the labourer, and there would be no surplus whatever for all the higher wants of society.*

It is necessary to insist here upon what is, I think, sometimes overlooked in considering this question, viz. that the "unearned increment" theory rests entirely

---

* I wish to draw particular attention to the demonstration of the statements of the last two paragraphs contained in the appendix (A) to this chapter. Fear of too much interrupting the argument has alone prevented me from inserting it in the text.—ED.

for its justification upon the so-called "loi d'airain" of Lassalle.*

* The so-called "loi d'airain" (jenes grausame eherne Gesetz) fathered by. Lassalle upon the English economists was stated as follows by Turgot : " En tout genre de travail il doit arriver et il arrive en effet que le salaire de l'ouvrier se borne à ce qui lui est nécessaire pour lui procurer sa subsistence."

M. LeRoy-Beaulieu (" Répartition des Richesses," p. 23) paraphrases this law by saying that it teaches that man is impelled by his nature to an inordinate multiplication of his kind as soon as he has more than enough to maintain life. This "law" would, as he justly observes, prevent all material progress ; but "since it is proved that such progress has taken place, the law must necessarily be a fiction, as it is not in accordance with the facts." Mr. Atkinson considers the "law" "an absolute fallacy, *except* in states *overburdened with armies and debts*."

I need only refer to the above summary, pp. 310–311, of the causes which have counteracted the working of the principles laid down by Malthus and Ricardo. It may at once be admitted that they failed to take account of the facts, (1) that there were and are vast tracts of cultivable and unoccupied land, to which men, and from which products, are daily becoming more easily transferable ; (2) that the higher the material condition, the less the population tends to increase ; (3) and, most important of all, of the progress of invention and discovery in agriculture and manufactures.

If this "loi d'airain" is not true, the gravamen of the charge brought by the socialists against the institution of private property falls to the ground, and their remedies are not only injurious but also unnecessary.

If it is true, either wholly or in part—and this is the question attacked in the text—how does socialism offer a remedy ? Does it not rather aggravate the evil ?

It is very important to note that the principle is not anywhere in the text attacked as a theory. It is merely asserted that other opposing tendencies have at certain periods and in certain circumstances kept it in check ; we need only look at cases of local congestion, such as exist in parts of Ireland and Scotland, in London, and other large cities, or in India, to see that they have not always succeeded in doing so. The succeeding argument in the text is, therefore, very far from having a merely abstract importance, even if it were applicable (as it is not) only to the case of the acceptance of the truth of the law—ED.

This seems to be the place for the following note :—

"In the late Mr. W. Bagehot's 'Economic Studies,' p. 136, there is an article on Malthus, of whom he speaks in very disparaging terms. There is, however, one respect, at all events, in which he seems to me totally to misapprehend the bearing of Malthus's 'Theory of Population.'

"In the first editions Malthus had, it seems, assumed that the only check to over-population were vice and misery ; but in the second edition he judiciously added, 'the principle of self-restraint, moral or prudential.'

"On this Bagehot observes that by this admission Malthus has cut away the ground of his whole argument. 'If there be this principle of virtuous self-restraint, he no longer answers Godwin's dreams of perfectibility. If it be

The advocates of socialistic methods of dealing with the unearned increment, of course, assume that this law will invariably operate, and that the process of the gradual absorption of the produce of the soil to the point at which it will be stopped by the fall of wages to the "minimum" of subsistence is in constant progress. If this position be accepted, we may be told that the laws of nature are unjust and oppressive ; but we cannot be informed by what other method than the creation of rents the whole produce of the soil will not gradually be absorbed by the labourer. Without the creation of rents the net produce, the fund out of which all civilization springs, will progressively diminish and ultimately disappear altogether, leaving nothing but gross produce to be consumed under the operation

possible for a perfectly virtuous community to limit their numbers, they will perform that duty just as they perform others ; there is no infallible principle that will break up the village community ; it can adjust its members to its food, and may last for ever.'

" 'Thus,' he says, 'in its first form, the essay was conclusive in argument, but based on untrue facts ; in the second form it was based on true facts, but inconclusive in argument.'

"Bagehot, as I have said, seems to me to miss Malthus's point. It may be freely admitted that if a community were wise and virtuous, population would not outstrip the means of subsistence ; but it nevertheless remains perfectly true (and this is the essential Malthusian doctrine) that as men individually are neither wise nor virtuous as a rule, there are only two ways by which the necessary restraints can be brought to bear upon them—one by throwing upon the individual the full responsibility of his actions, and suffering him to bear the penalty of improvidence ; the other, by depriving him of the liberty of action in this department altogether. The moral of Malthus's teaching I take to be, that if on the one hand society undertakes to support those who cannot or do not support themselves, and on the other leaves them free to multiply *ad libitum*, the growth of population will soon outstrip the means of subsistence. Malthus's second essay, therefore, is not open to Bagehot's very superficial criticisms. It is both true in fact and conclusive in argument.—L. M., December, 1884."

The appendix to this chapter, on "The Rate of Wages," and "The Law of Diminishing Returns," should be read in this connection.—ED.

of the "loi d'airain" by as many human beings as
the soil can be made to support in the lowest condition of human existence, which, it must be added,
will be found to be ultimately a much smaller number
than it now supports, in various degrees of comfort,
from the lowest to the very highest scale of refinement
and luxury.*

If, on the other hand, as is more probable, the
" loi d'airain " is repudiated as soon as it has served
its purpose in discrediting rent and capital, we have
a perfect right to deny its necessary operation now.

Accepting the truth of the law for the purpose of
the argument, we may now pursue the inquiry already
suggested, as to whether proposals like these, made by
the adherents of the theory we are considering, would
obviate or avert its operation, or whether, on the contrary, they would not aggravate it.

The question resolves itself into this. Supply
being limited, by what means can demand be limited
so as not to exceed the proportion which, in the interests of society or of mankind, will ensure the

---

* I suppose that, in discussing Political Economy, no one would deny that the
interests of society require the largest possible production of wealth ; but I greatly
doubt whether many would not be found who would dispute the proposition that
net produce is the object of all civilization, and yet this I conceive to be the key-
note of the Free Trade doctrine. " Man, they say, not wealth, should be the first
object of your regard " (Toynbee). Better, if so, a thousand men earning a bare
subsistence with no leisure, no culture, no refinement, than five hundred of
whom one hundred possessed all these advantages. I confess that I cannot argue
on this foundation. That mere numbers, the mere existence of a certain number
of human beings, with nothing to give dignity or interest to life, should be an
object of paramount concern, seems to me so absurd that I cannot suppose that it
is seriously and consciously entertained ; but I believe that unconsciously there is
a great confusion of thought in connection with this question of gross and net
produce.

maximum of well-being with the minimum of effort ?
Will the community at large receive a greater share
of these " natural gifts " (by the hypothesis there is
not enough for all) through the instrumentality of
private appropriation, or through that of State or
collective appropriation ? To these questions there
can be only one reply. The moment that a natural
gift acquires value in exchange, it is a sign that demand is encroaching on supply—that there is not
enough for all. As the supply cannot, *ex hypothesi*,
be increased, the only possible mode of checking progressive pauperization is to limit and check the
demand. Private appropriation at once supplies this
check by a progressive rise of price. Collective
appropriation, instead of checking it, directly stimu-
lates and aggravates the demand and makes things
worse than before, except on one condition. No Free
Trader would deny that if the State makes itself the
economic unit instead of the individual, it could perform the imperative task of adjusting supply and
demand as well as the individual ; but at what a cost ?
Only by the substitution of the most intolerable, the
most inquisitorial, the most impossible despotism, for
human freedom and personal responsibility.

For the purpose of adapting demand to supply, it
is indispensable that the control of the supply and the
demand should be in the same hands. Under the system
of private property and Free Exchange, every man is
in this position. He knows the precise limits of the
supply available to him—in other words, his income—

and he can adapt his demand accordingly. If the supply cannot be increased, he must either limit his demand or accept a lower reward. He can control his own destiny; but no industry, no providence, no self-denial on the part of the individual, could avail to avert the social doom, if he were always exposed to the idleness, the recklessness, and the selfishness of a neighbour, over whom he had no control.

How, indeed, can the demand of the whole community be limited and regulated without the sacrifice of personal freedom? If the State makes itself responsible for the supply, and become the land-holder and the employer of labour, it must also assume the responsibility of controlling the demand, and regulating the number of the population. Unless this be done, there can be no possible guarantee against universal pauperization.

Every socialist theory which presents itself to the world assumes that human nature, especially in the least-educated class, is endowed with every virtue, and always ignores the great truth which was very simply stated by Emerson, that " man is as lazy as he dares to be."

This difficulty does not appear to have been ever fairly faced by the Collectivists. Collective control over production and supply can be understood if the State is to possess all the land and capital and all the instruments of production; but no suggestion has been made to control the demand which does not involve the sacrifice of personal freedom.

Therefore it is that the equilibrium between demand and supply would be destroyed. No external authority, whether it be a government or a governing body of any kind, can possibly gauge the strength of individual desire or the amount of individual sacrifice —this can only be measured by each individual for himself; and thus it is essential that where alone power resides, responsibility should also be placed.

But in case it may still be thought that this obedience to the law of value, this equilibrium of demand and supply is, after all, unnecessary, and that society may exist without it, it may be well further briefly to explain my meaning. All values are utilities (utility being a condition of value), but all utilities are not values. If those utilities which are susceptible of value are allowed to be appropriated, they will not be exchanged save for equivalent values, and the equilibrium of supply and demand will be maintained ; but if these utilities are given gratuitously to the whole community, they will be substituted for values, and add to demand without in any way increasing supply. Society will be so much the poorer. The truth is that gratuities are values, because they are limited and difficult of attainment. And to treat a value as a gratuity or utility is to live on your capital, and must lead to bankruptcy. But why, it will be said, should it make any difference whether this utility which you call value is allowed (gratuitously, as we say) to such proprietors or to any number of collective owners ?

The difference appears to be this, and it is all-important: if this utility or unearned increment or rent remains in the hands of private proprietors (who for the sake of the argument we may call the producers), it cannot rise higher without a corresponding increase in the purchasing power of the consumers, which will maintain the equilibrium between demand and supply. The increased purchasing power must in this case be derived either from the increased productiveness of existing labour, or from an additional number of labourers, who have at least produced enough for their subsistence, *i.e.* within the limit of cost of production. Thus there will have been a distinct addition to the aggregate wealth of the community—in the first place indicating increased comfort to the existing population; in the second, a larger population earning the means of subsistence.

But if economic rent is taken from the private proprietors and appropriated by the community at large, the effect will be in the first place a transfer of this part of the national wealth from the former to the latter without any addition to it, thus not adding to production, but causing a different distribution.

If it is treated as the collective property of the whole community—if, in short, the supply and the demand are to be in the same hands—they, the collective proprietors of the supply, must regulate the collective demand. How can this be done? *Ex hypothesi*, the whole community will have a larger supply of utilities than before, with no additional labour or

Y

service. *If their numbers remain the same,* one of two
things will happen—either they will work less, and
produce less, substituting this increment to their earnings for a portion of their former earnings, in which
case they will be no better off than before, except in
leisure, and the community as a whole will have lost
the wealth before possessed by the private proprietary ;
or they will work as much as before, and have the
benefit of the unearned increment, in which case
the community as a whole will be neither richer nor
poorer, but the unearned increment will be diffused
among all its members instead of being confined to
some.

It might be thought that either of those alterna-
tives would be preferable to the result of private proprietorship, as in the first case the producing class
would have more leisure, in the second more comfort,[*]
and every man would have, in addition to his earnings,
a slice of the "unearned increment." But will or can
the numbers remain the same ? This the law of
population inexorably forbids ; and with an unlimited
demand and a limited supply, there is nothing possible
but progressive pauperization. The unearned incre-

---

[*] Even these suppositions are doubtful. If the surplus products of the soil
were divided among the whole population there would be little accumulation of
capital, and the fund out of which alone non-agricultural values can be created
would be seriously impaired. It is from the accumulation of rent that manufactures, industrial arts of all kinds, railroads, are rendered possible, and thus it
becomes possible to support a larger total population with a much higher average
of comfort and well-being. It is curious to reflect that if land had been unlimited,
the human race might have never advanced beyond the stage of a primitive civilization. The best proof that rent is one of those evils which is the germ of a
higher good, is that it is often better to pay rent than to take up new land.

ment would be substituted for wages, production would continue below cost, until starvation-point was reached, and the "loi d'airain" of Lassalle had asserted itself. It is strange that the advocates of this theory cannot see that if it is possible for the community at large to limit its numbers, the working classes have the remedy in their hands already; they could in a few years so force up the rate of wages as to obtain possession of the whole of the unearned increment, and leave nothing for the landlord.* .

So much for the economic objection to the unearned increment theory, and its logical application in the nationalization of the land. It seems to me insuperable. It has certainly never been faced by its advocates. Those among them who are at once able and candid have fully admitted that the doctrine of communism or collectivity is not possible without restrictions on population.

* The point may be put in a different way. The question to answer is this—and I am not aware that Mr. Mill had made any attempt to answer it—Would the possession of the land by the State diminish by a fraction the cost of food, or clothing, or lodging to the people? Certainly *not*, unless the rent taken over by the State, in other words, handed over to the consumers, added nothing to the demand. If this were to be so, no doubt the property of the rich might to this extent be divided among the people, and while the class specially possessing luxuries and refinements would disappear, there might be a less unequal diffusion of wealth, and less misery. But if it were true, not only do Ricardo's theory of wages and Lassalle's "loi d'airain" vanish into smoke, but also—and this must be insisted upon—the remedy for whatever misery is caused by the present system already exists, without any confiscation of existing property. If the masses are capable of arresting their progressive increase at any particular point, why not now? It is not necessary that a man should have land; what is necessary is that we should have the means of procuring whatever land affords—food, clothing, and houses, etc.—at the cheapest possible cost, and this, it is contended, under a free trade system, is absolutely assured.

Let us now briefly consider some general bearings of the adoption of the theory.

It is most remarkable that Mill, in his essay on "Land Tenure Reform," carefully and even ostentatiously avoids all attempt to show in what way the public at large, and the working-class in particular, would benefit by the appropriation of the land, or of the "unearned increment" in part or in whole. His solitary contribution to this question is a remark that such a measure would be a great relief to the tax-payer; but he entirely omits to add that the only effect of relieving the tax-payer, by making him a present of the rent of land, would be to increase his demand for its products, or for the land itself, and thereby counteract by the rise of price all the advantages which he might derive from remission of taxation. Nothing can be more feeble and more superficial than Mill's treatment of this question. There is no attempt to show in what manner the state proprietorship of land would benefit the people; no statement even (proof there could hardly be) that the cost of food and clothing or lodging would be reduced in the smallest degree. There is nothing but a reference to Oriental countries in which this system prevails, with results which are notoriously fatal to national progress, but which Mill implies, contrary to all evidence, to have been invaluable; and much loose declamation about abstract rights, without any reference to the principle upon which those assumed rights repose. It is difficult to conceive a less useful contribution to sound knowledge on a difficult and very important question.

Why, it may be asked, if a thing belongs to nobody, should it be given to everybody? and how can it be given to everybody when there is not enough for all?

Property and commonalty are not only inconsistent, they are antithetical ideas, and the phrase " nationalization of land," or other instruments of production, involves a very gross confusion of thought.

It is quite possible to vest the property of land in a Government, but it is absolutely impossible to vest it in the community at large. That which is common to all cannot be appropriated by any one. There can be no such thing as collective property in that which is common to all. Mill's language, therefore, does not admit of any rational construction. No scheme of social reconstruction is possible on such a foundation as he proposes.

It is quite competent to a society to vest the property in the soil, *e.g.* in one individual or any body called a Government, as in any larger number, but they must not hug the delusion that in doing so they are retaining it. They may, no doubt, retain a certain control over the administration of it, under popular institutions; but to speak of a property administered by a Government as the property of the people at large is an absurdity. It is conceivable and even probable that nearly half the people of a country might at any time object in the strongest manner to the distribution or disposal of this so-called property. And it is not only conceivable, but absolutely certain, that its disposal would take the form of the gravest inequalities between members of the community. Some would get infinitely less than others; and why? On what principle is the distribution of this common property to take place? If it is to be distributed on the principle of exchange of services with the different members of the community, how is the value of the service to be decided, except either by competition or by the arbitrary discretion of the Government? In either case the recipients will not have any share in the property of the community as property.

Practical proposals must, of course, be based, and as a matter of fact, in the case of Mr. Henry George and others, they have been based, on Mill's proposals that this fund derived by the State from the partial or total appropriation of economic rent should be devoted to relieve taxation. These proposals in no way attempt to recognize the equal claims of all its inhabitants to the rent of the land of a country, and proceed simply on the principle that the appropriation of the rent by the State instead of by the individual is in the interest of the community *as a whole.*

I will assume that by the State Mill meant a modern democratic Government, although his constant reference to the Government of India* might

---

* Thus Mr. Mill, with whose name the theory is chiefly identified, and who never succeeded in shaking off the tradition of Leadenhall Street, constantly refers to the land revenue system of British India as deserving of imitation (cf. " Dissertations and Discussions," vol. iv. p. 274). It is difficult for an economist to understand Mr. Mill's predilection for this system; the best that can be said for it is that it is an inheritance of Oriental despotism, that the people are

suggest something very different.   It is, at all events,
only on this assumption that it is worth while to

accustomed to it, and that, in the hands of a British administration, the revenue
which it yields consists in, and has assumed the character far more of, a land-
tax unequal and arbitrary it is true, both between the different occupiers and
the several provinces, than of economic rent, to which it does not even aspire
to approximate.   On whatever grounds it may be defended, it is as far removed
as possible from any ideal system, and could not be maintained in a free country
for a twelvemonth.   But the essential question to consider is the appropriation
of economic rent, if it is to be transferred from private ownership to the community at large as the "inheritance of all mankind."   There is no meaning
in the phrase unless it is understood as the equal inheritance of all mankind, or,
as Governments can only deal with their own people, of every member of each
particular community.   This principle at once bars the application of such a fund
to the relief of taxation, which Mr. Mill indicates as the object to which it should
be devoted, unless the sole tax levied by the State was a poll-tax.   If there is any
justice in the idea of taxation according to the means, however measured, of the
different members of a society, it would be very unjust to relieve the richer
members by giving them a larger share of a fund to which they have no more
right than the poorest of their fellow-creatures.   The appropriation of the
"unearned increment," therefore, in relief of taxation is quite inconsistent with
the principle that it is the inheritance of all mankind, and the common
property of the whole community.   The "unearned increment" cannot be
appropriated by its division among the community at large without disaster,
nor applied in relief of taxation without injustice.   But there is a third mode,
which, although evidently not contemplated by Mr. Mill, is nevertheless one
which is sometimes urged with a certain plausibility.   Why, it is asked, must it
be less in the interest of society that this fund should be appropriated by a Government, and devoted to public objects for which taxation cannot or ought not to be
imposed, than by private persons who spend it for private purposes, often of a
useless and even mischievous nature?   It may be admitted that, as a purely
economical question, it may be argued that so long as the fund in question is not
appropriated by the community at large, that is, vested in a government distinct
from the people, such as an Oriental despot, or an irresponsible oligarchy, the
only question would be whether by either of them the fund would be expended
more or less to the general social advantage than by private proprietors.   This
condition is fulfilled in the exceptional case of the Government of British India,
and it is perhaps intelligible that, impressed with the importance of this resource
to an Anglo-Indian administration, with which the interests of the native population are assumed to be identified, Mill and others should have favourably compared the administrations of this fund by the Government with the mode in which
it might be spent by rajahs and zemindars.   But even in India, it is probable
that there would be no more useful reform than the substitution of a well-devised
system of taxation for the present arbitrary and complicated methods of raising
the revenue from the land, while there can scarcely be two opinions as to its total
inapplicability to any self-governing community.

examine his theory ; and it has this advantage, that it lends itself more readily to our argument, by at once cutting away all the considerations derived from the idea of equal rights to the land as between all the members of the community. The only way by which any such claim as this could be satisfied would be by the equal division of the rent of the land between all its citizens —a process which Mill directly repudiates by his suggestion that this fund should go in relief of taxation. Now, it is at once apparent that if this were to be its destination there need be no taxes at all, for the rent of land and the ground rent of houses probably exceeds the whole existing amount of taxation in the United Kingdom, both general and local. The effect of this substitution of rent for taxes would be to divide the rent, not in equal shares between the members of the community, but in shares proportional to their *present* contributions to the taxes—an arrangement which would benefit the richer at the expense of the poorer members.

From another point of view it is difficult to understand how any sane politician could quietly contemplate a system under which the whole or part of the revenues of the State would be derived from sources independent of taxation, or fail to see that the strongest motive to economical and prudent administration would be thus removed, and the door opened to every form of wasteful and dangerous expenditure both in home and foreign policy, while, accompanied as it would be by placing at the disposal of the Government of the day

an ever-increasing army of paid agents and servants,
the political liberties of the country would be at the
mercy of any party which obtained its mandate from
the ballot-box. Under such a system, the country
would soon become the prey of contending factions,
struggling to get possession of enormous prizes and
opportunities of unlimited plunder; the flood-gates of
corruption would be unloosed, and after a period of
progressive disorder, society would seek a deliverer in
the first strong man who was prepared to play the
part of a modern Cæsar, from whom political liberty
would have again to be gradually extorted by return-
ing to the only method by which it can be secured, by
once more placing it on the only sound foundation,
that of private property and free exchange.

These considerations are so obvious that it is
impossible to regard the loose language so constantly
used at the present time even by responsible politicians
on this subject with much apprehension. There may
be foolish experiments, which would be far better
prevented if possible, but they will work their own
cure. In the case of agricultural land there can be
little immediate danger, for the unearned increment
on which Mill casts his envious eyes has not only
ceased for the most part to exist, but has become an
unearned decrement.* † But with urban land in the

---

* It is always assumed, and especially by Mill in the case of land ("Dissertations and Discussions," vol. iv. pp. 263, 275), that the exchange value of
natural monopolies *must* increase; but this is a very partial and incomplete opinion.
It is, of course, in the essence of their nature to increase in value whenever the
demand outstrips the supply, but taking the world as a whole (and political economy
is not only applicable to particular districts or towns in the United Kingdom), this

† Only ask agricultural rents.

great centres of population the process is still in operation which has given rise to this economical heresy, and special taxation of ground-rents seems to have taken its place in the new radical or reactionary programme.

It may be worth while to examine the remarkable character of this last suggestion. The evil which it is devised to remedy is the wretched nature of the house accommodation for the poor in our large cities, and the high rents which they are obliged to pay for it. The cause of this is notorious. It is the limited space available for building within a given area; in other words, the undue pressure of demand upon supply. For such an evil there can be only one remedy, viz. to increase the supply or to diminish the demand, or both. If it is impossible adequately to increase the supply,* there is nothing left but to diminish the

---

is by no means true. Population ebbs and flows, nations and races rise and fall, and if long periods of time and a sufficient area are taken into account, it is probable that on the average there is a tendency to a decrement and not to an increase in the value of natural monopolies. There is a note of a most misleading character in the essay of Professor Cairnes on "Land," in which he compares the case of land to that of consols, entirely omitting the consideration that whereas in the latter case the interest is fixed, in the case of land there is no security that it will yield any interest at all. It may safely be assumed that in the long run, taking into account all risks, the average return to an investment in land would be neither more nor less than in any other solid security. Those who look only at the enormous growth in the value of particular estates, either in this country or the colonies, entirely forget the length of time which usually elapses before this growth takes place, and the dead loss often incurred by a proprietor. If this is considered, and also the effect of compound interest in doubling capital every fifteen years, it will be found that an investment of £10,000 in consols at compound interest would in a hundred years yield on an average a larger return than any similar investment in land, because in the latter case speculation and social considerations often largely enter.

* M. LeRoy Beaulieu has pointed out how the improvement of means of

demand. How is this to be done? By improving the accommodation and lowering the rents, by thus stimulating instead of checking the influx of an excessive population into the towns, and aggravating all the consequences of overcrowded districts! *

There is no greater folly than the notion of an artificial interference with a natural monopoly. It is quite as gross a violation of free trade principles as the creation of an artificial ' monopoly. Both are equally the offspring of the doctrine of protection, and both are equally opposed to the well-being of the community, and especially fatal to the class upon ' which the ultimate burden of economic blundering invariably falls.

In this case, if the working classes in the great cities are to be housed below cost, the unearned increment which now goes to swell the capital which pays their labour will soon be absorbed in providing for a larger and larger population until it disappears altogether; the rich and well-to-do will become fewer and fewer, and there will be more poor than ever.

These are economic truisms upon which it is not the object of the present paper to enlarge, but at a time when from various causes of very unequal interest the political landmarks of the older generation are more and more disappearing, it is essential to insist that there can be no possible compromise between the socialistic doctrines of unearned increment,

locomotion may have an effect equivalent to increasing the supply, by enabling people to live at a greater distance from their work and from the centre.—ED.

    * See p. 337, Appendix A.

land nationalization, and special taxation of natural monopolies, and the principles of free exchange. The first may be all that their advocates claim for them, wise and just and politic. But men must choose between the two; they cannot support or connive at such measures as have been signalized, and at the same time stand forward, when it is convenient to do so, as the champions of Free Trade, without exposing themselves to the charge either of stupidity or dishonesty.

It is, in short, necessary to point out that, whether right or wrong, the theory on which these proposals rest, viz. that of the so-called "Unearned Increment," is absolutely inconsistent with the policy of Free Trade, and that men must choose between the two; for they cannot co-exist.

It is a misfortune that the term "Free Trade" has been adopted in English to designate this policy, instead of the far more comprehensive and accurate expression "Free Exchange," for it has led to its being chiefly considered with reference to one only, and that not the most important of its aspects. Many people think of it as a question of tariffs and protective duties, instead of recognizing it as the assertion in the broadest sense of the principle of private property, of which Free Exchange is only an attribute. There can be no property without the right of Free Exchange, and there can certainly be no Free Exchange without property; for a man must possess something before he can exchange it for something else.

All property is monopoly. The two ideas are inseparable. The only question is whether it is in the interests of society that this inevitable monopoly shall be kept within its natural limits by the competition, or whether it should be guarded against the effects of competition by artificial laws.

The Free Trade school hold that the limitation and inequality of natural gifts and favours must be accepted as a fact, and that all man can do in utilizing them as far as they will go, is to expose them to the greatest possible competition, which can only be done by complete freedom of exchange.

It is against this principle of free competition that in some form or other a perpetual resistance manifests itself. Sometimes it takes the form and assumes the name of Protection, sometimes of State Socialism in varying degrees, sometimes of Communism, or Collectivism. The forms and the names may differ; they are all the same. They all mean Privilege and Compulsion instead of Equal Rights and Freedom.

They all aim at creating a privileged class at the expense of the community at large.* Every class in turn, when possessed of political power, has tried, and usually with success, to secure such privileges for itself, and it is not surprising that the working classes should better the instruction given them by those who,

---

* The root of the evil is in both the same; it is the result of considering the producer instead of the consumer. The interest of the producer, whether landlord, capitalist, or workman, is to make things dear; the interest of the consumer is always to make things cheap. The interest of the producer is always opposed to that of society; that of the consumer is always identical with the interests of society (see pp. 266-7).

with far less excuse, have helped themselves in their turn out of the public purse by corn laws and protective tariffs. Fortunately, while partial protection to sectional and limited classes is unjust and mischievous, when it becomes general and assumes the form of communism, it becomes ruinous, and thus more speedily works its own cure. It is impossible to protect everybody.

While, therefore, it is even more necessary in the public interest that private property and free exchange should be recognized in natural monopolies than in cases where competition is supposed to operate freely, the interference of the state is perhaps, in these cases, less dangerous, because it is more futile.

APPENDIX A.

TABLES SHOWING FALLACY OF THE THEORY OF THE
UNEARNED INCREMENT.

THE fallacious nature of the unearned increment theory will
be seen from the following figures, which are founded on the
table given by Ricardo, quoted by De Quincey (Ricardo's
chapter on " Profits ") :— *

		Number of Men.	Quarters of Wheat.	Quarters per Man.
Five different qualities of soil.	1	10	180	18
	2	10	170	17
	3	10	160	16
	4	10	150	15
	5	10	140	14

From this table it will be seen that every additional 10 men
are supposed to produce 10 quarters less wheat, owing to the
inferiority of soils successively forced into cultivation by
pressure of population ; but as it is necessary that even on
the lowest the cultivators should live, it is obvious that 140
quarters are enough to provide subsistence for 10 men, *i.e.*
14 quarters per man.

If this be so, 18 quarters, the quantity produced per man
on soil No. 1, will be four quarters more than necessary to
support life ; 17 quarters on soil 2, three quarters more than
necessary ; and so on to the end of the series. This surplus
product is the result of the difference of soil between the

* Quoted above, p. 313.

four first and the last, which only yields the cost of subsistence of the cultivator. Mill calls this "unearned increment."

If this remains in the hands of the cultivators of the first four soils, it will constitute a fund, out of which they may gradually provide for their higher wants ; *e.g.* they may command the services of a schoolmaster, a doctor, a clergyman, artist, etc.

In varying degrees these services will be shared by 40 out of the 50 men who are supposed to form the producing class of the society. But Mill objects to this, and insists that the 10 men who cultivate No. 5 for bare subsistence should have an equal share.

Now, assuming the same order of degraduation of soils, let us trace the effects of Mill's proposal.

We have by our supposition a total unearned increment of 100 quarters of wheat—40 on the first soil, 30 on the second, 20 on the third, and 10 on the fourth. This, divided between 50 men, gives two quarters each. The cultivators, therefore, of No. 5 obtain 160 quarters instead of 140 quarters, *i.e.* they will have 20 quarters more than cost of subsistence.

But this will at once bring into the field 10 new men, who will cultivate soil No. 6, yielding 130 quarters only. There will then be 930 quarters to be divided between 60 men, or $15\frac{1}{2}$ quarters each. This is still $1\frac{1}{2}$ quarters each more than enough, and 10 more men will be called into life to cultivate soil No. 7, yielding 120 quarters. There will then be 1050 quarters for 70 men, or 15 quarters each ; but this is still more than cost. Another 10 men will appear and attack soil 8, yielding 110 quarters. There will then be 1160 quarters for 80 men, or $14\frac{1}{2}$ quarters each ; but this is still too much. Another 10 men will appear and attack soil No. 9, yielding 100 quarters. This will give a total of 1260 quarters for 90 men, or exactly 14 quarters each ; and here the process of descent upon inferior soils will cease, the whole society will subsist on the " minimum," all civilization will disappear, the schoolmaster, etc., will emigrate, and Mr. Mill's ideal will be attained.

But there is another class of property in which it is sometimes supposed that the unearned increment accrues in a manner injurious to society. I refer to the case of house property and ground-rents in large and populous centres. Very strange and subversive doctrines have been preached on this text by men whose positions lends a certain authority to their utterances.

I think it can be shown that the same reasoning which has led us to discard Mill's teaching on this head, in the case of agricultural land, equally applies to land used for building or for other purposes, factories, mines, and indeed to every kind of commodity (to use the term by which economists designate the subject-matter of exchange), of which the quantity, being limited and unequal to the demand for it, can give rise to the phenomenon of rent.

We have seen that, in the case of agricultural land, the effect of the appropriation and distribution (in equal shares between the members of the community) of the rent or unearned increment, is gradually to encroach upon the net product or surplus value produced by the progress of society on all but the last soil taken into cultivation, and ultimately to absorb it altogether, so as to leave nothing more than gross produce ; or, in other words, to cause a condition of things in which the whole community are compelled to live on the "minimum" product which will enable them to subsist in working efficiency, and to impose an effectual barrier, finally, against any further advance of population.

Precisely similar, though different in some of its accidents, will be the effect of such a measure (appropriation of ground-rents by the district or municipality) in the case of houses and buildings in towns. If the surplus value yielded by the rentals of town property were to be divided among the inhabitants (and this is what its appropriation by the municipality theoretically comes to), the effective demand for house accommodation would be to that extent increased, not by any addition to the wealth of the town, but because this surplus value would be transferred from those who have already got houses to those who have not, and who could not afford house accommodation without this subsidy. This process of transference would not be of long duration; it could only end by the absorption of the whole surplus value in providing house accommodation for a larger population, and leaving nothing for the other purposes to which it would previously have been applied, and which are, in short, all the higher purposes of a progressive civilization. Just as, in the case of agricultural land, we have seen that the appropriation and division among the whole society of the surplus or "unearned increment" would lead directly and inevitably to the absorption of the whole produce by the cost of subsistence of the population; so, in the case of towns, would a similar measure lead with equal certainty to the absorption of the whole rental or surplus value produced by the progress of society on all but the houses produced at the highest relative cost (*i.e.* the worst, in quality or situation, or both) in providing the lowest kind of house accommodation for all its members in the several classes into which society divides itself.

It is desirable to trace the process in rather more detail.

We will assume that in a given township there are three building blocks of different qualities, and in each three classes of house; that the houses on Nos. 1 and 2 pay rent, those on the first more and those on the second less, and that those on the third only repay their cost. If the rental of the two first is divided equally between all the inhabitants, it will be possible to build on a fourth block (4), on which it would not pay to build, unless part of the cost was supplied out of the rental of the more favoured houses; and this process would go on upon each of the three classes of houses, until, as pauperization proceeded, the new houses built would be more and more, and ultimately altogether, of the third or lowest class, so that the society would consist of the largest number of people whom it would be possible to provide with house and accommodation at the lowest cost compatible with the standard of comfort or decency of the lowest class of the population.

The radical vice of this theory is that it leaves out of account the inevitable effect of a progressive demand upon a decreasing quantity. The only foundation upon which it rests, the primary and necessary assumption on which it proceeds, is the limitation of supply. If land of equal fertility and houses equally well placed were unlimited, there would be no reason or pretext for the proposal; indeed, there could be no "unearned increment" at all. The fact that it exists is an unerring sign of scarcity, *i.e.* that the demand exceeds the supply. Now, wherever the demand exceeds the supply—by which I mean, of course, that it exceeds it in the existing ratio of exchange, whatsoever that may be— either the ratio must be changed, or no exchange can take place.

APPENDIX B.*

FURTHER AS TO THE WORKING OF THE THEORY.

HERE are certain natural monopolies, gifts of nature, or instruments of production limited in extent, given to the whole human race. How can they best be made available, how can they be rendered most useful to the whole human race?

Mill would vest property in them in the collective community as the representative of the race, only allowing to individuals the usufruct, to be obtained of course by free competition.

Bastiat would vest such property in any individual who is prepared to pay the market price for it. If at any time the whole or a part of the national domain is in the hands of the Government as trustee for the community, it should be sold for what it will fetch to any one who wishes to buy it, and thus acquire absolute ownership.

What will be the economic effect of these two systems respectively?

Under the first, the equilibrium between demand and supply will be destroyed. Under the second, it would be maintained.

Under both we have to deal with a limited supply (this is the essential condition of the problem) and an unlimited demand; but under the first, while nothing can be done to

---

* I print the following pages as an appendix because I have not been able to incorporate them in the text, where they might perhaps more properly have stood. They restate some of the positions of the last two chapters.

increase the supply, the demand will be progressively increased; while under the second, the demand will also be kept within strict limits by an increasing limitation of the supply.

Under Bastiat's system (which is the Free Trade system) the economic mechanism is made to depend on the free exchange of equivalent services. No man can acquire a value without contributing an equivalent, and the community can only gain by the exchange.

Under Mill's system a value is recognized to which men have a right without giving any equivalent for it. Every value so acquired, therefore, is a distinct loss to the community, and marks a constant progress towards increasing pauperization.

This may be made clearer by an illustration. The case of the private landlord is precisely analogous to that of the forestaller or regrator, who figures in all the text-books of Political Economy. In both cases the question is to adapt the limited supply to an unlimited demand, or rather a stationary supply to an increasing demand.

We will suppose that at a given time, in a particular country—and we need go no further than our own possessions in India to find the actual event—the food-supply of the poor. is inadequate to the ordinary consumption of the pauper, and cannot be increased. The only possible mode of averting famine, or confining its area as much as possible, is so to raise the price of the grain or other food as to compel the people strictly to limit their consumption. If trade is left perfectly free, this will be effected by the ordinary operation of the laws of supply and demand, which will ensure as far as possible an adaptation of the stock of food to the consumption of the population; the available supply will be husbanded to the greatest possible extent, and will be administered in the most economical manner.

But if the whole of the money paid by the people for their food were at once to be handed back to them again, after deducting the sum necessary to repay the actual cost of production and the profits of the dealers, the check on consumption would at once be neutralized, and as it would go on undiminished, would very soon lead to the absorption of the whole stock of food and the starvation of the people.

The effect would be precisely analogous if the State were to receive, and hand back to the people of a country the rent of land and houses. The natural check to the undue demand afforded by the action of private owners would be removed, no possible addition at a uniform cost could be made to the supply, which is, by our supposition and from the fact of the existence of rent, limited in amount, and the demand for the products of the land, and therefore for inferior soils, would be directly and dangerously stimulated. This may be put in another and perhaps even a still more striking way.

The theory of the unearned increment assumes that "economic rent" is due to the gift of nature, and is not a value which can be legitimately appropriated by a private person, but that it is the inheritance of all mankind, and ought to be distributed among all the members of the community, which for the time being represents the *human race.*

How is this to be done? It is impossible to make the producer of whatever is grown on the favoured soils sell his product at cost price, because this obliges him to sell below the market rate, which must be that of the products of the worst soil under cultivation. The law of indifference requires that there cannot be two prices for the same thing in the same market.

But in theory this is the process by which the advantage of the unearned increment of the better soils might be diffused among the whole community. The Government should make a general assessment of the value at cost price, or rather, the value of the products of each kind or quality of land, minus "economic rent." It should, for instance, on the assumption that with a population of 3000 there were three qualities of land, the first producing 1000 quarters of wheat at 60s. a quarter without rent, the second at 50s. a quarter and paying 10s. rent on each quarter, and the third at 40s. a quarter and paying 20s. of rent per quarter. Add together the 3000 quarters and divide the produce thus :—

1000 quarters of wheat at			...	...	60s.	=	£3000
1000	,,	,,	...	...	50s.	=	£2500
1000	,,	,,	...	...	40s.	=	£2000
3000 at average of		...	...	...	50s.	=	£7500

The 3000 quarters should then be sold in the market at 50s. per quarter, and the population would benefit by reduction of 10s. per quarter in the price of wheat, or from £9000 to £7500.

What would be the effect of such a measure? Simply this: the population would get their wheat at 10s. per quarter below cost price. The exchange value of wheat and money, determined by the cost of production on the worst soil (maximum cost), which is the law admitted even by the English school in this case, is one quarter of wheat = 60s.; *i.e.* this rate, or £3 per head (the population being 3000 in number), is that which represents the standard of living by the people. Unless this standard was raised, the reduction in price to £2 10s. per head would simply lead to an addition of 500 people to the population, in which case there would be 3500 people, and this would raise the price of wheat again to £3 per quarter.

It must be borne in mind that we are supposing a case in which the law of diminishing returns is in operation. Without this there can be no such thing as economic rent. If an indefinite quantity of wheat can be raised at a uniform cost, there can be no surplus value, or "unearned increment." In these circumstances, *i.e.* under the operation of the "law of diminishing returns," the reduction in price caused by the measures which have been described would lead to an increased demand for wheat. This could only be obtained at an increased cost, but it would now pay to produce wheat at say 70s. a quarter, because although this would exceed the cost of production on the worst soil previously under cultivation, viz. that at 60s., the difference would be made up by the saving in wages on the price of food. For instance, the grower of wheat at 70s. a quarter would receive from Government 60s. as the cost price on the worst soil as his share of the unearned increment on the better soils. Thus it would become worth while to grow under cost until the whole extra profit of the "unearned increment," or economic rent, was absorbed, when the difference between the two states of society would be that in the first there was a certain net product constituting a fund available for the higher purposes of civilization, and in the second the whole product would be gross, and would be entirely absorbed in providing the bare necessaries of life for the population.

All this is merely to say in a great many words that a limited supply cannot satisfy an unlimited demand ; that the supply being in the nature of things, *ex hypothesi*, limited, the only question is, how to limit the demand in the same proportion. If this be not done, the surplus value, or unearned increment, or economic rent (or "gratuitous gifts of nature limited in quantity," as Cairnes calls them), will soon disappear altogether, and the total product will be in exact correspondence with the actual cost of production, the surplus value being swallowed up in the minus value of that portion produced below cost.

There are only two possible ways in which the equilibrium between demand and supply, which we have seen to be an indispensable condition of civilization, can be maintained. The first is by the institution of private property and free exchange applied to all values ; the second by collective property and regulated exchange. The first rests on the principle of personal freedom ; the second on that of constraint.

Sir Henry Maine, in his " History of Early Institutions," remarks, "I believe I state the inference suggested by all human legal history, when I say that there can be no material advance in civilization unless landed property is held by groups at least as small as families."

Yet the second expedient is the one recommended by Mill, persistently advocated by Cairnes, and apparently accepted by most of the popular writers and speakers of the present time who deal with this question.

The same high authority, Sir Henry Maine, in his last

work on " Popular Government," comments on this tendency in modern democracies (p. 37) : " There is, in fact, just enough evidence to show that even now there is a marked antagonism between democratic opinion and scientific truth as applied to human societies. The central seat in all Political Economy was from the first occupied by the theory of population. This theory has now been generalized by Mr. Darwin and his followers, and stated as the principle of the survival of the fittest ; it has become the central truth of all biological science. Yet it is evidently disliked by the multitude, and thrust into the background by those whom the multitude permits to lead it. It has long been intensely unpopular in France and the continent of Europe ; and, among ourselves, proposals for recognizing it through the relief of distress by emigration are visibly being supplanted by schemes founded on the assumption that, through legislative experiments on society, a given space of land may always be made to support in comfort the population which, from historical causes, has come to be settled on it."

APPENDIX C.

The Rate of Wages—Law of Diminishing Returns— Mill's Stationary State.

WHAT makes the rate of wages? This is the question discussed by Mr. Edward Atkinson, of Boston, one of the most eminent authorities in the United States on questions of trade and economy, in a very interesting treatise, read before the United Association at Montreal, in August, 1884.*

It is hardly necessary to observe that the question is one of vital significance. If it be accepted as an axiom that the aim of all governments should be the greatest happiness of the greatest number, it follows, beyond all possibility of dispute, that in modern societies the rate of wages is the test and measure of its success. It is estimated that about 70 per cent. of the population of the United Kingdom belong to what are called the working classes, of whom the largest proportion are dependent on wages. In the United States the percentage is, according to Mr. Atkinson, over 80 per cent. Upon the rate of wages, by which, of course, is meant not the mere money amount, but the quantity of food, clothing, shelter, and other commodities which it commands, must therefore depend the well-being or the misery of the vast majority of the people.

What are the causes which tend to raise or to depress the rate of wages? If these can be discovered, it remains to ask, What are the human institutions, what are the laws, what is

---

* Republished under the title of "The Distribution of Products." This work has gone through four editions in the United States.

the policy, which tends to promote or to retard the operation of those causes ?

The well-known wages fund theory, discarded by all, was derived from the general notion that the rate of wages depends upon the relation of labour to capital, without any reference to the resulting product of these instruments of production—a notion which pervades most of the writings of the earlier English economists, from Ricardo's memorable chapters on "Profits and Wages" downwards ; but, to avoid useless repetition, it will be enough to state the doctrine in the language of Mill, who has been happily described by Bagehot as the "Secrétaire de la Rédaction" of his school, and who certainly presents it in its least unfavourable light.

"Wages depend mainly on the demand and supply of labour, or, as it is often expressed, on the proportion between population and capital. . . .

"There is, unfortunately, no mode of expressing by one familiar term the aggregate of what may be called the wages fund of a country, and as the wages of productive labour form nearly the whole of that fund, it is usual to overlook the smaller and less important part, and to say that wages depend upon population and capital. It will be convenient to employ this expression, remembering, however, to consider it as elliptical, and not as a literal statement of the entire truth.

"With these limitations of the terms, wages not only depend on the relative amount of capital and population, but cannot, under the rule of competition, be affected by anything else. Wages (meaning, of course, the general rate) cannot rise but by an increase of the aggregate funds employed in hiring labourers, or a diminution in the number of competitors for hire ; nor fall except either by a diminution of the funds devoted to paying labour, or by an increase in the number of labourers to be paid." *

The rate of wages is in no sense dependent on the rate of profits, as Ricardo says, rising or falling inversely as the rise or fall of the latter, but will depend—

* Mill, "Principles," bk. ii. ch. ii. § 1.

1. On the quantity of work to be done—*the demand.*

2. On the quantity of productive force, combined capital and labour, available to do it—*the supply.*

The ratio between these two quantities will determine the value of the product, and the value of the product constitutes the fund to be divided between capital and labour. The proportion falling to each will again depend on the ratio of the capital and labour available.

It is a commonly received doctrine among economists that in the industrial progress of society there are two conflicting tendencies always discernible—the one towards a diminished cost of production, an increased return to human effort, *i.e.* towards cheapness and abundance ; the other towards an increased cost of production, a proportionately diminished return to capital and labour, *i.e.* towards dearness or scarcity.

Everything which contributes to increase the power of man over nature, all the agencies which augment the efficiency of labour, tend necessarily in the first direction ; the counteracting tendency is the result of the pressure of population upon the soil, which brings into play what Mr. Mill calls the fundamental law, that increased labour in any given state of agricultural progress is attended with a less than proportional increase of produce. It is obvious that these tendencies are not constant in their operation at all times and places, and that their action is often suspended and occasionally even reversed ; but the question is whether they are so apparent in large spaces of terms as to constitute what are called economic laws.

Some writers have gone so far as to assert as an inherent law—Mr. Senior among them—that in manufacturing industry increased production takes place at a diminished cost, and an equally inherent law of agricultural industry at an increased cost. These have been called respectively the laws of increasing and of diminishing returns.

It is significant that Mr. Mill, while accepting the latter, denies the former, and doubts whether even in manufactures increased cheapness follows increased production by anything amounting to a law. It is, he says, a probable and usual, but not a necessary, consequence.

On the other hand, some eminent economists, such as Bastiat and Carey, have suggested serious doubts whether the tendency to a decreasing return in the case of agriculture can be accepted as a law, except in a sense so abstract and so remote from actual conditions as to be beyond the sphere of practical speculation.

There is, then, a wide divergence of opinion upon a question of vital importance ; for upon the issue it is not too much to say that, so far as can be predicated from conditions now known to us, the future of the human race must depend.

It is not surprising, therefore, that the aspirations of those who, on the one hand, have adopted the theory of progressive scarcity, and those who, on the other, have been able to believe in progressive abundance should have taken a very different direction. In a world where there is not enough for all, the superfluities of the rich appear to be the only provision for the deficient necessaries of the poor, especially if it be true that, as the rich grow richer, the poor grow poorer. But in a world where there is not only enough but to spare for all, and in which the rich cannot grow richer without making the poor less poor, especially if it be true that the poor cannot become less poor without making the rich richer, no attempt to redress the balance is necessary, and indeed could only be mischievous.

From these opposing views of the relations of man to nature, it is easy to trace the apparently hopeless conflict of opinion as to the best mode of attempting the solution of what is called the social problem—whether this should be sought in the principle of constraint or in that of freedom. From the first view have naturally proceeded the various schemes of socialism, from class protection to full-blown communism ; from the second has been derived with greater reason the policy of free exchange.

I say with greater reason, because even on the assumption of those who take the darkest view of the limitations within

which human progress is confined, it may be found that no
social arrangements have yet been proposed which afford so
good a prospect of averting the worst consequences of a
stationary state (see the whole tendency of the argument
in the chapter on "The Unearned Increment") as those
presented by freedom of exchange.

As an economist, Mill was not an original or powerful
thinker, and as his latent apologist, Mr. H. Sidgwick, admits,
he always manifests the "piety of a disciple" towards
Ricardo's teaching; but it is still difficult to account, after the
extraordinary changes which had taken place before his eyes
in the economic conditions of the world, and especially in
those of England, for the very contracted view which he takes
of the possibilities of human progress.

There is nothing in the whole range of economic literature
so depressing and so inadequate, in a treatise dealing with the
science of wealth, as Mill's chapter on "The Stationary State."
Having been unable to shake off the "mazy and preposterous
assumptions of the Ricardian school," and perpetually haunted
by the apprehension of the constantly impending approach of
the final term of industrial progress, he is compelled to con-
sole himself with the reflection that after all it may not be
desirable for wealth to increase beyond a certain point, and that
the solution of social problems is rather to be sought in some
fancied ideal state, in which the upper classes will be satisfied
with a moderate competence, and the working classes be led
so to restrain their numbers as to avoid an undue pressure
upon the means of subsistence. No better proof can be afforded
of the morbid habit of mind engendered by this vein of speculation than the unworthy sneers in which he indulges at the
great nation, which by its strenuous efforts has extended
man's conquest over nature throughout a vast continent, and
placed at the disposal of the human race resources offering possibilities of progress which, for many generations at
all events, must render the gloomy forecasts of writers such as
Mill mere idle abstractions. But idle though they may be,
they are not innocuous. They are responsible to a great
degree for the false direction in which the minds of the pre-

sent generation have of late been moving. They have diverted interest and energy from the agencies of international progress. They have overturned confidence in the great principles of private property and free exchange, and given a new impetus to schemes of social regeneration by false and artificial methods. They have brought into an unnatural and sinister alliance the teachings of the English universities, and of Proudhon and Karl Marx.

Very different has been the conception of the destiny of the human race formed by those economists who regard the so-called law of diminishing returns as entirely local and temporary at the present stage of industrial progress, and believe that for as long a period of time as it is rational to take into account, the countervailing tendency will cause an ever-increasing proportionate return to human effort. It is observed by the adherents of this school that the "law of diminishing returns" rests on certain assumptions which are, to say the least, doubtful.

Who can say that the cultivable area of the world is a fixed quantity,* or set a limit to the progress of invention and discovery in agriculture and in manufacture? Who can affirm, in view of physiological and social facts already becoming apparent, that the human race is destined by an inexorable law to multiply indefinitely, and for ever keep pace with or outstrip the possibilities of increased production?

So far from accepting Mill's statement that society in advanced communities is perpetually on the verge of the stationary state, they believe that, in view of the innumerable agencies in active or latent operation which tend to increase production and facilitate exchanges, the advance of knowledge, the discoveries of science, the enormous economies which might be effected by improved commercial relations of countries politically distinct, the internationalization, so to speak, of

---

* "Land itself," says, for instance, Mr. Atkinson ("Industrial Progress of the Nation, 1890," p. 157), "may be exhausted when treated as a mine; it may be maintained when worked as a laboratory. Its potential in the increase of fertility and production, when used as a tool or instrument for diverting nitrogen and carbon from the atmosphere and converting these elements into food for man and beast, *is as yet an unknown quantity.*"—ED.

industrial forces—that period, if it is ever reached, is so remote as to be beyond the range of rational speculation and the domain of practical politics.

In this connection the investigations of Mr. Atkinson are very important and suggestive.

APPENDIX D.

CAPITAL AND LABOUR.

IN Bastiat's "Harmonies Economiques" the following passage occurs, thus translated by Mr. Atkinson: "In proportion to the increase of capital, the *absolute* share of the total product falling to the capitalist is augmented, but his *relative* share is diminished; while, on the contrary, the share of the labourer is increased both relatively and absolutely." *

This proposition, which if true is of vital and fundamental importance, Mr. Atkinson, "whose conclusions have," as he says, "been based almost wholly upon facts and deductions from business experiences rather than from books," entirely confirms.

He repeats it in the following form :—

1. In all the arts, including agriculture, to which modern machinery and improved tools have been applied, a less number of persons compass a constantly increasing product in ratio to the time which they devote to the work.

2. In proportion to the increase of the product, and to the efficiency of the capital applied thereto, this lessening number of persons have received decade by decade higher rates of wages in money, or in what money will buy. They earn for themselves a constantly increasing share of an increasing product, or its equivalent in money.

3. As a necessary result of this increasing efficiency of both capital and labour, the joint product is served to the

* This position is still further illustrated and supported by Mr. Atkinson and Mr. Wells in their recently published works mentioned in the Introduction.—ED.

consumers at constantly increasing prices, or at less cost to them.

4. As capital itself increases in efficiency, its value in ratio to the product of capital and labour becomes less. Capital, therefore, is forced to be satisfied with a lessening share of an increasing product. Of course capital includes credit.

This view seems to be correct. The increased efficiency of capital must be the same thing as an increase of capital. If £1000 can be made to do the same work as £2000, it is the same thing as if £2000 were substituted for £1000.* Now, without going beyond Mill's definition of capital, viz. that it is "whatever of the produce of the country is devoted to production," it is evident that, as he says, "every addition to capital gives to labour *either* additional employment *or* additional remuneration. In either case labour must gain." But Mill, as usual, is not exhaustive. He might have added that every addition to capital gives additional employment *and* additional remuneration in many cases. Let us, then, suppose that the efficiency of capital is doubled by improved processes. This is the same thing as a double capital. There is no reason why this should increase the share of profits earned by capital, or the interest paid on it—on the contrary, it would probably diminish both; the supply being double, the gain must therefore fall to labour. On the other hand, let us suppose that the efficiency of labour is double. This means that every man produces twice as much as before. Here it is clear that labour would also gain. In any case, therefore, the tendency of progress must be to increase the share of labour in the total product, as stated by Bastiat and Atkinson.

Of course this tendency may be neutralized by an increase in the working population more than equivalent to the

---

* N.B.—There is, however, this difference. An addition of £1000 to the capital of £1000 would no doubt be the same thing as the doubled efficiency of £1000, but it is improbable that any large addition to the capital of a country could find employment without bringing into play the law of "diminishing returns," whereas the double efficiency of existing capital would imply that the converse process was in operation.

increase of capital. If population outstrips capital, it is im-⸱
possible to provide for increasing remuneration under any
system ; but the argument is that, other things being equal,
the tendency must be in the direction of an increased share
to labour in the total product. It must be assumed that,
whatever may be the case with capital, population will
advance in a certain ratio; and if this be so, every extra
addition to capital will tend to increase the share of labour.

This supposition, be it observed, meets the case of
"diminishing returns" should this phenomenon present itself,
for the pressure of population on the means of subsistence
will be the same, whether capital increases or not ; but, as
Bastiat points out ("Harmonies Economiques : Capital"), the
operation of the law of diminishing returns is energetically
balanced by an opposite tendency, viz. the constant progress
in industrial arts, which, by ameliorating the processes of
labour, perpetually diminishes the value and remuneration of
fixed capital, and transfers to the domain of utility, which is
the common property of all, that which was before a value
only to be obtained by an equivalent human effort. This
law is one of immense importance and is often overlooked,
especially in estimating the value of land. For instance, the
purchaser of a piece of land worth £1000 in one year (1870)
may lay out £1000 in fixed instruments, buildings, machines,
etc., and calculate on getting 3 per cent. on his £2000. In
another year (1880) the cost of these instruments may have
been reduced by, say, £500 ; and, other things being the same,
this would have the effect of diminishing his rent so as to
reduce it to an amount which would only pay 3 per cent. on
£1500.

I think, therefore, that the proposition of Bastiat, adopted
by Atkinson, may be accepted as true, as a condition of
normal progress. Certainly, if it is questioned on theoretic
grounds, it may well be retorted that if the historical or inductive method be applied, the confirmation is complete ; for
no one can deny that profits and interest are lower in all
countries where capital abounds than in those where it is
scarce. The actual facts of life, therefore, absolutely justify

the position taken up, and make it clear that the one thing needful in the interest of labour is the greatest possible increase of capital. If this is once admitted, all the socialistic schemes with which we are afflicted must suffer an ignominious collapse.

THE END.

PRINTED BY WILLIAM CLOWES AND SONS, LIMITED, LONDON AND BECCLES.